Chasing
POINTS

Chasing
POINTS

A SEASON ON THE PRO TENNIS CIRCUIT

GREGORY HOWE

First published by Pitch Publishing, 2018

Pitch Publishing
A2 Yeoman Gate
Yeoman Way
Worthing
Sussex
BN13 3QZ
www.pitchpublishing.co.uk
info@pitchpublishing.co.uk

ISBN 978-1-78531-383-7

Typesetting and origination by Pitch Publishing
Printed by TJ International, Padstow, Cornwall, UK

Contents

For Mr Munckton.
Thanks for everything, Fred.

Acknowledgements

IF I was to look for a parallel between my experiences of being on the tennis tour to writing this book, it would simply be that – while both often appear (and are, at times) solitary, lonely pursuits – what is often not visible is the great support team working behind the scenes, without whom nothing would be possible. As I never got the opportunity to make an acceptance speech on tour, then I guess here is my chance now –

A massive thanks to the great team at Pitch Publishing – as professional as any team I've encountered in the sporting world. To Jane and Paul Camillin for backing a tennis book not about one of the big stars, and to Derek Hammond and Margaret Murray for their help. To Duncan Olner for the great book cover – a fitting visual metaphor for a tennis adventure. And to Gareth Davis for editing, Dean Rockett for proofreading and Graham Hales for typesetting. Really, it was a pleasure.

To Ian McMechan for his help with my early drafts and advice in navigating through the mysterious world of publishing. I'm forever grateful that your language expertise is far superior to that bloody, sliced forehand of yours. And to Amy Hanlon, who scrutinised my story from a non-tennis fan's point of view. Your brutal feedback led to months of redrafting, but the story is so much the better for it.

On the tennis front, thanks to Jake Baluyut, Mark Robinson, Daniel Lazaro and John Tashiro in helping me prepare for the tennis tour and listening to my ideas. And to the players and officials in the tennis world, who knowingly or unknowingly became part of the story. I hope you find my comments fair.

To the aficionados (my term) from britishtennis.active board.com for following me – and other unknown journeymen – on tour, and agreeing to their comments being used in the book. With special thanks to Steven Trezise (aka Steven @ GBtennis) for his selfless help in getting me in contact with a world I know little about.

To my brother Andrew, for joining me on tour and making the whole adventure something special. To share a lifelong love of a sport with a sibling is something I wish everyone could experience.

And most importantly, to my wife, Sylvie, whose unending support for all my crazy ideas meant that my tennis tour, and now this book, was even possible to try for. Hopefully, I have a little credit left for a few more ideas …

Introduction

'Dreams do come true sometimes.'

Andy Murray's Facebook, on Marcus Willis

ON PAPER, Marcus Willis had no right to be there. Here was a part-time coach – a player who used to be so out of shape his nickname was 'Cartman' (the fat character from the cartoon, *South Park*). Yet, there he was, in the second round of Wimbledon facing the G.O.A.T. – Roger Federer.

You couldn't make it up. Any of the spectators who had bought centre court tickets for the 2016 Wimbledon Championships could have watched Willis for free, only a year before, in small English towns like Felixstowe or Frinton-on-Sea. I bet none of them had.

The British tabloids had a field day. The *Daily Express* ran the headline 'The Fairytale of Wimbledon's Underdog'. Romance, surreal and dream were words used to describe his journey. Roger Federer summed it up, 'It is what our sport needs, where guys come from nowhere.' To the majority of the public, it must have felt like Marcus Willis had indeed emerged from nowhere. Inevitably, people started to ask, what had he been doing?

Reporters attempted to tell Willis's Wimbledon back-story. Obscure facts began to emerge: he had to qualify for the qualifying; he was 772 in the world; his best 2016 result was a quarter-final in a Tunisian Futures event; and so far in 2016, he had won a grand total of £258.

You could imagine the average fan's confusion. Futures… qualifying…a player ranked 772…they play tennis in Tunisia? For them, a whole new world had opened up – a world outside of the Grand Slams and marquee players.

This is *my* world.

* * * * *

Every year, well over 10,000 players will try their hand on the men's professional tennis circuit. They will compete en masse, often in huge qualifying draws in far-flung corners of the world. It is a win – or go home – survival of the fittest where most don't survive. This is tennis's version of baseball's minor leagues – the Futures circuit.

To become a world-ranked professional, a player must battle through the qualifying rounds, and then win their opening match in the main draw of a Futures event, all the time beating established ranked players along the way. By doing this, they earn *one* precious ATP (Association of Tennis Professionals) point and a world ranking beginning around 1,500.

From here they must fight their way through the next two levels of the pro game – the Challenger circuit, and finally the rarefied air of the ATP tour. On the weekend before any tournament, a qualifying competition allows lowly ranked players the chance to fight for a few places in the main tournament.

The weekend qualifying competitions prior to ATP tournaments are brutal: journeymen, rising stars, and top players whose careers are on the slide desperately compete, knowing they are within touching distance of the huge pay cheques, crowds and top stars. When fans turn on their televisions and watch the pros, they are watching the survivors.

The game's big four – Federer, Nadal, Djokovic and Murray – all began their careers early: playing Futures by age 15; at 16, all were world ranked; by 18 they had already moved through the Challengers to play exclusively on the ATP tour. These are truly special players, shooting stars rocketing towards the top of the game. In reality, most aspiring pros will never achieve a world ranking, while most who do stall well before ever reaching the ATP tour.

Making it as a pro is tough, but at least the professional tennis circuit is a meritocracy. *Anyone* can enter the qualifying of a Futures tournament. Then, all you have to do is keep winning and you'll soon end up on the ATP tour.

If you don't believe me – just look at Marcus Willis. In his first tournament of 2016, he had to qualify for a Futures tournament in Tunisia. In his second tournament of the year – the Wimbledon Championships – he pre-qualified, qualified, and ended up playing Federer on centre court. Willis just kept on winning.

With this in mind, if a 34-year-old schoolteacher – who played a bit of tennis – quit his job and threw himself on the professional tennis circuit, how far could he reach? Could he earn a world ranking? Could he fight his way through to the elite ATP level and play alongside the likes of Federer, Nadal, Djokovic and Murray?

Marcus Willis could do it.

Why *not* me?

Prologue

The Holy Grail, and a Crack in a Window

COME BACK in time to 1988. September to be precise: literally decades ago to an iconic era in tennis. The cool Swede, Mats Wilander, had just become world number one by beating Ivan Lendl in the US Open Final. A brash Las Vegan with denim shorts, long hair and earrings was making his move, while the glow of tennis's glory days could still be felt every time a fading John McEnroe or Jimmy Connors took to the stage.

I was 16 years old at the time, and about to begin my pro career – if you could call it that (and *no one* ever has). Unfortunately, it wasn't at the US Open, but rather in a low-level event on the other side of the world in Australia, namely in my hometown of Gladstone.

Gladstone was anything but a tennis town. It was a tough industrial city, rugby league territory, with no time for a white-collar sport like tennis. It made no difference that the legendary Rod Laver came from a city just up the road; no one good ever came out of Gladstone. The city did have brand new tennis courts though – a gift from the nearby aluminium refinery – and this meant we were awarded a pro tournament.

My coach, Fred Munckton, just so happened to be the tournament director. He awarded both myself, and my younger brother, Andrew, wildcards into the qualifying draw. Andrew had just turned 15 and was the city's men's champion – the best prospect in years. Although I was a year older, my game was full of holes. If anyone had even noticed my name in the draw, they would have simply assumed I was there to keep my brother company.

Memories from my first pro tournament are still vivid today. For that week, the city burst with international flavour – US college players mixed with tanned Europeans, exotic Mexicans and the best tennis players in Australia. On match day, overly eager to get down to the courts, the Howe brothers turned up at daybreak only to find themselves locked out of the complex. Once the matches got underway, I watched Andrew compete well against a world-ranked pro. Club members had turned out to watch him, with his loss deemed a credible one.

I would prefer not to talk about my match. After hanging around all day, my pro debut began under the floodlights. They might as well have been metaphorical headlights blinding me; I was wiped off the court in about half an hour (including an injury time-out when I almost threw up due to nerves). My opponent, Neil Prickett from Western Australia, was at least nice enough to allow me one game to escape a double bagel.

It wouldn't deter me. This was a glimpse into another world, and I was hooked. In the clubhouse, I discovered tennis's version of the Holy Grail. Taped to the brick wall was the entire men's professional ranking list from number one down to number 990: Wilander, Lendl, McEnroe, Connors, Becker, Edberg and Agassi were at its peak. In these pre-internet days, to find a complete list of the world rankings was virtually impossible.

I spent an eternity scanning through the list, fascinated with each name and what it represented. To be on this list meant something – it was proof of being a world-class player, to be a little part of tennis history. There was permanence to it all, even if it was held to the wall by sticky tape.

The sight of this list changed my life. I vowed then and there to one day see my name on the world-ranking list. What I didn't realise at the time, was that it was to become my own personal Holy Grail – to fascinate, haunt and motivate me for the next two decades of my life.

* * * * *

During the next five years I finished my schooling and attended university. I worked hard at my game. Each year, I continued to play the professional events on the Queensland circuit, eventually winning an occasional match in the qualifying, but never coming close to escaping the huge qualifying draws. To earn an ATP point and a ranking was never a reality. In these events, I saw future stars such as Pat Rafter and Mark Philippoussis start at the lowest rung. They were soon gone – on their way to the very top of the game.

After university, I graduated as an English teacher, moving straight to London to begin my schoolteaching career. Since I was now living in London, I started playing tennis for Great Britain, making use of my British passport (I was born in Derbyshire, England, to Australian parents).

The European summers became my opportunity to dream again of tennis glory. With Andrew, and my best friend in London, Jake Baluyut, we used tennis as a passport to see the world…or at least north Africa and eastern Europe where our money went further. It was like backpacking with a tennis racquet. Chasing Futures tournaments, we slept in Moroccan airports, shared rooms in the fleapits of Cairo and braved earthquakes in eastern Turkey.

It was an amazing experience. Yet, I never got close to earning that ATP point that would give me a world ranking. I figured it was just not meant to be. I told myself it was *okay*. To see the world, travel with my brother and friends, and play the circuit was *reward enough*.

As I turned 30, the tours slowly trickled to a halt. My life was heading places: doing all the things that you were meant to be doing at that age. I moved into a London flat with the girl of my dreams, Sylvie, from the French Caribbean. I got promotions at work, rising quickly to run an English department in a school in north London. I was in charge of ten people, many of whom were much older than myself with mortgages, children and baggage. With more work and stress, I put on weight and was

10kg heavier than in my playing days. I still played the smaller amateur events around London, but year after year my British ranking fell; I slowly slipped out of the top 1,000 in the country.

After one first-round loss, the tournament director asked me, 'What happened? You used to win these events.' His comments stung, and I considered his words for a while. I told myself it was *okay*. Tennis was my hobby; going so well at work and at home was *reward enough*.

* * * * *

Fast-forward four years.

One evening, I found myself working alone in the English department office in the same north London school. Winter had set in, leaving a grey darkness to envelop the city of London. The students had left hours ago, the other teachers not long after them. However, I was middle management, with responsibility, and *accountability* – education's new buzz word.

Through the office window, the concrete back wall of the Tottenham Hotspur football ground could be seen, along with the barbed wire fence that separated the stadium from the real world. Abandoned, looted cars lined the road leading towards the school's front gate. A huge crack had appeared in the window – courtesy of a student who had seen his English teacher in the office, and hurled a rock in his direction.

On the lone computer terminal, I started surfing the internet. Like any other tennis enthusiast around the world (bored at work), I checked the ATP world rankings, seeing who was trailing Roger Federer in the order of merit. After scrolling through the top ten, and then the top 100 players in the world, I did something that separated me from other tennis enthusiasts.

I kept on going: past the journeymen, past good players who had fallen on hard times, and well past the unknowns struggling in the minor leagues. I went all the way to the end, to the players with a lone ATP point who were hanging on to the coat-tails of the pro circuit with everything they had, living the dream – once upon a time, *my* dream.

The crack in the window seemed to be mocking me. Everything else in the office was brand new, but the crack ruined everything. Unable to be fixed or replaced, they said. It would have been better to just kick the whole thing in.

I looked back at the ranking list on the computer screen. I pictured my name on the end of the rankings. I would take any ranking, no matter how low. I pictured being 16 years old again, transfixed by the list of names taped to a brick wall.

There and then I made my decision.

'You're making a big mistake,' the principal of the school told me a few days later. 'Your career in management will be over.'

I was 34 years of age; for my tennis dreams, it was now or *never*. I had unfinished business. He could take his job in management…and shove it.

I was heading for the men's professional tennis tour.

1

The Futures Tour
Bangkok

SIX MONTHS later…

August 2006

My tour had begun. It didn't matter that I was only in the immigration queue at Bangkok International Airport. What had been an abstract idea was suddenly real, very real.

Now, I know what you're thinking. This guy quits his job on the premise of 'playing tennis' and heads on a year-long journey around the world, starting in the hedonistic capital of the world: parties, sex and *The Hangover Part 2*. However, Bangkok is precisely the kind of place that the third-tier Futures tour is found – places that people assume have no connection to tennis.

As for the typical Futures player, they're the kind of person who'll fly halfway around the world to a third-world party place to hit a fuzzy, yellow ball. Like myself, I bet there'd be nothing else in life they'd rather be doing.

Starting this tour was a special moment; its significance was not lost on me. Sure, I had just quit my job, landed in the Far East, and held a round-the-world ticket in my hand. That's got to make anyone feel like an adventurer on some kind of spiritual journey. But I'm sure the backpackers ahead of me in the queue, their hair in braids and colourful bracelets on their wrists, were feeling just the same.

It was much more than that.

For the first time in as long as I could remember, I looked out into the future and saw no horizon. There was no job waiting – no place I had to be anytime soon. I had given myself a year to play on the pro circuit, but if things went well, really well, then there was nothing forcing me to stop.

Before, I had always played in my holidays. I'd felt like a bit of a tennis tourist, just seeing the world, playing for fun before I had to return to the day job. This time was different. Now, for the first time, I felt like I was on the pro tour, about to join the thousands of other hopefuls with only one thing in mind – to make it to the ATP tour.

In tennis speak: I was *seriously* pumped.

Returning to reality, my first job was to get out of the airport (not always the easiest task in some countries). After handing over a small fortune in Thai baht for a limousine airport transfer, I was led to a battered white station wagon around the back of the terminal. My driver gave me a cigarette-stained smile. I sat in the back.

It was late evening by the time we left the airport. There was coolness in the air, the kind that follows a torrential downpour of rain. The smell of a nearby swamp mixed with exhaust fumes. A motorcycle raced by – a girl perched elegantly behind her male driver, both legs balancing over one side as she sat sideways. Bicycles fought with motorcycles and cars. They weaved around each other, their lights illuminating the pitch-black road. If I hadn't known it beforehand, then the chaos of the traffic alone would have told me I was in a third-world country.

Gradually the traffic disappeared into silent back roads. The yellow street lamps gave everything a soft, somewhat eerie glow. Stray dogs sleeping beside the road casually eyed the car as it passed by.

The taxi driver turned around flashing his trademark smile. He passed me a worn pamphlet (that I tried not to touch). 'Good girls, only good girls,' he said while smiling again. He opened the pamphlet to reveal rows of girls holding up numbers and a girl in a bikini about to step into a Jacuzzi. 'You want massage? I use all time,' the driver said proudly.

Strangely, when I dreamt about being on tour, I hadn't pictured dealing with these kinds of people. Maybe *The Hangover Part 2* was more realistic than I had first realised.

After politely declining the taxi driver's offer, we arrived a few minutes later in the car park of the Eastern Lakes hotel: a blandly modern four-storey hotel with palm trees out front. It backed on to a man-made lake that looked a perfect breeding ground for mosquitoes. The Eastern Lakes was the closest hotel to the tennis courts, so it was this bit of luxury or the tennis academy's dorm rooms. At 34 years of age, I was done with dorm rooms.

In the hotel reception, a heavily made-up Thai girl in her early 20s sat chatting to the male receptionist. Behind them, taped on the lift doors, a notice read, 'Don't bring mosquitoes in on your back'. Perhaps the world's biggest gecko hung from the ceiling, its bulging eyes staring at me intently.

The moment I reached my room, I put on my trainers, picked up my skipping rope and headed outside. The giant gecko had disappeared. The girl and the receptionist both looked bewildered as I jogged past them into the hotel parking lot and slowly began jumping rope. Another stray dog popped its head out of a bush to see what was going on.

The clock hit midnight: I didn't care. I remembered once reading an article about the legendary Jimmy Connors, how he would religiously exercise upon landing in a city. It didn't matter if it was two in the morning – they would open the tennis courts if necessary so he could train, preparing his mind for the battles ahead. If Connors – the game's ultimate warrior – was in my shoes, I bet you he would be jumping rope in Bangkok, after midnight, surrounded by stray dogs.

* * * * *

Tennis in Thailand was booming. They had two players in the world's top 100 – unprecedented for a nation where the sport was traditionally a rich man's pastime. Their national hero, Paradorn Srichaphan, was so popular that his matches were televised live in Bangkok's nightclubs (I couldn't imagine walking into a London nightclub to find Andy Murray posturing on a big screen).

The Thai government wanted to capitalise on tennis's newfound popularity. They bought the rights for an ATP event and built a state-of-the-art national training centre. Their goal was simple: bring in elite coaches from around the world and turn Thailand into Asia's tennis powerhouse.

I had arrived in Bangkok a day early with the idea of training with the elite squad based at the centre. What better way to start my tour – get some advice from a world-class teaching pro and train with Asia's top juniors. You know what they say; if you want to be a pro, train like one.

At least the idea was good.

It was an underwhelming ten-minute walk from the hotel to this new beacon of success. The road was a crumbling bitumen strip. The ever-present pack of stray dogs eyed me sleepily from the dirt roadside. Only when I reached a huge iron gate and a security guard let me in, did I realise how serious the Thai government was. A flower-lined driveway led me to a three-storey glass clubhouse surrounded with manicured gardens, flowing streams and brand new hard courts further than my eye could see. It was hard to believe that just outside the tennis grounds, it had smelt like a swamp.

Juniors from all over Asia – Vietnam, Uzbekistan and Kazakhstan – were beginning to assemble outside the stadium court. An Indian coach stood near a flip chart where the theme of the day was written, 'Hit with CONFIDENCE!' It was like Nick Bollettieri's Florida academy had been transplanted straight into south-east Asia.

One of the older players strode confidently across, flashing a smile, and offered his hand in greeting. 'My name's Kevin. Pleased to meet you,' he said with a slight American accent – adding that he was from Hong Kong.

Chatting to Kevin, it became abundantly clear how different his situation was to mine. Although only 17, he was already a fringe player in Hong Kong's Davis Cup team. Being a nation's brightest prospects brought benefits. Kevin had two personal coaches: a technical coach *and* a hitting coach. Hearing this made me realise the last time I'd had a tennis lesson was 16 years ago...a year after Kevin was born.

I became more astounded when Kevin then told me his hitting coach was the former Aussie pro, Andrew Ilie (who himself was five years younger than me). I told Kevin that Ilie had a reputation in Australia as a temperamental hothead – an image helped when, during one run at Roland-Garros, he would tear his shirt in half in a crazed frenzy after each win.

'Andrew Ilie is a very calm person – very together,' Kevin assured me. 'He was going to come across to these Futures and play doubles with me if the organisers promised a wildcard. They didn't, so he didn't come. I originally came with my dad, but he went back. Now my girlfriend is over here. She's not into sports, but writing and English – and probably shopping now.'

It appeared that Kevin wasn't a full-time member of the squad. The Hong Kong federation had paid for him to come across before the Futures event for two weeks specifically to train with the Swiss performance coach in the academy. I guess, like myself, he was just a drop-in touring pro (I'll admit, I liked the sound of that title).

'If you're from Hong Kong, then why do you have an American accent?' I asked him.

'I go to an American school in Hong Kong. I'm hoping to go well enough to get into a college in the States and combine tennis with study. Hong Kong schools are very good, but tough. Every time I come back from a tournament, they give me an exam immediately as punishment for having days off.'

I had always wondered how elite juniors, trying to combine training with school studies, managed to juggle both. It appeared that for Kevin, being intelligent was more of a hindrance to his tennis career than anything else. The tennis world rarely considered anything outside of the tennis world, while schoolteachers and academics often saw tennis as simply a recreation to be enjoyed before afternoon tea. I wanted to give Kevin my thoughts on teachers, but quietness fell over the squad. Players turned towards an approaching figure.

Dominik Utzinger looked across the assembled players. He was the academy's top performance coach, brought across from Switzerland. At 6ft 4in tall, with small glasses and long, wavy hair held in place by a plastic hairband, Utzinger appeared a charismatic figure. He had the lean, wiry frame of an ex-professional, which he had been during the 1980s. He spent most of his time on tour as a journeyman, before finding some success as a doubles specialist towards the end of his career. However, it was his time as a coach for the Swiss Tennis Federation that established his aura. In Switzerland at the time was a 14-year-old junior called Roger Federer.

When Thailand created its new tennis academy for the future, it needed an expert to develop the best juniors and to teach the coaches. Dominik Utzinger was that man. His first task of the morning was to give Thailand's best 14-year-old junior a stern lecture.

'Why aren't you in qualies? It is a 32-qualifying draw and there were byes last week. I want you to come and talk to me about your tournaments.' His voice had a calm, almost soothing authority to it that forced everybody around to listen. For added effect, he leaned forward when he talked, although the junior was too busy staring at the ground to notice.

'Oh, I'm only 14,' Utzinger continued, mimicking the Thai boy's voice. 'You play one under-14 tournament a year – this is rubbish. This is not professional. You are now a tennis apprentice. If you think what I'm saying is rubbish, then you must say so.'

When the training session began, it was a brutal affair. It was continual drills of four balls where you were moved behind the baseline, before turning defence into attack and ending up at the net. If you missed a shot, you started again. If you pushed the ball, you started again. I seemed to be starting again a lot.

Within minutes I was drenched in sweat. Neither Kevin nor the Thai junior appeared to be perspiring at all, yet as I sat down, a puddle of perspiration began to form under the chair. My light-blue grip had turned a dark colour and squeezing the handle of the racquet made streams of water splash on to the court.

'How old are you?' Kevin asked during an early break.

'In my 30s,' I replied. I had been *dreading* this question.

'So how old are you, exactly?' Kevin went on.

'Too old to say – but I'm younger than Andre Agassi!'

A couple of minutes later, I smacked an outright winner past Kevin, causing him to shout, 'Are you sure you're 30?'

Kevin, the Thai junior and myself took it in turns until the shopping trolley of balls were exhausted. As we collected the mountain of balls, Kevin mentioned his guitar playing. Utzinger told him something about Dire Straits' Mark Knopfler and then drifted off into anecdotes from the tour. Then the drills began again.

After 45 minutes my legs had turned to jelly. By the end of the hour, I felt like throwing up; I simply wasn't used to this kind of punishment. As the balls were collected, I lay on the ground and promptly told Roger Federer's ex-coach that I couldn't finish – a humiliating acknowledgement.

'When did you fly in?' asked Utzinger, looking down at me as I lay prostrate on the court.

'Last night.'

'It could be jet lag. What are you drinking?' Utzinger asked me.

'Water and Gatorade.'

'In Thailand, water and Gatorade is not enough. I know it's hot in Europe at the moment, but it is different here. You lose so much more water. You need to go to the pharmacy – there is stuff that is safe. I just can't remember the name.'

I replied that maybe I had been a little dehydrated – it was the only way to save face. I thought I was fit, but I couldn't even finish the morning drill session in this humidity. I pathetically sat in the court-side chairs as Kevin and the Thai junior finished the session without me.

The morning session ended 30 minutes later. I was still glued to the chair listening to Utzinger telling stories from his training days with Federer. I asked him if, at 14 years old, Federer looked like he was going to be this good. He must have been asked the exact question countless times over the past decade, but he paused, and looked at the sky in thought, before returning his gaze towards me and speaking in a tone I can only describe as a kind of hushed urgency.

'I cannot tell you who will make it at that age. I can tell you who cannot make it, and who may make it, but I cannot tell you for certain that they will make it. There are so many factors to be considered. When Federer was 14, his father came to me and said Roger would like to make it as a professional. He was then small and skinny.'

He held up his little finger for emphasis. 'When he used to hit a high topspin backhand, it was like this.' Utzinger pretended to swing with an imaginary racquet that was so heavy that his wrist was limp. 'But he had this amazing timing – it was all timing.' At this point Utzinger paused and looked at me sternly. 'Back then, he was talented, but a lazy, little brat. I told his father he would have to work harder if he was going to make it. Then he came back every two years and the progress he made was amazing. By the time he was 17, he was a physical monster – just the same as he is today.'

With the story over, he turned to Kevin. 'When do you fly out? Before you go I want you to come and talk to me about your tournaments and what you're doing next year.' Kevin nodded. Then Dominik Utzinger wished us good luck before walking off to lunch.

I walked slowly back to my hotel, trying to make sense of what had just happened. Had I been a fool to think I could compete with talented full-time players half my age? Kevin didn't even have a professional ranking, yet he had outlasted me and looked like he could have continued for hours. To rub salt in the wounds, Kevin and the rest of the squad still had the afternoon session to look forward to. There was no way I was attending that. What would be the point? I'd probably end up lying on the ground halfway through the session...again. This time the stray dogs didn't even bother to look at me; they just sauntered by.

Loser.

The qualifying rounds for the event began tomorrow. It was no time to feel sorry for myself. I was already committed.

* * * * *

Pro tennis is run by two organisations. My personal favourite is the ITF (International Tennis Federation). They are the last bastion of tradition, running the third-tier Futures circuit, the Grand Slams and the Davis Cup. I'm fascinated with the history of the game, and tennis's frontiers, so it's logical I relate to them. Their antithesis is the ATP (Association of Tennis Professionals) who control the ATP and Challenger tours. For them, everything is about *the product*. They care about the top stars...and not much else, and that's fair enough.

What's important is that, despite their hang-ups, they work together so that all professional tennis events give *only* ATP points, towards *only* one world ranking list. What this means is that the number one player on the ATP rankings list is the number one player in the world – without question. Failure to agree on this would have rendered tennis like boxing, which has God knows how many world champions.

Thailand, being a Futures event, was thus run by the ITF. It had a 64-man qualifying draw, so I would need three wins to progress to the main draw where the possibility of ATP points and prize money began.

My first match was against Nat Sornsamran, a local Thai player.

After spending months visualising hungry opponents across the net ready to destroy me, my opening match was...

slightly underwhelming. Actually, it was more than that – it was downright bizarre.

For a start, Nat Sornsamran kept addressing me as 'sir'. I've heard of respecting one's opponent but this level of humility was unnerving. Then, in the warm-up, as the morning wind picked up, the image of my opponent manically chasing an uprooted umbrella around the court became surreal.

The wind soon became a gale, making the opening games an erratic affair strewn with errors. However, it didn't take too long to realise Nat really didn't have a backhand; he swatted it rather than hit it. His game wasn't up to the Futures level and it slowly unravelled in the wind. Before the hour, the match was over 6-1, 6-2 with my opponent performing a traditional Thai bow before shaking hands.

This was tennis's meritocracy at work – *anybody* is allowed to enter the Futures qualifying and have a go at a professional career. In most cases, players have worked their way through the tennis system and know when they are ready. However, there are always a few outliers – players new to the game – who throw themselves in at the deep end, usually to drown.

After the match, a devastated Nat lay down in a corner of the complex with his racquet bag draped across his face. He stayed motionless for over an hour as players walked past him. No one bothered speaking to him, no one particularly cared how he felt. This is just the way it is in the tennis world; the quality of your game determines the level of respect you earn. At a professional level, Nat didn't earn much. I never saw him the rest of the week, and he never played a professional event again.

For lunch, I ate pad Thai in the modern glass clubhouse. From my seat, I could see the Argentinian number five seed in my section of the draw being clubbed off the court by a left-handed Australian with an aggressive game. It was a classic contrast of styles. The top-spinning Argentinian was pinned so deep he was nearly touching the fence, while the burly Australian charged the net at every opportunity. The South American smashed his racquet into the back fence and screamed 'fuck!' as he crashed out of the tournament. With the seeded player gone, my section of the draw had just opened up (at least this is what I tried to convince myself).

By late afternoon, the wind had gone. The day's oppressive humidity was now a balmy pleasantness for my second-round match against the Korean, Gook-Hee Lee. A whole squad of Koreans had descended upon Bangkok, ranging from their Davis Cup team to the nation's promising juniors – all playing identical games. It was as if a factory line had run off a batch of superbly fit, baseline grinders, all with perfect techniques and grim expressions.

When I walked on court, two Korean coaches had already taken their positions in the small, metallic stand. Caps and dark sunglasses masked their thoughts. They made endless notes on clipboards, using pens that hung from strings around their necks. Of course, I couldn't know it at the time, but I would see one of these coaches again a year later, when the pressure – and the stakes – would be much, much higher.

In the warm-up, the Korean didn't miss a ball with his smooth groundstrokes. He was young, fit and deeply tanned. My plan was simple: rush him, hit him off the court and break his rhythm – do anything but let him get into his drilling routine.

I served and volleyed four times. I held to love. I was going to do everything the Korean least expected, and it seemed to set the tone for the next hour where I could do no wrong. It turned into one of those days where the sport seems so easy.

By the second set, my opponent was on the ropes. I even rushed the net behind my returns, anything to keep him under pressure. I served aces – a rarity for me – and my volleys raced off the green hard court for crisp winners. Lee looked confused, while his coaches let their pens hang from their necks and shouted encouragement.

I didn't dare blink until the last point was over (I was scared to think about winning…and choke). When the chair umpire called the final score 6-0, 6-1, I turned to the stand and gave a clenched fist to one of the academy coaches who had turned up to watch.

My Korean opponent silently shook my hand. Unlike the end of my match with Nat, this time there was no 'sir' and no traditional Thai bow. He slung his enormous Babolat racquet bag over his back and quietly left the court looking a beaten man. I assumed that Gook-Hee Lee would put this match behind him and find success in the future, but like Nat Sornsamran, he would never play another professional tennis match again.

This was a little hard to understand. Lee had all the strokes and had clearly been honing his game for years – so why throw the towel in so early? Maybe, in retrospect, some of the players weren't like me at all – weren't so enamoured with the idea of playing the circuit that they weren't in it for the long haul, no matter what.

I spoke to Andrew that evening, replaying the day's matches for him. 'The next one is the match that will show if you can get points. The others don't mean a thing!' he told me. I realised he was right. To fall in the last round of qualifying, even if I had won a couple of matches, would still mean *no* money and *no* opportunity to play for ATP points. Perhaps that is why they say to lose in the final round of Wimbledon qualifying is the most heartbreaking of all – instead of the fame and glory, you get…*nothing*.

* * * * *

The next morning, I was scheduled to play Dayne Kelly of Australia in the first match of the day. When the officials' morning briefing overran I found myself sitting on the court with my opponent. Whether it was to calm nerves, or simply finding himself alone with a fellow Antipodean in the middle of south-east Asia, my opponent wanted to chat. I was focused – I didn't want to make small talk. But how do you ignore someone talking directly to you?

'I just lost in the final of the junior ITF event in Darwin,' Kelly told me.

He was wearing a sleeveless shirt, revealing muscular arms that looked like they had seen hours in a gym. 'You're a junior?' I asked, genuinely surprised.

'Yeh, I'm only 16. My father works in construction, so I help out when I can. Also, I want to play in Europe and it gives me some money.'

The umpire eventually sauntered on to the court wearing sports sunglasses, regulation beige trousers and a dark polo shirt. He paused, surveyed his domain, and then promptly demanded that the local workmen repair his wind-beaten umbrella. This meant another ten-minute delay.

Word in the locker room was that, while Kelly was a good player, he had a suspect temperament and he could anger quickly. Having heard this, I made my plan: play him from the baseline, pin him back with topspin, and wait for his groundstrokes to break down. Did I not realise in the pros you don't get things for free?

Perhaps.

I never got the chance to find out. The glaring sun baked the court and turned the balls into missiles. From the opening, he pounded huge, leftie topspin serves, while his groundstrokes created angles, kicking away at speed once they left the court. I changed racquets three times looking for a tightly strung one to control the ball.

The metallic stands were empty; there would be no academy coaches to look to for support today.

At 6-1, 3-1 down, I realised months of preparation were going down the drain. I knew my game had limitations, but I didn't envisage being blown off the court like this, especially by a guy less than half my age. I changed my plan, hoping that it wasn't too late to get back into the match. I attacked the net myself (finally) – anything to keep the burly Australian from getting there first, but to no avail. He was simply too good.

Yesterday's wins seemed far away. They might as well not have happened. All my optimism before the match had been destroyed within an hour. There would be no dream start to my tour: no ATP points, and more tellingly, no illusion that it would be an easy ride up the rankings to the higher echelons of the game. I had to wonder if this was the realisation that made Nat Sornsamran and Gook-Hee Lee quit the game, there and then.

When we shook hands, I told Kelly, 'If you play like that in the main draw, you'll go well.'

My prediction was correct. Kelly earned his first ATP point and world ranking the next day when he beat my training partner, Kevin Kung, in the main draw. He had achieved a world ranking in only his third professional tournament, whereas I was still struggling after a lifetime of trying.

It was a sobering thought.

* * * * *

Later that evening killing time on the internet, I stumbled upon my name on a tennis forum. In some kind of underground tennis society, it seemed a group of tennis fanatics scoured the internet for results from professional tournaments, posting and discussing the performance of every British player on the circuit. They prided themselves in knowing obscure details and facts about the players – even giving some nicknames.

On their website, BritishTennis.activeboard.com, I read comments about my performance in Bangkok:

Johnnylad, '34-year-old Briton Gregory Howe (with no world ranking) attempted to qualify and won two rounds, but lost in round of 16. I wonder why he bothered?'

Drew, 'Probably on holiday and thought what the heck!!!'

There were no clues about their identities. I wondered what kind of person would devote their time to tracking down unknown players in remote corners of the world? I saw people hunched over laptops in darkened rooms in the dead of night, the sound of their keyboards the only noise. Reading other posts, it was clear they would often be at tournaments, providing live commentary to the rest of the society.

In a way, they reminded me of the bullfighting fans from Ernest Hemingway's first novel, *The Sun Also Rises*. These true fans, *aficionados*, sat apart from the masses and their simple fascination with the killing of the bull. Hemingway's *aficionados* were instead found away from the crowds, debating the finer points of a matador's style and daring. If Hemingway's novel had been based in today's tennis world rather than 1920s bullfighting, without a doubt, his *aficionados* would be the kind of fans who followed obscure British players around the world, obsessing about their results on internet forums.

* * * * *

A day later, Kevin Kung and I played in the first round of the doubles draw. Instead of playing with former top pro Andrew Ilie, Kevin had *me* as a doubles partner. We drew the number one players from the nearby Asian countries of Malaysia and Vietnam. Okay, not exactly tennis powerhouses, but the best player in any country was usually good. They would have years of Davis Cup experience to draw on and would benefit from a nation's funding and best coaches.

Our match was played in the stadium court. Rows of empty seats circled the playing arena – a grand total of six spectators sparsely spread out created an eerie silence. A couple of players sat in the stands, shirtless, working on their tans.

The dead atmosphere matched my energy. After training with the academy and playing three singles matches, I was exhausted and played a truly awful match. On one shot, I mis-hit and it went straight up into the air; there was laughter from the stands. Being mocked by one's peers wasn't a great feeling.

Afterwards, Kevin and I were left sitting on the centre court. The palm trees in the corner of the stadium swayed gently in the warm afternoon breeze. 'It's a shame Andrew Ilie couldn't have played with you,' I told Kevin.

Kevin smiled, 'Yeh – it would have been fun. Still, it's my first main-draw doubles match. I really enjoyed it. Don't worry, I'll see you in the locker room.' He picked up his black racquet bag and headed out of the stadium.

The kid had class.

* * * * *

In the handful of days I had been in Bangkok, I had seen the hotel, the tennis complex, the road and a lot of stray dogs. I didn't mind.

I craved to live the life of a touring pro – sightseeing wasn't on my to-do list. After my doubles loss, I had no more reason to be in south-east Asia. The tour was moving on – to another tournament, in another part of the world. I booked my flight for that evening.

As chance would have it, Kevin Kung wasn't hanging around Bangkok either. We shared one of the tennis academy's buses to the Bangkok International Airport, and loitered together in the airport waiting for our respective flights to be called. While sitting on the polished floor of gate 73 in the departure terminal, I asked Kevin how he found juggling school with his budding pro tennis career.

'I missed the first day of school yesterday,' Kevin explained. 'It was important. You find out what courses you're doing.'

Kevin explained how he took his studies seriously; he aimed to go to Columbia University in New York, one of the top-ten academic universities in the USA. 'I plan to combine my studies with tennis. I'm sure I'll get ATP points in the future.'

I told him he sounded like James Blake, who had studied at Harvard. 'But he only finished one year,' Kevin responded quickly. I wanted to point out Blake had completed two years of his degree, but with Kevin, it seemed a moot point. To not finish a university course was unthinkable. When I asked Kevin if he wanted to try to play on the tour, he replied, 'I'd rather go to university. I wouldn't like the continual struggle for money.'

I had to admire his maturity towards everything he did – when I was Kevin's age, the last thing on my mind was worrying about making money.

Kevin stood up, 'I've got to go.' He held out his hand and flashed his trademark smile. I watched him briskly walk away without turning back. It had been a real pleasure, and in some ways, an inspiration. He played aggressively – *without* fear. He went for his shots, fully believing he would make them, both on and off the court.

2

Rod Laver Country

Queensland

AUSTRALIA WAS next, and I was returning home. How could it be anything else? Sure, I played pro tennis with the initials of GBR (Great Britain) after my name, and I was born in the industrial city of Derby in midlands England. Yet, between the ages of 3 and 22 I had not left Australia's shores (save for a couple of brief trips to New Zealand). The country's psyche was deeply engrained within everything I did, including my tennis.

There was a delicious symbolism to the possibility of making ATP points in my hometown. Imagine that. Almost two decades since first seeing the ATP world rankings taped to the wall in the Gladstone clubhouse, I return to finally fulfil my dream: to put things right. It couldn't happen perfectly to script as Gladstone was not hosting any of the Futures events, but the nearby cities would do.

Yet, playing again in Australia after such a long time away brought mixed emotions. All my peers – the likes of former world number one, Pat Rafter – had moved on: were done with competitive tennis and had moved on to the next stages of their lives. Yet here I was, 34 and never a great player to start with, playing the Futures again. *He must be having a mid-life crisis.*

The following afternoon after leaving Bangkok, I walked into the Gladstone tennis club. It was where my tennis journey had begun, all those years ago. Andrew was with me – he was back home on holiday. I saw it as us turning back the clock, playing tennis together again on *our* courts. I'm sure Andrew just saw it as tennis training; he isn't into symbolic meanings.

Inside the club's small, brick office, Ken Hick was organising the day's coaching programme. Our old coach, Fred Munckton, had passed on, leaving Ken to solely lead tennis in Gladstone.

Ken was universally known as 'Hickey' (Australians need to abbreviate everything). A big man, he leaned back in his chair and placed his hands behind his head. Now in his late 40s, he had a permanently sunburnt complexion with the skin on his forearms freckled after a lifetime under the harsh Australian sun. Dressed in a white tennis outfit, his shirt tucked tightly over his stomach and into his shorts, old-school style, I had known this man my entire life and I swear I had never seen him dressed in anything else.

'Queensland is becoming the new Spain,' Ken said matter-of-factly when I queried him about what was happening with the game in Australia. 'Players will play tournaments every week. Every local tennis club will get money, but it will be based on *performance* (the *new* buzz word from Tennis Australia). So many juniors will have to be ranked if you want to get money.' His flat hand hovered in the air, as if to emphasise that this could go up...or down.

I was still considering the 'new Spain' comment. When I was growing up in the 1980s, if an Australian tennis coach had dared compare Australian tennis to the sport in Spain, they would have been lynched: burnt at the stake as a heretic. Nowadays, no one would blink an eye. In the tennis world's view, Aussie tennis was an old-world afterthought.

With his hands still behind his head, Ken continued. 'This year, the Australian Open made a loss. The states got no money and the staff in various states got cut, except Queensland. It's all down to the success of the women's WTA event in Brisbane,' Ken said proudly. 'At the start, like most tournaments, it ran at a loss, but this year it broke even. We had Sharapova, and

Hingis on her comeback made the semis. All the tickets were sold in advance, and all the sponsors jumped on board. It was a *big* success.'

I found it scary to think that just breaking even qualified as a major success in today's Australia. Had the sport fallen that far in the nation's sporting psyche?

Ken epitomised the local sporting hero: cricket, squash, tennis – he excelled at them all. He even had the ability to push the top Australian players whenever they turned up to play in his backyard. He was therefore my yardstick, one of the first adults for me to emulate – and aim for. However, he retired from playing before I got the chance to catch him; the sporting equivalent of trying to climb a ladder only to find the next rung had disappeared.

Ken walked into the small cafeteria and helped himself to a sports drink. 'It's good you're still playing,' he nodded to me while opening the lid of the bottle. 'You've got to play…while you've still got wheels.'

Andrew and I headed out to practise. Ken's comments hung in my thoughts. He had retired from playing as soon as he had sensed his 'wheels' were going; timing his departure before being caught by both time and the approaching pack. I was 34 years of age and had been mauled by a teenager only days ago. I had to wonder if I had left my run too late.

* * * * *

We were on the road two days later. Andrew and I borrowed our father's Mercedes for the four-hour journey north to Mackay. Along the way, the dry grasslands slowly changed to palm trees and dark green foliage as we crossed the Tropic of Capricorn into the wet and humid tropics. The drive was a good opportunity for me to persuade Andrew to play.

'I'm not signing in. I'm not playing Futures anymore unless I'm prepared. You're playing terrible, you're going to get killed anyway. So, *you* can sign in.'

It didn't look good.

Mackay was one of those places where nothing ever went right for me. As a junior cricketer, our city team travelled by bus to compete in a regional carnival. I got a terrible case of food poisoning. If I wasn't on the toilet, then I was feverishly standing for hours under a scorching sun. Then there was the tennis tournament where I played all day and gave myself a minor case of heat exhaustion. Once again, arriving into the humidity of Mackay, I'm not sure why I thought this time would be any different.

The sign-in for the qualifying draw always closes at precisely six o'clock the day before the matches begin. With five minutes to go, I went to find Andrew. He was refusing to go anywhere near the tournament desk. 'There are still a few spaces left. You can still sign in.' I think he was sick of hearing my pestering voice; he was the last player to register with about a minute to go before it closed.

We drew Australian players for our first matches. There was a good chance you would play an Australian, for the simple fact that only 11 foreigners had bothered to make the journey halfway across the world to a remote country town. As I signed in under Great Britain, I was officially one of these 11. Holding Futures tournaments in the middle of nowhere was often a deliberate attempt by federations to dissuade foreigners to make the effort. The more ATP points for local players, the better.

The aficionados on the internet tennis forum had spotted the Brits in the draw, with Johnnylad posting, 'Ed Corrie, Iain Atkinson and Gregory Howe trying their luck in qualifying here. Howe is the veteran that tried to qualify in Thailand a couple of weeks ago. Maybe he's on a round the world holiday!'

Thanks for that Johnnylad: veteran…holiday …*smart ass*.

* * * * *

My match the next day began in blazing midday heat. Although Australian, Michael Massih was of Lebanese background and eventually he would play for Lebanon in Davis Cup competitions.

Short in stature, he looked like he could run all day playing the role of a retriever.

From the warm-up I realised I was in trouble. When I held my racquet to serve, my hand was shaking, not from nerves but rather pure exhaustion. I had yet to recover from Bangkok and had flattened myself with days of plane and car travel. My legs were dead with lactic acid, making movement feel like running in quicksand. The sun was high in the sky, baking my head and back.

Michael Massih ran from side to side, flicking the ball back high over the net and deep into the court. I couldn't help but do the same, turning the rallies into tense, drawn-out affairs. The worse I felt, the fresher he looked. I lost the first set 6-4 with sweat pouring down my cap into my eyes. I knew I could win, but I just couldn't do anything about it. He would only kick his first serve in, sensing I was struggling – better for him to turn every point into a marathon.

I couldn't even tell you how long the match went – it seemed never ending. I inevitably lost, and by the end felt like getting every racquet I had…and smashing them into little pieces. I could handle losing, but being unable to give your best was beyond frustrating.

I was still simmering inside when Andrew walked on court for the last match of the day. Perhaps he could save the day; I was as excited for his match as for my own. If he could get a couple of wins under his belt, then maybe he'd join me on my travels. Just like old times: the Howe brothers on tour again.

From the beginning, I was shouting encouragement from behind the wire fence, sensing Andrew was struggling. His game was rusty, his feet always half a step behind.

At 4-1 down in the first set, Andrew was pulled wide. He tried to muscle his forehand and immediately clutched his side. 'I told you I shouldn't have played!' he shouted in my direction. 'I'm not listening to you anymore!' He angrily swung his racquet at the air in frustration – the racquet making a deep swooshing sound.

I watched helplessly as Andrew strode towards the net, shook his opponent's hand, and promptly walked off court straight to the car. As he was playing on the court at the far end of the complex beside the car park, I suddenly found myself sitting in the car and driving within the minute. We left the city limits of Mackay shortly after, hopefully not to return anytime soon.

* * * * *

Exactly a week later, I drove to the nearby city of Rockhampton for the second Futures event. Andrew was refusing to even come and watch, so I had driven up alone in the Mercedes that morning.

Rockhampton is synonymous with Rod Laver, one of the legends of the sport, and the only man to win the coveted 'Grand Slam' (all four majors in a calendar year) in the open era. Nicknamed 'The Rockhampton Rocket', he is tennis's equivalent of Babe Ruth. As long as no current man can perform the Grand Slam, then his aura and mystique will only continue to grow.

The city is country Australia at its roots. It is the beef capital of the nation – the surrounding areas home to cattle ranches and dairy farms. Driving down the main road that morning, I passed a huge statue of a bull raised on a pedestal in the centre island. The whole feel is one of laid-back, farmer country; you could understand why Laver turned out the way he did – honest, hardworking and unassuming. There is no statue of Laver on any pedestal to be found in the city.

In the tennis club itself, the front four courts remained a wonderful throwback to an era when the likes of Laver graced the playing areas. Behind the courts, an ancient corrugated iron roof shaded rows of seats. It wasn't difficult to imagine spectators dressed in grey suits and fedora hats, politely clapping players wielding antique wooden racquets while playing on the traditional crushed anthill courts of outback Australia.

Today the courts are hard, concrete and blue.

For my first-round match, I walked on to the first show court with my opponent, Michael Look from Australia. He was a modern Australian player – a grinding baseliner, wiry in build and America-bound. In a month, he was heading to UCLA in California on a tennis scholarship (if you want to combine academics with high-level tennis, there are *no* opportunities in Australia).

It's hard for me to describe this match; Michael Look was a confusing player. He defused any power I created with timing and efficiency, deflecting the ball at strange angles into the corners of the court. A comparison to the 'big cat', Miloslav Mecir, from the 1980s would be fair.

I ended up losing 6-4, 6-2. Every game felt close, yet games seemed to slip away. A break here, a break there, and then we were shaking hands at the net. I hadn't played badly but my opponent was always that little bit better on everything. Look – who would eventually reach 300 in the world – didn't blow you off court, but rather he deflected you off court, so that by the end I wasn't really sure how close the match actually was. It was an uncomfortable feeling.

After the match, I sat in the car for a while. The courts where Rod Laver had learnt the game sat directly in front. If they say you learn more from losses (like losing means you go home), then I'd now had three losses in a row, so I should have been learning lots. It wasn't time to panic – my opponents were good players and they weren't out of reach – but in the matches so far I was always a step behind.

Something would need to change, and soon. I didn't want to be a 34-year-old player with a ten-match losing streak on my hands. I could only imagine what the aficionados online would be saying then.

* * * * *

Back in Gladstone, I had a week to regroup.

Andrew had recorded my Mackay match on video. Watching, I mentioned that I thought I was playing pretty good. 'Who are you kidding?' came the reply. 'Look. You're leaning back on your forehand – you're trying to hit heavy and it's not working on these fast, hard courts. Your volleys stink and your footwork is lumbering. You're slow to the ball, so you're hitting a defensive slice – you've got to hit on the rise.'

We went to the local supermarket and bought a box of balls. Every day for that week, we took it in turns to do attacking drills: *Hit the short ball! Punch the volley! Keep moving forward. Why are you so slow?* We chose a court in the far corner of the Gladstone complex. It wouldn't have made any difference – the courts were always empty. We trained for two hours in the morning, and then an hour in the late afternoon. With every session, I could feel my confidence return.

The 2006 US Open was on television. Andre Agassi played his last match, losing to the German, Benjamin Becker. The denim shorts and the long hair were long gone. He looked old on court; his back had seized up and he hobbled between the points. It felt strange to watch Agassi wave to the crowd with tears in his eyes. He was only one year older than myself. I was still at school when the teenage Agassi had started on the tour. Now he was retired, while I felt I was just starting.

Every day after tennis I went to the local gym, called Lavers. Rod Laver's brother, Trevor, owned it. It was a squash complex in the 1980s. Now one squash court was the aerobic studio, while the second court and the upper viewing deck housed weight machines, stationary bikes and running machines.

I had known Trevor since my days as a junior; he used to help out on the Saturday morning fixtures. Like his famous sibling, Trevor had red hair and freckles. He had a thin, wiry build and had the reputation of being an amazing squash player in his youth.

'Do you get to go to Wimbledon?' Trevor asked me in the slow, laconic drawl of someone who had grown up in the Australian country. When I told him Andrew and I had been on centre court this year, and seen Roger Federer play, his eyes lit up. 'Rodney was over there this year too. They invited him. They also asked him to go to the US Open.' It was strange to hear the legendary Rod Laver being referred to as Rodney.

'He doesn't play so much anymore. He had a hip replacement, but he is doing an exhibition for Martina Navratilova in America after the US Open. We don't see him very often, but after the Australian Open he's coming back and we're going fishing for three days. He doesn't like to travel much if he can help it.'

The pride for his brother's achievements was obvious. There was never a hint of brotherly rivalry or jealousy from Trevor. If anything, I detected more of a sadness that his brother's fame meant he rarely saw his famous sibling.

Before I left, I asked Trevor if they were actually from Rockhampton – the inspiration behind his brother's famous nickname. 'Actually, we all grew up in a little place called Malborough,' Trevor replied. 'It was only when I was 12 that the family moved to nearby Rockhampton.'

So, the iconic Rod Laver, known around the world as the Rockhampton Rocket, was actually from Malborough. I guess the alliterations just worked better with the 'r' sound.

* * * * *

The final leg of the Queensland circuit was to be held near the Gold Coast. This was Australia's version of Miami and Los Angeles all rolled into one: platinum blonde hair, fake tans, cosmetic surgery, golden beaches and an underworld, drug problem. It was a seven-hour drive from Gladstone and like being on another planet. The tournament would be played at the Pat Cash Tennis Academy. Originally called the Cash-Hopper Academy, the second name was dropped two years previously after Gavin Hopper, the elite trainer and co-founder of the academy, was caught up in a highly public scandal.

My idol Pat Cash (the 1987 Wimbledon champion) was not around during the week, although the chequered headbands he once wore were on sale in the pro shop. I decided not to buy a Pat Cash headband; I'd once worn one as a kid in the 1980s, and was ridiculed mercilessly for wearing it.

On the day of the sign-in, all the practice courts were full. There were four players to a court, and the small gym and clubhouse housed a multitude of racquet bags, players, officials and hangers-on. There was more of an international feel to this event with players from Korea, Hong Kong, Barbados and the Pacific Islands joining the fair-skinned Brits from the previous weeks. The Gold Coast's nightlife and beaches were obviously a lot more alluring than the remote country towns of Mackay and Rockhampton.

With an hour to go in the qualifying sign-in, the queue was so long it ran outside the clubhouse. For the 64-man draw, over 100 players had signed in. I didn't bother waiting to watch the draw being made. Andrew and I found an empty court and had a quick hit – made quick because I had left my tennis shoes back in the hotel. Much to Andrew's disgust, I hit in my flip-flops. His side strain still didn't allow him to serve fully, so he didn't sign in. It wouldn't have made much difference; he would have missed the cut anyway.

I rang the tournament director that evening praying for a good draw, needing a win for my confidence. The Tennis Australia official cheerfully told me I would play the number five seed and 1,325 in the world, Stephen Donald. Perhaps the universe was testing me.

* * * * *

The next morning, Andrew and I ordered a coffee from the Pat Cash café and sat in the car. There was a chill in the air. The grey sky looked nothing like the postcard pictures of the sunny Gold Coast beaches with its iconic names like Surfers' Paradise. With the car park backing on to the courts, we had a view of all the early qualifying matches. One player stood out, rushing the net in a classic serve and volley style.

Luke Bourgeois was ranked 281 in the world – making him number eight in Australia behind the likes of Lleyton Hewitt, Mark Philippoussis and Wayne Arthurs. He had lost the previous week in the qualifying event for the US Open, and decided at the last minute to ask for a wildcard into the qualifying of the Hope Island event.

From the moment he walked on court, he looked like a seasoned pro. His face was partially covered by the hood from his dark grey warm-up jacket, while headphones blocked out the rest of the world. He looked like former world number one Patrick Rafter. The resemblance was uncanny, even down to the white zinc sunscreen spread across his nose. He appeared focused and purposeful as he strode on court to face a young English player, Ed Corrie.

I had played Bourgeois many years ago in a tournament in Melbourne when he was a promising junior. A decade later, I was still chasing my first ATP point, while he currently had 139 of them.

In the past couple of years, Tony Roche, who was coaching Roger Federer, had recruited him as a practice partner for the world number one. Training with Federer and staying in five-star hotels must have rubbed off on Bourgeois. Earlier on in the year in the Sydney ATP event, he had won through three qualifying rounds before losing a close match in the main draw to Romania's Andrei Pavel. After a decade on the tour, he was finally starting to make his move.

Sitting in the car looking down a row of courts, Bourgeois's quality stood out. While all the other players were rooted to the baseline – locked in a war of attrition with their opponent – he attacked every short ball with deliberate aggression. While the young Brit ran everything down, eventually the pressure was too overwhelming and the experience of the 28-year-old veteran paid off.

At midday, the loudspeaker announced the Howe–Donald match. We were scheduled on court ten, right in front of the clubhouse. I was first into the referee's office to collect the Wilson Australian Open balls, then first on to the court to secure the chair closest to the clubhouse (tennis players are superstitious – just ask Rafael Nadal). I arranged my water, sports drink, towel and racquets as I waited for my opponent to arrive.

Eventually Stephen Donald walked out on court dressed from head to toe in his matching Diadora tennis outfit: Italian designer shoes, socks, headband and sweatband. His outfit looked freshly pressed. Donald was the ninth-ranked junior in the world; he looked like a player going places.

Before he had even sat down, Donald had pulled out his mobile phone and was making a call. An official wearing dark sunglasses and a Tennis Australia hat promptly strode on to the court. In Australia, the land of 'fair play' and 'no bullshit', the official was having none of this prima donna behaviour on his court. What began as a quiet discussion suddenly became an audible drama for everyone in the clubhouse.

'The rule clearly states you can't talk on a mobile on the court!'

'Well, what do you want me to do? There are 15 Tourna grips sitting in the clubhouse.'

'You shouldn't even have the phone out here!'

'Where do you want me to leave it then?' Donald raised his hands in exasperation, looking for support from the growing number of spectators behind the fence.

'Leave it off the court!' The official, in a statement of finality, had already turned mid-sentence and was walking off the court.

Before the warm-up could begin, my opponent needed to change his clothes. He had obviously decided today could not be an all-white day. He promptly dropped his white Diadora shorts on court and changed them for a brown pair, albeit with exactly the same matching pattern. If it was indeed possible, he looked even better than before.

Behind the court, a muscular figure sat down on the grass in a cross-legged yoga position. A former world number 19, Jason Stoltenberg was employed by Tennis Australia as one of its performance coaches and had recently taken on the reins of Stephen Donald. At 36 years old, he still looked remarkably fit. His sports car with alloy wheels and spoiler was positioned prominently in the car park. In the juniors in Australia he was only a year older than myself, and I held him in the kind of awe a kid has for his peers who make it to the big time.

The match began as an edgy affair. Donald was a confidence player; when he was nervous he would push the ball, but with a lead his well-drilled groundstrokes became long and smooth. When he broke my serve at 2-2, his whole demeanour changed. He started chatting to players passing by behind the fence. His one-handed backhand began to resemble Stoltenberg's, with an impressive shoulder turn and a full follow-through. He hit with authority as I was dragged from one corner of the court to the other.

Things had changed though. After all the drilling with Andrew, I could stay with his baseline slugging. When he served for the first set, a subtle shift occurred. Point after point, the rallies grew longer and longer. Just as I had practised with Andrew, I then hit the short ball as hard as I could and charged the net. At break point, he slammed a backhand passing shot halfway up the net. In one fluid motion, Donald pulled a ball from his pocket, and launched it high over the car park (it was a beautiful follow-through).

While the ball was in mid-air, the same official in his floppy Tennis Australia hat nonchalantly opened the gate and strode across the court. In a voice loud enough for anyone in the clubhouse to hear, he stated matter-of-factly, 'Code violation, warning, ball abuse.' This time there was no reply as he turned and walked away.

Behind the court, the presence of Stoltenberg had become a magnet for the rest of the Australian coaching fraternity. While he stayed cross-legged on the ground, other state and national coaches grabbed chairs from the clubhouse and joined him in scrutinising one of the nation's top juniors. They looked on as every point became a slugfest with no one willing to back off.

At 3-3 in the tiebreak, I hit a passing shot I was sure would be a clean winner. Somehow, at full stretch, my opponent reached it and angled a volley winner. The iconic Australians of the past would have been proud of such a shot. 'Come on!' Donald shouted. He pumped his fist and turned to his coach. He screamed again, although more in my direction, when he won the first set moments later.

Although I had lost the first set, psychologically I felt I was edging ahead. When I approached the net again and hit a volley winner to break him, now it was my time to scream in his direction, 'Come on!'

His confident demeanour had gone. Ominous dark grey clouds loomed in the sky as thunder rumbled in the distance. After each lost point, my opponent started berating himself and throwing his racquet in disgust. 'Unbelievable,' he screamed after one missed shot. When I won the second set 6-3, Jason Stoltenberg quietly wrote in his notepad. The assortment of other Tennis Australia coaches looked on stony-faced.

Sitting down at one set all, the ninth best junior in the world looked slightly lost. Point for point, I was now outplaying my opponent. Then the dark clouds opened and flooded the court, abandoning play for the day.

* * * * *

I would like to report a fairytale ending to the match, but it did not happen. The next morning, Stephen Donald arrived on court looking visibly relaxed, even looking to chat as we walked on court. There were no coaches behind the court to scrutinise his play, and the dark skies of yesterday had been replaced with a crisp, sunny autumn day. The slow build-up of tension had vanished, meaning it was now simply his strokes versus mine. Donald won the final set 6-1 in 20 minutes. Today, he had worn his classic all-white outfit.

There is nothing set in stone to say how many losses it takes to officially be called a losing streak. And when you're in the middle of one, there's no way of knowing if you're at the beginning or the end: just ask American Vince Spadea who holds the ATP record of 21 straight defeats. I wasn't anywhere near his record, but I'll admit to being a little frightened of looking over my shoulder, just in case there was a Spadea-like losing streak lurking there with my name on it.

3

Operation Entebbe
East Africa

EMIRATES FLIGHT EK721 sat on the runway in Nairobi International Airport, Kenya. All of the European tourists, and most of the Africans, had departed in Nairobi. A dozen Ugandans were left waiting for the final leg of the journey. As the night sky slowly closed around the plane, the remaining passengers congregated into small groups throughout the aircraft and sung melancholic African harmonies.

Looking at the tennis calendar before my tour had begun, this was the circuit where I figured my best chance of a break-through lay: weaker African players, Europeans out of their comfort zones, and the hardships of the third world. If I could just keep it together, somewhere in the next few weeks an opportunity would present itself. When it came, I had better be ready.

When leaving Australia, I had an awful vision of arriving in the middle of the night in a dangerous African airport, alone, the only Westerner, with a bright green tennis bag on my back acting like a beacon for unwanted attention. I was so worried that I rang the tournament director in advance, a man named John Kasule. He said that he would meet me at the airport, 'Just to make sure that nothing happened at night.'

It was already 7pm. The Entebbe-bound plane was scheduled to arrive in Uganda in another three hours. Unlike my premonition though, I was not alone. At the last minute, my long-time girlfriend Sylvie (who was now working in Dubai for Emirates) managed to use her cabin crew status to get on to my flight. She would be with me for two days – hopefully long enough to see my first match.

I felt a little better...but not much.

A male Emirates cabin crew tapped me on my shoulder to get my attention. 'You're going to play a tennis event in Uganda, aren't you?' He looked excited and didn't even wait for my reply. 'There's another passenger who just got on. He's going to play the tour too!' He motioned to a young guy in his mid-20s a couple of rows back, who looked up suddenly. Maybe he too had visions of arriving in Africa alone.

'Are you playing the Futures in Uganda?' I asked him. Stupid question really, considering he was sitting beside a huge, bright blue racquet bag.

'Yeh. Are you playing the Futures too?' he asked – another stupid question (who, outside of the tennis world, knew about the Futures circuit?), but we were both just breaking the ice.

He came up and introduced himself as Aly Zaver, and said he was from Canada. His trip was worse than mine: Toronto, New York, Amsterdam, Nairobi, then seven hours in the airport before boarding the Emirates flight to Uganda.

'I only booked my flights a couple of days ago,' Aly told me. 'I didn't have time for the yellow fever injection, or to get malaria tablets.' He looked worried when I told him I had both. 'I'll just put loads of repellent on,' he reassured himself.

He explained that both his parents were from Uganda, but were forced to flee in the 1970s when the dictator Idi Amin demanded all Ugandans of Indian origin leave within 90 days... or die. When he saw the east African circuit on the calendar, it was an opportunity for him to see a bit of his heritage. I guess he didn't feel like he was returning home though; he too had rung John Kasule before his departure.

I was impressed with Aly. For me, he epitomised all the best values of the Futures player – a young man who was using tennis as a passport to see the world, compete, and along the way get a wealth of life experiences. Whether these experiences would be good or bad, it didn't necessarily matter. He would have good stories to tell the grandkids.

The brief flight from Kenya to Uganda flew across Lake Victoria, into Entebbe International Airport. The name Entebbe was synonymous with the 1973 hijacking of an Israeli airliner, a daring commando raid codenamed 'Operation Entebbe', and the pompous arrogance of Amin – the perfect ingredients for future Hollywood films.

Our plane taxied into the airport's only terminal. From my porthole window, I could see a small propeller plane descending through the darkness, the words Rwanda Express emblazoned on its side.

Waiting in the eerie fluorescent glow of the immigration queue at Entebbe Airport – with Sylvie and Aly from Canada – we stood amazed as one tennis player after another emerged from the small plane into the immigration queue. By the time the plane had emptied, there were as many tennis players in the airport as regular passengers – all of them coming from last week's Futures event in Rwanda.

John Kasule was waiting after immigration. He had expected a total of three people to be transported to the player hotel. Beside him, a shorter man eagerly held a little sign, 'Tennis Player – Gregory Howe'. Suddenly, 40km away from the capital city of Kampala, they were swamped with over a dozen tired tennis players demanding to know where their transport was to the player hotel. Did anyone care that no one had even rung for transport, or tell anybody in Uganda that they were coming? Hell no – that's the tournament's responsibility to be flexible… isn't it?

Half an hour later some taxis arrived and the players were divided among them. Sharing the taxi with Sylvie and I was a tall, 6ft 5in American, named George Barth. I had first met George way back in the late 1990s, and we had bumped into each other sporadically since.

I got on well with George; he was a kindred spirit. Two years older than myself at 36 (although you'd never know it with his youthful, clean-cut features), neither of us had to justify our lives to each other. While working as a tennis coach in Ohio, every year for the past two decades, he would pick a handful of far-off Futures in search of ATP points: Bangladesh, Senegal and Central America to name a few.

Tennis friendships are different than those you have in ordinary life. With people like George, I would practise and hang out with him for a few days and then we would say bye, see you around. No stress, no *we'll keep in touch* or any other heaviness. Just, see you around. A couple of years later in another corner of the world, we would unexpectedly run into each other again and the conversation and friendship would be picked up from where we had left it.

'Rwanda was a pretty boring place – nothing much happening,' George stated in his American Midwest accent. 'But, I'm still going to watch the film *Hotel Rwanda* when I get back to the States.'

The taxi raced along in the dark, swerving violently to miss pedestrians walking along the roadside and oncoming traffic. Maybe the road once had a centre line, but it certainly didn't any more. The driver weaved in and out of the traffic making sure he dodged the oncoming lights. Sylvie was so tired from overnight flights that she slept the whole journey, her head nodding to the rhythm of the road. But George, in the front seat, and myself behind the driver, kept our eyes glued to the road, pausing our conversation every time our taxi overtook a dilapidated truck.

'Where have you played this year?' I asked over the whine of the engine. It was always good to pick other players' ideas on their itineraries, so in the future you would know yourself which tournaments to play.

'I played Costa Rica at the start of the year – it was okay, nothing special. And I went well in Senegal a couple of months ago.' I asked George if he recommended the west African country. 'Yeh. It was fine – a typical African country. I didn't have any problems.' I took this comment with a pinch of salt. If players played well in the tournament, then they might feel the biggest hellhole on earth was good.

'Do you know any French?' I asked him.

'No. Everybody speaks English wherever you go.'

The driver managed to get stuck close behind an ancient truck pumping out black exhaust fumes. George was getting a face full of it. The taxi bobbed back and forth, looking for an opportunity to overtake. George pulled his shirt up over his nose, 'Can you move away from the truck?' Our driver looked bewildered. 'Move away! Move away!' George made a pushing gesture with his hand. This time he understood and the taxi decelerated.

'Are you going to Kenya too?' I asked George.

'No. Two weeks is enough. I figure that if it hasn't happened for me in two weeks, then it's not going to happen. I might play Ghana next month though. It's on its own, so it might be pretty weak. And I was looking at Iran after that.' I told him I thought Americans were banned from entering the Islamic Republic. 'I don't know, probably. I don't even know if we even have an embassy over there. One thing's for sure though – I'm going nowhere near Nigeria.' Among the locker room banter, stories of violence and muggings of tennis players in Lagos and Benin City had been circulating.

The battered white taxi eventually pulled in front of a sign saying 'Holiday Express Hotel'. The centre of Kampala was utter mayhem. Mopeds weaved in and out of the gridlock with everyone beeping their car horns at once. The pavements were packed with people, while armed soldiers in camouflaged fatigues stood on street corners. A Ugandan teenage girl boldly walked up to one of the Romanian players, taking his arm, 'I'll be your escort tonight!' A moment of panic spread across the Romanian's face as he shrugged his arm free.

The scene in the hotel foyer matched the chaos of the street outside. John Kasule stood in the semi-darkness, shrugging his shoulders, remonstrating with the hotel staff. The eastern

Europeans stood around giving dark looks and cursing under their breath. 'This is fucking shit,' came an English accent.

'Well, where the hell are we meant to sleep tonight?' George asked me, sauntering over with a resigned smile on his face that suggested he knew all along this would happen. 'They forgot to book hotel rooms. There are no rooms left. What are you going to do?'

I knew what I was going to do. I had booked a double room over a week ago and confirmed it – to hell with everyone else if they couldn't organise themselves. I forced my way through the crowd to the reception desk.

'I've got a room booked.'

The hotel receptionist put out his hand and gave me a cold, weak handshake. He looked nervous, as if awaiting another tirade of abuse.

'I'm sorry. We're full tonight.'

'But I made my booking a week ago!'

'I'm sorry. We didn't know how many of you were coming. We just gave it away.' The players in the lead taxis had raced to the hotel and had been given my room. If I had learnt anything in my brief time in Africa so far, it was that being well organised counted for nothing.

It was beyond midnight by the time we reached a second hotel, the College Inn, after another chaotic ride through night-time Kampala. Sylvie fell asleep on the bed in her travel clothes. I lay on my bed, listening to the noise from the street below. Trucks roared past and the car horns never wavered.

Just keep it together.

* * * * *

A full day later, all three of us were together in a taxi again heading to the Lugogo Tennis Club for the first round of qualifying. The Lugogo sports complex was reputedly Kampala's sporting jewel with football fields, basketball courts and even a cricket oval. This was pretty impressive considering the country couldn't even repair the crater-sized potholes on their roads.

Consistent with my African experience so far, we predictably got the only taxi driver in Kampala who couldn't find it.

'Lugogo! Lu-go-go!' George demanded of the driver, resorting to the anglophile stereotype of breaking words into syllables and speaking louder to get his point across.

'Yes. Lugogo. No problem.'

George turned around to me and spoke loudly enough so the driver could hear, 'He hasn't got a clue, has he?'

We eventually spotted the Lugogo Tennis Club's concrete walls in the distance. It could only have been a tennis club – the walls and corrugated iron roofs were painted a traditional dark green. Even in Uganda, tennis clubs like to imagine they are Wimbledon.

Beside the tennis courts was the green expanse of a cricket oval: a nostalgic throwback to the days of the British Empire. A billboard advertised an international cricket match between Uganda and Kenya scheduled for Sunday. I thought of how nice it would be to have the refined atmosphere of a cricket game drifting across from next door.

The Kenyan cricketers were warming up on the oval. Their bodies were different than those of the tennis players: thick and muscular, but heavier and slower too. It was hard to gauge who were the better athletes – like comparing an Arabian to a Thoroughbred. Cricket was my first sport as a youth before tennis took over. If I had continued as an opening bowler, perhaps now I would be thicker and more muscular, heavier and slower.

By midday, I had seen Aly and big George both dumped out in round one of qualifying. It was a long way to travel for both of them, only to be knocked out in the first morning's play. After my recent string of losses, I desperately did not want to join them.

A small crowd of Ugandans had settled in on centre court for the upcoming match between local boy, Ronald Semanda, and one Gregory Howe of Great Britain. Sylvie sat alone in the rear stand. If that section had been designated for the 'away' crowd, then Sylvie was my lone supporter. Aly Zaver dejectedly sat alone in a corner of the concrete stand, wondering what had gone wrong.

Semanda walked on court clutching two blue Babolat racquets (likely the equivalent of a small fortune in Uganda). Like many of the locals I had seen, he was short and stocky in build. At 17 years old, he was a real Ugandan fairytale. A coach had told me that as an orphan, both himself and his siblings had their tennis and schooling funded by a foreign benefactor. Next week, he would go to England to further his education and tennis. The small crowd was already trying to get behind him, shouting encouragement.

My opponent won the toss, elected to serve, and promptly won the first eight points of the match. Everything I hit flew long in the dry, rarefied air of Kampala. After the last of these sprayed over the baseline, I turned to Sylvie, sitting in the stands in the position of what would have been the royal box at Wimbledon, and sarcastically told her, 'It's looking good again.' Sylvie had obviously been studying the tennis girlfriends on television – looking back without emotion.

The small crowd were getting behind the local player at every opportunity. But, their boy was nervous too. His serve deserted him and that allowed me equalise, and then pull ahead. I was a heavyweight squaring up against a flyweight; my extra weight of shot meant I was controlling every rally. By the time I had won the first set the crowd had gone silent. I gave Sylvie a clenched fist and got a smile in return.

Three European girls, stereotypical backpackers with short shorts (and backpacks) joined the crowd from the street. With the Ugandan tennis player struggling, the local men's attention quickly turned to the new spectators with every male in the stand suddenly peacocking. Most likely the foreign girls would have gotten their attention even if Semanda had suddenly metamorphosed into Roger Federer.

Serving for the match at 5-2 in the second set, I rushed the net. Twisting to drive a forehand volley, out of nowhere I felt a flash of pain in my abdomen. Semanda raced over and whipped the ball past me. The crowd erupted, their shouting reverberating loudly off the corrugated iron roof. A shy smile appeared on my opponent's face.

I gingerly walked back to the baseline, careful not to appear injured to either the crowd or my opponent. The pain had disappeared as quickly as it had arrived, like a lightning bolt that never touched the ground. *Perhaps it was nothing.* I had a match to win and five weeks in Africa ahead of me. *Yeh…it was nothing.*

When Semanda's high backhand return floated in the air on my first match point, I raced in again and smashed as hard as I could. The ball spun off my opponent's racquet, floating wide into the stands. Relief swept over me – my first win in over a month. A couple more first-round losses and the panic would have really set in.

'Tough match,' I told the teenage Ugandan at the traditional handshake. Several of the Ugandan coaches would later tell me that they thought he had played the best out of the local players. Apparently, the crowd hadn't finished with the match. When I went to fetch my sports towel from the end of the court, it had disappeared – a souvenir for one of the spectators.

George had watched the last few games. 'Good job,' he congratulated me. He was obviously disappointed with his first-round exit, but sportingly said his Russian opponent had played well. 'Hey, do you want to go get some food?'

At this point, a top pro would have been in the physio room getting the injury checked. But not me – I was too high on emotion, feeling pretty good about myself. Instead, George, Sylvie and myself headed across the street to an upmarket coffee shop.

After coffee, George rushed off to change his flights. He couldn't wait to get back to the States, and while I didn't see him again, I figured that we would catch up again soon somewhere on tour. Sylvie also left that evening to return to her cabin crew job, John Kasule organising her a 'safe' taxi to take her to the airport.

Although I was now alone, at least I would have my old sports towel for tomorrow's match. It magically reappeared on centre court, five hours later in the exact same spot that I had left it. Strange things seemed to happen in Africa.

* * * * *

Waking up the next morning, I couldn't get out of bed without rolling over and sort of falling over the side. Trying to raise my legs brought a disturbingly dull pain. *It'll be okay: the physio will fix it.*

At the Lugogo club, the doctor and physiotherapist shared the same concrete hut as the re-stringer, an old bed sheet hanging off the ceiling separating everyone. The sheet was ridiculously short, so anyone waiting for a re-string could see the patient as they lay on the treatment table.

The physiotherapist was a short, muscular man with a completely shaven head and a soft, innocent-looking face. He spoke his English in a quiet whisper. As I lay on the bench behind the sheet, he started poking his fingers into the side of the muscle in rapid movements. This was just what I needed – African witchcraft (still, it made my old towel reappear). It was so painful I had to clench my teeth and hold my hand over my mouth to stop myself from swearing. But it worked and I tipped him well in Ugandan shillings.

I hopped off the treatment table and walked straight out on to court. Here I was again – just like in Bangkok – in the last round of qualifying. Only this time I was up against Ed Seator of Great Britain: world number 1,323.

It was a typically hot, steamy African day. On the outside courts, there was no stand or seating, so the local spectators clung on to the fences. In Africa, watching tennis was treated the same as watching a football match – spectator involvement would be high. The international cricket match next door was underway. Unbelievably loud rap music blared out of the huge speakers on top of the concrete stadium, aiming for the couple of hundred spectators in the concrete stands, but probably reaching distant neighbourhoods.

Seator strode past me to the far chair. He pulled out two oversize sweatbands from an enormous red kit bag. There was a sense of urgency about him, a hurried, forward-leaning way of doing things. He approached the umpire, shouting over the din coming from the cricket. 'Can you do something about the music?' The chair umpire was the oldest in the Ugandan umpiring cohort on show today – doing a good Morgan Freeman impression.

'I'm sorry,' came the umpire's unhurried and calm response. 'It's not in our control.'

Seator was crafty. I felt I was overpowering him, but somehow always found myself down in every game. He didn't have a big shot, instead relying on subtle changes of direction and pace: quiet weapons that were hard to pinpoint among the deafening noise. Twenty minutes later the first set had gone: 6-1. I wasn't even sweating.

Sitting down at the change of ends, I had visions of Bangkok all over again where the match slipped away before I knew it. I pictured Andrew laughing at me over the phone as I tried to explain another last-round-of-qualifying collapse. *The same thing happened – the guy was just too good!*

A 50 Cent album commenced on the loudspeaker, regularly mixing profanities with lyrics. The locals clung to the fence behind the baseline. 'Come on!' a local teenager urged me as I walked to the baseline. 'I'm coming! I'm coming!' I replied, not making any sense, but getting the idea across.

The second set turned about half an hour later. On a break point, Seator served wide and a long, slow rally began. Out of nowhere, his forehand flew about three metres long. He pulled a ball out of his pocket and smashed it into the side fence, then hurled his racquet into his chair, watching it bounce off. 'Can't you do something about the music!' he screamed. The old umpire shrugged his shoulders.

Seator didn't sit down. Instead, he stormed past the umpire screaming something inaudible above the music. His racquet was flung horizontally as hard as he could into the fence. He reached the gate and ripped it open, forcing the locals hanging on to the fence to jump back surprised. He then walked straight off the court.

'What's going on?' I asked the umpire, who was staring transfixed at the open gate.

'I don't know. Maybe he's going to the referee's office.'

Moments later, Seator came storming back on court in furious conversation with the Slovenian ITF referee. It was hard to tell who was looking more irritated. Today had seen a series of blow-ups and warnings, and by now the referee was looking thoroughly fed up with constantly being called on court. With Seator still following him screaming about the music, the referee in mid-court shouted to the umpire, 'Did he have permission to leave the court?'

'No.'

At this, my opponent threw his arms about as he clutched his hat. He too turned to the umpire. 'What do you mean? I yelled it as I walked past you. I said I was getting the referee!' 50 Cent's chorus kicked in. Seator was shouting. The referee was looking stern. I sat on my chair along with the locals clinging to the fence waiting for the word 'default' to be issued.

The referee turned to Seator, who perhaps now was wondering exactly what possessed him to walk off court. 'You did *not* have permission to leave the court. It's clear.' He turned to the chair umpire, 'Issue him with a warning for unsportsmanlike behaviour.'

I caught up with the departing Slovenian referee at the service line. 'What exactly is the rule for leaving the court *without permission*?' I demanded, stressing the final two words. 'It's unsportsmanlike conduct,' he said, his face now red in contrast with his white hair. 'And that's why it's *only* a warning!' With that, he left the court and bolted the gate shut. I wasn't entirely convinced, but I was up a break with an opponent who was going crazy.

Shortly after, on set point, Seator blasted his return about four metres long; I'm not sure he believed it would ever go in.

In the third set, there was no more shouting. The match turned into a tight baseline duel with long defensive rallies and no one willing to give an inch. At two games apiece, I had a break point – this was my moment. Here was my chance to move into the main draw, to be within one step of my dream.

Whatever happens, be aggressive.

On Seator's serve, I gave myself room and ripped a forehand. He had moved in expecting a weak return and was caught in no-man's land. My ball sailed past him…' Out!' Morgan Freeman in the chair was holding up two fingers about an inch apart. The Englishman turned his hat backwards and beat his clenched fist on to his chest.

I had my opportunity…and had blown it. Quality opponents don't give second chances and Seator was one hell of a rugged competitor. He won the final set 6-3 to qualify for the main draw.

Later that night, I phoned Andrew in Australia and tried to explain the failure. 'You're just throwing away points!' came his reply. 'I can picture what happened. In the third set, he played aggressively, and you began to push the ball. It happens every time.' I tried in vain to tell him if only my big forehand had gone in.

If only.

* * * * *

Two days later, I arrived at the Lugogo Club to find Seator destroying the Ugandan number one, Patrick Ochan, 6-0, 6-1. The nervous Ochan sprayed balls all over the court in front of his home supporters. I couldn't help picturing myself out there, playing and winning my first ATP point.

I left quickly to the coffee shop, my sanctuary amid the chaos of Kampala. The Ugandan waiters watched the tennis during their lunch breaks, treating players as minor celebrities whenever one of them ventured into their workplace. Over a decadently Western cappuccino, I scanned the local newspapers looking for articles about the tennis.

In today's *Daily Monitor – Truth Every Day*, the bold headline 'The Death of Tennis in Uganda' cast a dark shadow over Uganda's first professional tournament. The paper seemed to be east Africa's answer to the *News of the World* or *The Sun* in England – sensationalist and trashy.

It appeared there was a whistle-blower within the Ugandan Tennis Federation (UTA). The whole article accused the federation of corruption and incompetence (not a great surprise, to be honest). It reported that the UTA got $4,000 from the ITF annually in the form of money and equipment, but that 'reports have…been making rounds that some of this ITF equipment ends up in Kampala's top sports equipment stores.' The attack continued, 'UTA carries out its activities in a room… no computer, one wonders how they keep their records and they have no telephone line. This, it has been revealed, keeps away top officials from sitting in the office.'

I knew this room as the referee's office. The *Daily Monitor* wasn't lying – it was indeed a sparse room with only a large wooden table that held an enormous, archaic printer that looked like it had served time under Idi Amin's reign. Ironically, that morning all the players had turned up to find the ITF referee sitting glumly outside the office. There was a huge padlock on the door and he was locked out. The only person with a key was running late after someone had smashed into his car in the traffic chaos. Once the door was opened, the lone printer then died, forcing the Slovenian referee to write the order of play out by hand and pin it on the notice board.

It was hard to disagree with the *Daily Monitor – Truth Every Day*'s comments.

* * * * *

I didn't touch my racquets again in Uganda. My abdominal strain felt like someone sticking in a knife every time I moved. I signed into the doubles with Aly Zaver (more out of hope than anything else) and it was probably a good thing that we didn't get into the draw.

I booked a taxi for the rest of the day to travel all over Kampala, getting money changed and flights moved forward. The taxi was constantly searched for bombs – mirrors attached to sticks would be routinely passed under the car. In Uganda, there was a constant sense that something was about to happen; military trucks transporting camouflaged soldiers were a common sight. I often wondered what was happening that I didn't know about.

* * * * *

I checked out of the Holiday Express Hotel in the early morning of the next day. I found Aly sitting in a pitch-black hotel foyer, waiting for a taxi to the bus station. A tennis coach promised him that the bus journey to Mombasa, on the Kenyan coast, was first-rate. In passing through the African bush, he would see lots of exotic wildlife. He paid $80 for his round-trip bus ticket that would take almost a whole day's travel.

My taxi driver to Entebbe International Airport, named Jimmy, was actually a tennis coach at the Lugogo Tennis Club. He was moonlighting as a taxi driver for the tournament's duration to earn some extra money (giving players the premium rate). He drove through the dark complaining about life in Uganda and telling me his plans to leave to England.

At the airport security barrier, the soldiers spotted that Jimmy wasn't wearing his seatbelt – pulling the car over and questioning him, looking for money as a bribe. Jimmy told them that the chief of police owned the car and that he was a regular at the Lugogo Tennis Club. They begrudgingly waved us through.

Once in the terminal, I asked the Kenyan Airways girl at the check-in counter to look at her copy of the *New Vision*, another national newspaper. Turning to the back page, there was a colour picture of Ed Seator and his first-round victim, the Ugandan Patrick Ochan. I couldn't believe it – the image could have been of me with the article reporting a Gregory Howe victory. I handed the paper back. I didn't need any more reminders of my constant failure to escape the qualifying.

* * * * *

Thirty minutes later, I was sitting on a plastic chair in Entebbe International Airport. I could see the single runway, flanked by lush green grass as it ran towards the banks of Lake Victoria. In the film, *The Last King of Scotland*, this scene was one of the final shots as the fictional English doctor escaped from Idi Amin's Uganda.

My contemplations were broken when two young English players, Joe Cooper and Alex Johnston, strolled across with their huge tennis bags strapped to their backs. We were all on the one flight heading towards Kenya this morning and decided to travel together. Barely out of their teens, they were new to international travel. Everything they did seemed to be either a fascinating discovery or an accidental mishap (usually more of the latter).

'Hey, look. They forgot our eating trays,' Alex pointed out to me once we were in the Kenyan Airways plane. We were all sitting in the exit aisle where the trays were hidden in the armrests. 'What's behind that curtain?' came the next question. Directly in front of us was the business-class section.

'I've heard in business class they've got seats that go flat, so you can completely lie down,' informed Joe.

'Yeh – if you're a midget,' joked Alex.

These guys were amazing. They couldn't locate business class in an aeroplane, but in the last month they had travelled throughout Africa in countries like Sudan, Rwanda and Uganda without a second thought – a journey that would send even experienced travellers into a panic. This was one of the wonderful things about the Futures tour; it gave people who didn't have a clue about travel, a purpose, and then the sense that nothing could ever go wrong. *No problem. It's a pro tournament – the ITF will take care of everything.*

That said, the rest of the journey was ridiculous: a little girl tried to pickpocket Alex's mobile phone; neither of them had enough cash to pay for the onward visa; my bag was temporarily lost in Nairobi Airport and then only thrown into the hold after the plane was taxiing to the runway; and after finally making it to Mombasa, on the Kenyan coast, we then got lost in the maze of streets that made up Mombasa and had to twice double back to the hotel for directions.

I have to admit though, in the end, we made it.

By the afternoon, Alex, Joe and myself finally arrived in front of the green-walled Mombasa Sports Club. Entering the clubhouse was like stepping back in time to an era when the British ruled most of Africa. The clubhouse was first built in the 1890s. Not much had changed since. Large fans swung lazily from high ceilings and everything from the clubhouse to the changing rooms was made of a dark, brown wood. Framed black and white photographs lined the corridors, freezing the clubhouse and its members from the 19th century in time.

Outside the clubhouse were cane chairs and tables overlooking an immaculate cricket oval. I had heard that it was the only international cricket ground that had a tree within its playing area, and sure enough, a huge oak tree sat in the middle of the clipped green lawns. It wasn't too difficult in one's mind to travel back a century to a time when local servants served English gentlemen and their ladies afternoon tea as they watched a cricket match unfold before them. I couldn't imagine them blaring out 50 Cent lyrics like in Uganda.

If the clubhouse and cricket oval were elegant, then the tennis courts were most definitely not. One wall was all corrugated iron, standing vertically and being held together by wire, like something you would find in a shanty town. As for the tennis courts, the ITF fact sheet had stated 'hard court', but this was slightly misleading. I had heard of stories of Futures in Africa being played on dried cow manure that stunk when it got wet, and Mombasa's sandpaper-rough, patchy-grey courts were just as unique. Each court had obviously been laid in huge blocks as large gaps ran throughout the court. For the rest of the week, players would have to jump over the gaps for fear of twisting an ankle.

We had barely started hitting when a heavily set African woman emerged through the corrugated iron fence, approaching us holding an arm up in the air.

'What do you think she wants?' asked Joe.

The woman came closer, slightly out of breath. 'I'm sorry to interrupt your practice…I heard there were tennis players here…and I wanted to ask you a few…questions.' She broke the myth that all Kenyans were natural runners.

'I'm a reporter with *The Standard* – Kenya's *biggest* paper [there was a pause, whether for dramatic effect or to allow her to catch her breath, I wasn't sure] and I'm covering the tennis this week.' Upon hearing this, Alex joined Joe and myself, grinning at the prospect of an interview.

'How you find the heat?' the woman asked straight away. Clearly, she already had her angle.

Joe looked puzzled and peered up at the sky. It was overcast and quite cool. 'Hey?' Alex muttered.

The reporter continued, 'Often players from Europe come here, and they can't cope with the heat. It gets very hot here you know.'

Joe and Alex looked at each other, lost for words. The interview was going nowhere. I wanted to see our comments in the sports section…not the waste paper bin.

'Well, you have to understand that we've been in Africa for weeks. We're used to the conditions,' I stated. The reporter scribbled frantically, making me feel pleased with my explanation.

'Do you think you'll make it then?' she asked.

This caught me by surprise. What did she mean – make it as a professional? 'No chance,' I laughed.

'So, you don't believe you'll make it through the week?' I was confused – was she talking about the heat again? Joe and Alex started sniggering in the background (like they did any better).

'That's fine. I'll let you get back to your practice.' As she turned to go, I asked her if my comments would be in the newspaper. 'Definitely, in tomorrow's *Standard*.' She confirmed this with a nod. 'There'll be a photographer. He'll be here in 30 minutes.' She left through the corrugated iron exit.

The photographer failed to materialise, and there would be no mention of us in the following day's *Standard*. In hindsight, I realised I should have told her that we thought we were going to die in Mombasa's heat, or at least go missing in one of the ravines running under our feet. Instead, the only tennis article would state that Christian Vitulli, Kenyan number one and the son of the tournament director, would receive a wildcard into the main draw.

After hitting with Joe and Alex for a couple of minutes on perhaps the world's slowest courts, I left for the fitness room. Past the cricket oval, yet before the rugby and hockey fields, I found a small hut. There was a large office fan and an assortment of free weights. I sat on an ancient, steel stationary bike that looked like it should have been in the club's black and white photographs. For the next hour, I reflected on my day that had begun in Uganda. It had been organised chaos, but at least I was here. Aly Zaver would just be leaving Nairobi on his bus with a night of travel to look forward to.

I wondered which *wild* animals he had seen.

* * * * *

The next morning, I arrived early in the Mombasa Sporting Club to find Aly sitting alone in the middle of the clubhouse, surrounded by his bags. He was still dressed in his jeans and long white sports shirt. After he had discovered that malaria was prevalent on the Kenyan coast, he wore his long sleeves everywhere and threw a fit if a mosquito came close by.

When he saw me, he jumped up, 'Hey dude. Oh, thank God I've found someone. I haven't seen anyone, and I've been here since dawn. I was starting to get worried.' His words poured out and he looked stressed after his travels. He put his palm to his temple as if to stop a headache.

'Dude, I tell you,' Aly blurted out when I asked which animals he'd seen. 'The whole trip I saw a goat…and a chicken.'

He was literally spitting out his words. 'Wait till I get back to Uganda and speak to that coach.' He threw his hands up in exasperation before going on.

'Twenty-four hours, and the whole time I was scared stiff. I tried to sleep, and I opened my eyes and this guy was this far from my face, just staring at me.' He demonstrated by separating his hands a couple of inches apart. 'I tell you dude – I freaked out and raced to the back of the bus. The rest of the trip I held my racquet bag strapped to my chest and kept my eyes wide open.'

Aly and I went to practise. Predictably, the hit was a mess. He had a James Blake kind of game where he tried to run around and hit everything with rapid-fire forehands. Like the flashy American, if his main weapon was misfiring, then things got bad…real quick. The grey, sandpaper-rough courts in Mombasa were so slow that the ball just seemed to sit up and hover in mid-air. On many shots, Aly was already through his swing before the ball had reached him, shanking the ball into the next court. After every mishit, he got more and more agitated – threatening to hurl his classic, burgundy-coloured Head Prestige racquet into the concrete wall behind the baseline.

I signalled to him to stop and get a drink. He was too wound up to drink. 'I get down on myself too quickly,' Aly admitted while violently plucking the strings on his racquet. After a week to stew over his first-round loss in Uganda, followed by solitary confinement on an African bus, Aly's confidence was gone and his nerves were frayed. I changed the subject, asking him about his Head Prestige racquets that looked like the early prototypes from the 1980s.

'I've had them since I was 14 years old. They're great – a lot of the top players still use them, and they just paint them up to look like other racquets.' I told him I had recently seen Tommy Haas's racquet, which was identical to Aly's.

'I had those blue Babolats until about a month ago. But, I lost a match in a Canadian tournament, went nuts, and smashed them. These Heads were all I had left, so I started using them. They still feel pretty good.'

Aly pulled a small book from his racquet bag. 'My uncle is sort of a motivational guru back in Canada. I've been following his steps for goal setting.' He showed me how the little book took you step by step through goal setting, visualisation and being positive. The pages became blank after the goal-setting section. 'I was doing them up until I came to Africa. Then, I don't know…I'm just finding it hard to stay positive at the moment.'

We returned to the clubhouse where a local power failure had left it in darkness. As we sat in the shadows looking out for mosquitoes, perhaps we both sensed that the writing was on the wall for us in Kenya. Every time I moved, I could feel a sharp pull in my abdomen. As for Aly, his day got even worse. The player hotel was fully booked for the next two days, forcing him to sleep on the floor between the beds of two Indian players. It would be hard for him to visualise positive images while sleeping on a cold, concrete floor.

* * * * *

I had entered the qualifying draw hoping to play a Kenyan and bluff my way through. Instead, I got an experienced Romanian on centre court. When tennis draws are made, the universe always seems to know when you're taking short-cuts.

The Mombasa Sports Club's stadium court was no different than any of the other concrete courts, except it had a small, metallic stand running alongside one side of the court. Playing on the show court wasn't what I wanted; I hadn't even tried running since my match a week ago in Uganda. I didn't wish to embarrass myself in front of spectators expecting to see professional tennis.

Everything about my Romanian opponent, Viorel-Catalin Ciobanu, looked tough: a short, serious haircut, muscular walk and a typical eastern European demeanour. His racquet bag was faded and worn, looking battle-hardened. He had made the quarter-finals in the Rwandan tournament a fortnight ago and was slowly moving up the rankings.

My bluffing lasted as long as the warm-up. As soon as the match began and my opponent hit the ball into the corners, I could only watch it go by. The first set was gone in about 15 minutes. My opponent looked disgusted – perhaps he thought I had just given up. The few spectators had disappeared and even the ball boys looked disinterested. At one stage, the two ball boys were together at the back of the court, playing football with the ball as Ciobanu waited for the balls to serve.

The ball boys were the poorest kids I had ever witnessed in all my travels. None had shoes and their clothes looked old and ragged. The club had recruited them from the poor neighbourhoods in Mombasa to give them an opportunity to earn tips and money for their families. After a whole day in the sun throwing balls back and forth, the quality of their service matched the quality of my play.

If I hadn't scraped a couple of games early in the second set, I would have retired before the end (not wanting a double bagel on my record). Instead I had to endure a no-look handshake from the Romanian after losing 6-0, 6-2.

My whole African tour was in tatters. This was the circuit I had targeted to make ATP points on, and now two tournaments were gone and I was struggling just to run.

Aly Zaver didn't fare any better. He'd lost earlier that day, and had now taken two bad losses in his African adventure. He looked thoroughly disenchanted by the end of his match. I doubt he wrote any more in his uncle's little goal-setting book; he still had his return bus journey back to Uganda to look forward to.

Some of the players were heading to White Sands, the tourist beaches of Mombasa. I didn't join them – being injured had ruined my spirits. Instead, I decided to head to the internet café to change flights and get out immediately.

In Mombasa, a trip to the internet café meant outrunning the well-organised groups of child beggars who patrolled the city's main street. Some were badly disabled, using wooden crutches and little makeshift karts to mobilise themselves.

Early on in my stay, I couldn't understand how I always managed to find myself surrounded by them; there weren't enough of them to watch the entire street. Then I discovered that perched on a concrete block in the centre traffic island was an older, taller boy. Whenever he spotted a Westerner approaching, he would point in their direction – directing the groups of beggars towards them like a general marshalling his troops.

I was already in a foul mood with my precious first-world problems to deal with; I didn't need this now. When I saw the spotter pointing in my direction, I upped my pace as the child beggars surged in my direction. With my abdominal strain, I could only move at a fast walk, so the chase became a longer, more drawn-out affair lasting two street blocks before they gave up. It dawned on me that my professional tennis tour had descended into a race…to outlast begging children.

Wretched.

I'm not sure who left Mombasa first, Aly or myself, but I'm sure we were both gone by that evening. I meet people who tell me how beautiful the beaches and resorts of Mombasa are, and I'm sure they are wonderful. But when the little white bus cleared the shanty towns of Mombasa heading for the airport, let me assure you, the feeling was one of relief.

4

Edge of the World

Namibia

ANDREW DECIDED he was bored in Australia. After claiming two weeks ago that he wasn't playing professional tennis ever again, within 24 hours he had gotten all his vaccinations at once and had booked his ticket to Namibia – via Singapore and Johannesburg.

To be honest, it didn't surprise me. Whereas I enjoyed planning things months in advance, Andrew worked on last-minute spur-of-the-moment decisions. It didn't matter – we both arrived in the same destination. We were together on tour again. I saw him waiting for me as I left the terminal.

'What took you so long? I've been here for two hours!'

Bloody hell. Hadn't we just coordinated trans-continental travel itineraries? To get from Mombasa to Windhoek had taken me four flights (Mombasa–Nairobi–Dubai–Johannesburg–Windhoek), and he's complaining about two *bloody* hours.

'The pilot kept aborting the landing due to wind,' I told him.

I didn't mind the criticism – that's what brothers are for. They don't hold back; they tell you as they see it and they tell you the things you need to hear, without the sugar coating. And you believe it because you know they have your back when it really counts.

When I thought about it later, maybe I wasn't the only one chasing a dream. After all, Andrew was always the better junior player...by a mile. Everyone in Gladstone expected him to push on, and he had the ability to, but his tennis faded into the background. He was too good at everything, including academics, and soon his studies and career took precedence. Yet maybe, without announcing it, he was quietly sneaking in the back door, also giving himself one final roll of the dice to achieve a world ranking.

We left the airport in a taxi driven by a man who looked like the great Namibian sprinter, Frankie Fredericks. This was ironic as the guy drove so slowly that I wondered if there was something wrong with the car. There wasn't, so I guessed this was just the pace at which Namibia moved.

After two weeks of nerve-fraying bedlam in east Africa, Namibia felt vacantly quiet – a vast space in the far corner of the world map where not many people lived. The taxi cruised along the highway past savannah and mountain peaks: a landscape painted in shades of brown and green. The dry, mountain air and the warm sun seemed to remove any sense of urgency from the world.

We arrived at the Safari Hotel an hour later. In the hotel reception, a squad of football players wearing green and yellow tracksuits stood about. Kitbags were piled in a corner. The Ethiopian national team were in town for an African Nations Cup qualifier against the Namibians: the 112th-ranked team versus the 164th (the football rankings went down to 206, so Namibia could also be said to be the 43rd worst team in the world). The Ethiopian footballers were small in stature – they made some of the tall European tennis players look like giants. In a sporting sense, their football match would be around the same level of tennis's Futures circuit. Professional in name: sometimes less than that in terms of performance.

'Let's walk to the club. It's just over there,' Andrew told me, looking vaguely into the distance. His sense of spontaneous adventure had kicked in. I voted to wait for a taxi, but what do I know. Only after we arrived did he find a section in his Namibian *Lonely Planet* guidebook warning tourists not to walk through this particular grassland as muggings were common.

After we had made it through the grassland without seeing a living thing (we each held a racquet in case of wild animals), we passed the rugby stadium on Rugby Street, and a hockey field on Hockey Street. The tennis stadium was on the corner of Frankie Fredericks Street and Tennis Street. Perhaps hinting at Namibia's apathy towards tennis, the club was surrounded by bush and was so remote and isolated that even passing taxi drivers couldn't tell us where it was.

'You'll have to buy your own Dunlop balls from the upstairs bar,' the South African ITF referee told us once we had found the club. 'Whoever is responsible in Tennis Namibia for the tennis balls hasn't given us enough, so there aren't any for practice.' The South African admitted that, if there were more than 15 three-set matches in the tournament, they would run out of balls before the final. It seemed Namibia's systematic way of thinking didn't go beyond street names.

Andrew and I walked down a steep hill to a bowl-shaped stadium court. African shrubs protruded from the rows of concrete seats in the stadium. Namibia hadn't had a pro tournament for quite some time and the shrubs appeared deep-rooted and comfortable in their existence. Down on the court, you could see nothing apart from the clear blue sky after the final row of seats, giving the feeling that you were playing on the roof of the world. In a way, this was true – Windhoek sat on a plateau surrounded by mountains and was Africa's highest capital city at an altitude of 1,800m. The sun felt close.

Playing at altitude was definitely different, the ball literally flying through the thin air. A slice shot seemed to continue on its horizontal course without being affected by gravity – occasionally thudding into the concrete wall at the back without bouncing. Breathing became a deliberate act where I felt like I had to *suck* in the oxygen after every point. After an hour, we'd had enough.

Andrew decided we should return to the Safari Hotel by taxi. It was becoming dark outside and the deserted African grassland was starting to look scary.

* * * * *

Andrew started the Saturday morning's schedule against Elmarco Hoff. He was one of Namibia's better juniors, but considering Namibia wasn't exactly a tennis powerhouse, it was hard to predict exactly how good he would be.

Andrew steamrolled him 6-0 in the first set. Under a scorching sun and a gusty wind that blew across the court, Andrew blasted down heavy serves. One serve exploded off the court so violently that the Namibian cut the ball into the middle of the next court. Once he calmed down, Hoff's groundstrokes became consistent, but he lost his serve once and never looked like breaking Andrew's.

'I can see points in this tournament,' Andrew beamed after coming off the court with a bit of a swagger. 'Did you see those serves? Oh boy – Max Mirnyi serves!' He proceeded to show me how he put away his forehand volleys. Wasn't it only a month ago that he was done with tennis?

I was given a day off – courtesy of a bye as the draw wasn't full. We went down to the bowl-shaped stadium court to see who I would play tomorrow, either Joe Cooper or a player from Portugal. The stands were vacant except for two African workers wielding shovels, noisily removing shrubs from the concrete stands. Huge piles of uprooted plants lay around the stadium.

Joe had been struggling for weeks on the slow clay courts of the east African circuit. His confidence had taken a battering. He could only chip his backhand against the neat, but underpowered Portuguese, taking him two hours to get past his opponent in a tight affair. Joe's win meant that one of us would be qualifying for the main draw, with the chance to play for ATP points.

* * * * *

It was still dark when I awoke the next morning, unable to get the upcoming match out of my head. Andrew kept reminding me, 'This is a huge opportunity. If you don't qualify this time, you probably never will.' Okay, perhaps he was right, but hearing it over and over again certainly didn't help the sinking feeling in the pit of my stomach.

My match with Joe was scheduled for ten in the morning. By the time I had walked on court I had gone to the toilet three times. I was taking a cocktail of drugs: malaria tablets, anti-inflammatory pills for my abdominal injury, and now Imodium for an upset stomach. When you factor in the Voltaren cream and pain relief patches, I couldn't feel a thing. Whether it was the drugs or my injury healing, I wasn't entirely sure, but I could play…and that was all I cared about.

Against Joe, I had a clear strategy in mind – at every opportunity I would direct the ball to his backhand and race to the net. After practising with him in Uganda and Kenya, I knew his topspin backhand had deserted him, so surely it would break down now.

In the opening game, I got a short ball and hit a beautiful approach shot. Joe locked two hands on his racquet, cocked his wrist…and flicked the ball past me for a winner. I felt like vomiting – *this can't be happening*.

My ears were blocked and my heart was thumping in my chest. I soon got another short ball, and approached again. A few minutes in and here was a major turning point. If Joe made this shot, his confidence on his backhand wing could reappear. Miss it, and I'd be coming in on every point.

Joe launched his topspin backhand halfway up the net. He stood there with a bewildered look on his face, trying to figure out how it had happened.

At the hour mark, I was leading 6-1, 3-1. I had attacked on every ball, every serve, and any return I could. It then got worse for Joe. As he stood to serve, he appeared disorientated, a moment before blood began to pour from his nose.

It took the doctor an eternity to find his way down the hill to the court, and then several more minutes of squeezing Joe's nose with a handkerchief to make the blood stop. By the end, the Englishman's face and hand were smeared with blood and the cloth had turned crimson in colour. The South African ITF referee walked on court. 'Why is it taking so long?' he demanded of the doctor. He turned to me. 'You Aussies are all the same. What did you do to the poor bloke?'

'He's dehydrated,' I could hear the doctor telling the referee. 'He hasn't drunk any electrolytes since Thursday and hasn't had enough water.' Joe wasn't playing in a hat and he had trained with his shirt off that morning; his pale English skin still visibly flaking after being sunburnt in Kenya.

I won the match 6-1, 6-2 feeling relieved, but somewhat underwhelmed, to finally qualify for the main draw. Joe looked terrible and headed straight to the doctor's office.

On a court further down the hill in the sloping complex, Andrew was playing a ponytailed South African, Gregg Le Sueur. By the time I got there it was one set all. If Andrew could join me in the main draw it would be the perfect day for the Howe brothers.

Even though the match was tight, it didn't look promising as Andrew started to muscle the ball – expending huge amounts of energy to attack the net. After each point, his hands went on his hips as he gasped for air, perspiration pouring down his face and arms.

'Don't come in unless you're set,' I told him in a hushed voice through the fence. 'You're starting to rush things.' Technically, giving advice is illegal. But, it is so regularly and blatantly abused at all levels of the game that players are genuinely shocked if an umpire ever warns them for it. And, in my defence, Andrew never listens to me anyway.

'I've got to keep coming in – that's how I'm going to win,' he replied.

I headed towards the small stand behind the court where Le Sueur's coach, Raven Klaasen, sat chewing on a long piece of biltong. He had dark brown skin and the slightly curly black hair of someone from a mixed-race background. He wore his hair in a tight ponytail that only seemed to accentuate his wiry physique.

Nowadays, Klaasen is one of the world's best doubles players, appearing in Grand Slam finals and end-of-year Masters events. However, that day in Namibia, his career looked as washed-up as one could possibly imagine – he had damaged the ligaments in both knees and had just had a series of operations.

'Look at the difference,' he told me as he straightened both legs out in front of him. After months in plaster following his operation, one leg was stick thin with no noticeable quadriceps muscle above the kneecap. 'I've been hitting for the past month with Gregg. Just groundstrokes. I'll start to play points next month and then tournaments after that. I've got to give it one more go – if the knee gives way, then I'll have to do something else. I'll probably coach. But I have to try again, even if it's just for my peace of mind.'

While watching the match, Klaasen explained how he had been selected in the South African Davis Cup squads in the past. However, there had always been two top singles players around who got first preference for the live singles matches. As those players had since retired, this should have been his opportunity.

When I asked him if the South African Tennis Federation had funded him, he held up his fingers in a circle. He paused for a moment, then laughed, 'This is not a Roman C for a hundred; it's a zero for *nothing*.' As for his coaching arrangement, he explained how Gregg Le Sueur was a friend of the family, and that Le Sueur's parents asked if he could accompany him on the seven-week African Futures circuit. While they would cover all his expenses, the budget was tight. Klaasen was trying to make the packet of biltong last all day.

Andrew went down a break in the third set after an exhausting rally in the energy-sapping altitude. 'Gregg has all the shots in the book, but he gets really tight and starts to push the ball,' Klaasen explained. In the altitude, that was all one needed to do. Le Sueur eventually won the final set 6-2 after Andrew ran out of gas. It would have been special to see both our names in the main draw, but it just wasn't meant to be.

Having two Howes in the draw seemed to be causing confusion when the aficionados on BritishTennis.activeboard. com started posting the qualifying results:

Johnnylad, 'So two Brits qualify. I wonder if the Howes are related. Gregory is 33 I believe.'

Sheddie, 'The nationalities are wrong. Andrew Howe is an Australian. Congrats to Gregory for qualifying, he's started playing futures again this August and has had some pretty decent wins, this'll be one of his best chances for getting his first ever ranking point.'

* * * * *

The main draw was supposed to be posted on the bulletin board in the foyer of the Safari Hotel. When Andrew and I went to dinner, it still wasn't up. At dinner Alex Johnston, who had also qualified, strolled across. He was always with Joe, but this time was alone.

'I'm playing the Namibian club coach,' he told us, clearly pleased with his draw. He could see ATP points. The coach at the Central Tennis Club was Namibia's number two, and a good shot-maker. However, he was clearly overweight when compared to the full-time professionals found in the main draw. When we asked where Joe was, Alex replied, 'Oh, he's in hospital. I don't know what's wrong with him. He went in this afternoon and he's not back yet.'

Joe would eventually reappear the following afternoon, praising the Namibian hospital after they had given him a *special* injection. Joe later admitted he had no idea what it was made up of.

Alex scratched his head. 'I remember seeing your name, but I just can't remember who you got.' I wasn't sure if this was a good omen or not. In the draw would be four local wildcards – other local coaches, and even the club re-stringer, were given one. Whoever played these would be almost guaranteed an ATP point.

By the time we left dinner, the draw was on display. Scanning down the list of names, I found my name paired with Jurgens Strydom of Namibia. He was the number one player in the country and their only travelling professional at 1,156 in the world. The previous year, he had advanced to the semi-finals of the doubles in the 2005 junior Wimbledon event. Playing on his home courts with a game developed in the country's high altitude, it certainly wasn't the easy match I had hoped for. If I were going to earn my first ATP point, it would be the hard way.

The doubles draw was also there, showing both Andrew and myself. We had gotten lucky, sneaking into one of the remaining spots in the 16-team draw. Unfortunately, I'd be facing Jurgens Strydom again, and this time paired with the number one seed for the entire tournament, Bogdan-Victor Leonte from Romania.

* * * * *

There was a palpable air of tension on the player bus the next morning. It was the first day of the main draw and the higher world-ranked professionals were mentally preparing themselves for their matches. Every win from now on guaranteed ATP points and more prize money. It was a great feeling to be among them, with everything still to gain and a precious world ranking within reach.

The main draw in Windhoek kicked off in a wonderfully laid-back fashion, matching the atmosphere of the country. The first match got underway when the umpire, two players and a dog walked on court. No one seemed to overly mind the animal's appearance, and as the warm-up began, the dog was still casually making its way off court.

At midday, Alex Johnston played the club coach. Alex was younger, and vastly fitter, but the experienced Namibian number two kept the ball in play long enough for nerves to set in for his English opponent. In the end, Alex lost and the possibility of a world ranking slipped away. 'I had so many chances, but it was a good experience. I'm sure I'll get more opportunities in the future,' Alex told Andrew and I. He was speaking with the innocence of youth where the future feels limitless. However, tennis is an unforgiving sport, with a history of players who live a lifetime ruefully regretting not taking an opportunity when it presented itself.

On the court in front of the clubhouse, our doubles match would soon begin. Even on good days, our doubles play was streaky at best. There were patches of sublime play, resembling the brotherly comradeship of the Bryan brothers. However, when it went bad, it went *really* bad. As matches slid away, we would remind each other of stupid errors that cost us previous doubles matches (often from decades ago).

Our experienced and fancied opponents followed us on court. Leonte was an absolute giant from Romania with a touch of Ilie Nastase's craziness about him – without the nasty streak. He smiled and said 'hello' as he loped past. He was the number one seed in the singles and ranked in the top 400 in the world.

His partner, Strydom, was much shorter and stockier, with a serious demeanour about him. He looked like the spitting image of the Australian football player Harry Kewell, which for some reason annoyed me immensely (I'll admit, this was slightly irrational).

Strydom's girlfriend sat directly behind, and above the court, on the wooden balcony. During the warm-up, she let out a loud whoop and then a prolonged, 'Let's go ba-by!'

'I can see I'm going to get really pissed off,' I told Andrew as we warmed up our serves. 'You're always getting worked up,' came his reply. 'Why don't you just play?'

And we did…for about three games. Then I lost my opening serve. Andrew blamed my weak service. I pointed out my serve didn't affect the volleys he had dumped into the net. Meanwhile, Leonte's serve was rocketing down aces, while Strydom was serving and volleying effectively. With his crisp, neat volleys, it was easy to see why the Namibian had made it so far in the Wimbledon junior tournament on England's grass courts.

'Come on ba-by!' cried the voice from behind the court as we dropped the first set 6-2. This was followed by a series of ever increasing whoops that gave Leonte a fit of giggles. I had managed to work myself into a silent rage, which certainly didn't help the quality of my play. Andrew and I changed our serving ends so I would have the wind behind my serve (apparently my serve was that slow).

The strategy failed.

Andrew promptly lost his serve in the opening game of the second set, and I lost my own serve two games later – even with the wind behind me. By this time the rot had set in. 'You're shit at doubles. I'm not playing with you any more,' Andrew helpfully pointed out (I'm sure I'd heard it before). We managed to win one game in the second set. Everyone shook hands and I left straight for the physiotherapist, grateful to get off the court.

The physio's office was a large tent erected beside the club-house on a grassy hill overlooking the courts. The local hospital sent a different physio each day, and today was a pretty girl named Christine. The charge was about ten dollars for massage, back manipulation and ultrasound therapy. The Namibian physios were a lot better equipped than their counterparts in Uganda, surrounding themselves with the latest machines and equipment brought from the nearby hospital. She was also a lot gentler than the muscular Ugandan from a fortnight ago.

'I was the physio yesterday for the Namibian national football team with their match against Ethiopia,' Christine explained to me, while massaging my abdominal injury. She told how she was constantly running on to the field to treat players who had fallen over. 'They are so unfit. In the second half they all started cramping. It's their off-season at the moment, so they haven't been training.'

I asked if the tennis players were fitter than their footballing counterparts. 'I don't know about that, but the footballers are cry-babies,' she said in a lilting accent similar to Afrikaans.

'They are always asking for painkillers and injections for sprained ankles. They never let their injuries heal.'

In the newspapers later in the week, it revealed that the football players had threatened to strike. They received the Namibian equivalent of about $300 per match, and that had been their official match fee for several years without a raise.

Christine then asked me if I would be taking a break after this tournament – to rest the injury. 'Sort of,' I lied.

* * * * *

The next day, my injury felt better. This was more than could be said of Joe. Following his mystery injection, he began to feel unwell again and during the night started to vomit blood. Joe was back in the same Namibian hospital with a drip in his arm. He felt so ill that he was convinced his African tour was over, and booked the next available flight back to London.

In the clubhouse before my match, a white man in his 50s approached me. He introduced himself as Bob, the president of the Namibian Tennis Federation, adding that he was here to support Namibia's top player. He told me how Namibian tennis had received three years' sponsorship from MTC, the Namibian mobile network. This included funding for the Futures event, the Davis Cup team, and Jurgens Strydom's attempt to break into the elite of world tennis. As there were only 8,000 mobile phones in the entirety of Namibia, then this funding was seen as a major commitment by the relatively small company.

'In the 1970s and 1980s, Namibia had been on the pro tennis map,' Bob told me, with more than a hint of pride and nostalgia in his voice. 'World-ranked players like Guillermo Vilas would make the trip to Windhoek after they had played in the South African Open. They used it as a stopover on the way back to the European circuit. But when politics killed off the South African Open, Namibian tennis suffered as well.'

The whole complex had a kind of 'end of the earth' feel to it, so it was difficult for me to imagine a time when Namibia was anything but in the tennis wilderness.

For his singles match, Strydom had enlisted the support of his whole family, sitting alongside his girlfriend and other onlookers on the balcony overlooking the court. There was a strong local interest in seeing how Namibia's brightest prospect would fare in his hometown event.

The tension was palpable as the match began. Strydom had the more refined technique and the better pedigree, but as we slugged it out from the back of the court – pound for pound – I was physically bigger, hitting a heavier ball.

The first set was crucial. Whoever won it would be heavy favourite to take the match. When I reached break point at 4-4, my chances to become a world-ranked pro looked good. Strydom's girlfriend's encouragement was getting louder and more desperate. When he served in a slow spinner that sat up in the middle of the court, I threw everything I had into my forehand – launching it crosscourt. I looked up to see the Namibian caught off balance with the ball speeding off the court, forcing an error. 'Come on!' I screamed, loud enough for the entire complex to hear.

Sitting down at the change of ends, I looked up to the balcony. Andrew and Alex, sitting on the far side of the balcony, nodded their heads. Strydom's entourage had gone quiet. Other players were standing in the upstairs bar. A player fighting for their first ATP point is fascinating: everybody knows the pressure they are under, its significance. They wait to see whether the player can push through, or capitulate.

Serving for the first set, my ball toss went to pieces. If a player has a technical problem, then real pressure will find it… and expose it. When I toss the ball up, it somehow comes out the back of my hand. I've done it all my life and it is never a problem – until it *really* counts. With my heart racing, the ball seemed to get stuck on my fingers, making it go all over the place.

'Let's go baby. Whoaa!' the girlfriend screamed as her boyfriend launched into my second serves with relish, realising his opponent was choking. At break point down, I hit two serves into the middle of the net. Strydom's father was out of his seat. 'Come on Jurgens,' he urged to his son across the entire court.

Before I knew it, I had lost the first set in a blur. My head was a mess. I was seething – angry with myself, and pissed off at the entire Namibian tennis community who were still shouting from the balcony.

During one point in the second set, Strydom smashed a winner past me. The crowd burst into applause. I picked up the balls from the back fence under where they sat, and slowly walked to the service line.

'Let's go baby! Whoaa!'

I snapped.

'Can you tell the crowd to shut up!' I screamed at the umpire.

The young Welsh umpire looked startled. He was in Africa for three weeks to umpire the entire southern African circuit. In order for an umpire to move up to the top echelons of the game – the Grand Slams and ATP tour – they first have to work their way through the minor leagues. Often, they would have no linesmen to help them, forcing them to call all the lines, while at the same time dealing with irate players desperate to get out of the Futures.

'Er…were they talking while you were serving?' the Welshman asked calmly.

Good point umpire. Okay – so they weren't – but they were pissing me off, and that was enough justification for me.

On the next point, I bounced the ball and…ace! I turned to face the crowd, giving them my best Lleyton Hewitt fist pump. 'Let's go baby!' I screamed at the top of my voice. In hindsight, I'll admit it was rather juvenile. At least with anger replacing my nerves, the ball was no longer getting stuck in my hand and I reeled off a succession of winners. I walked past the umpire's chair for the change of ends when my opponent strode towards me.

'You don't speak to the girl like that.' He pointed his finger at me for effect.

'I wasn't talking to the girl. I was speaking to your *whole* family.'

If this were a rugby or football match, we would start pushing and grabbing each other with things getting physical. However, in tennis, there is a net separating opponents, so everyone feels satisfied throwing insults until the umpire tells them to stop. Also, in tennis, to touch an opponent risks default, fines and lengthy bans – rarely does anybody cross that line. It's like two dogs on either side of a fence – squaring up – knowing they'll never have to meet.

As my opponent walked away, he said something I couldn't quite make out.

'Can you tell the player to stop talking to me?' I told the umpire. 'He's trying to intimidate me.'

The Welshman raised his eyebrows, brushing his hand against his blonde, spiky hair. 'Gentlemen. Please, etiquette.' It sounded like the umpire from Wales was rehearsing his lines for a future Wimbledon appearance. 'Gentlemen: let's play.' It was the time-honoured line used by umpires over the years, which effectively translates to, 'Stop acting like *prats* and get on with it.'

The confrontation seemed to affect the Namibian's play. Was this the reason why John McEnroe was always creating arguments with his opponents? I didn't start playing better, but my opponent's game became strewn with errors as I levelled the match at one set all.

Sitting in my court-side chair, I felt exhausted – all the nervous energy and rage had drained me. I told myself to keep going. I'd waited a lifetime for this opportunity – it was time to dig deep.

In the third set, the Namibian changed his strategy and attacked the net at every opportunity. I was a step behind, chasing lost causes as he punched his volleys away for winners. He raced to a 5-1 lead.

'Make all the balls,' I told myself, staring at defeat. 'Make him beat you. He might get nervous.'

Strydom obligingly tightened up. He tried to finish it too early – spraying balls long, or hitting hopeful chips and running to the net. With the pressure off I started to pass him. When I got back to 5-4, he launched a ball out of the complex.

'Code violation. Ball abuse. Mr Strydom,' came the predictable response from the chair. After all the aggression, this was the first warning given in the match. The fine would cost him U$50.

With Strydom serving for the match at 5-4, 30-all, the result hung in the balance. After almost two decades chasing the same dream, an ATP point was tantalisingly close. My opponent served and raced to the net, floating a backhand volley crosscourt. I couldn't reach it, but could only hope it would land wide. It landed perfectly on the line.

My heart sank.

When I missed a passing shot on his match point, it was over. I had *nothing* left. 'Well played,' I said as I shook his hand. 'Sorry about all that before.'

'Thanks a lot. No, no. It's nothing.' He waved his hand to dismiss any ill feelings. No one had any energy left to argue. Anyway, the match was over. There was nothing left to argue about.

I saw Andrew as I left the court. 'I couldn't do it,' was all I could offer. For once he didn't say anything. He knew how long I'd been waiting for a chance at ATP points.

I lay on the Namibian grass, staring at the sky. Had this been my chance to achieve a world ranking? Would there be another one? I had already accepted the match was gone. No matter how many times I could replay the points – or ask myself *what if* – the match was never coming back. I knew the disappointment of this lost chance would be etched deep in my psyche.

I collected my U$117.50 prize money in cash. If I were lucky, it'd cover two days' worth of expenses. The Namibian official asked if I would be staying for Wednesday evening's player barbecue. I said no – I would now be flying out on tomorrow evening's plane.

* * * * *

On the morning of our flight, Andrew and I visited Windhoek's centre. It was a beautiful city: a real old-world throwback with wide, tree-lined streets creating an atmosphere of refinement and history. We had lunch in what looked like a civilised outdoors bar. Most of the patrons turned out to be older white men who surrounded themselves with heavily made-up African prostitutes. We guessed the ageing men didn't care that Namibia had one of the highest rates of HIV/AIDS infections in the world, where one adult in every five had the virus.

After lunch, I sought out one of Windhoek's many jewellery shops. I didn't want the prize money I had earned to be simply used covering travel expenses, so I decided on buying Sylvie some African jewellery. Namibia was famous for its gems. Ironically, the owner of the store turned out to be a close friend of the Strydom family, who had followed Jurgens' tennis career closely. He said he and his wife used to babysit the young Jurgens and his sibling. I decided not to mention that I had recently told the entire family to 'shut up'.

The jewellery store had a copy of the Afrikaans newspaper, *Republikein*, dated 'Woensday 11 Oktober'. On the back page was a large picture of Strydom serving. I asked the assistant from the jewellery shop to translate it for me. She dutifully translated it into the following:

'Namibian Jurgens Strydom, sponsored by MTC, progressed to the next round with a *naelbyter* win over Gregory Howe from Great Britain. Jurgens had to work very hard to overcome the Englishman and the hot Namibian sun. Strydom won the first set 6-3, but lost the second set 4-6. The Englishman looked in top form and looked like he was going to win. But after a loss of concentration when up 5-1, Jurgens won the final set 6-4.'

I vowed not to read any more local newspapers. At least, not until they were reporting a Gregory Howe win.

5

Heart of Darkness
Southern Africa

ONE WEEK later.

The light blinked. Red or black: I had to make a decision.

My tour of Africa had turned into my own *Heart of Darkness*. Like the characters in Joseph Conrad's novel, the further I pushed into the dark continent in search of elusive ATP points, the more I descended into madness: third-tier Futures madness.

During my first-round match in the qualifying of the Botswana Futures event, Gregg Le Sueur had hit the ball into the corner of the court. The ball kicked wildly, I made a last-second lunge, and my abdominal wall tore – completely – like a knife going into my side. I ended up prostrate on the court. Raven Klaasen, watching from a court-side stand, thought I had run into the fence. The physiotherapist had failed to turn up: it wouldn't have mattered. I *knew* my tour was over.

Now, days later, I sat in the casino of Botswana's Gaborone Sun. Red or black? The light on the giant electronic roulette machine blinked faster, awaiting my decision. It was mindless entertainment, but as long as it stopped me from thinking about tennis, then it would do.

Andrew sat beside me. He reckoned he had devised a winning strategy and had been testing it for the past few evenings. Joe (who had recovered from his misadventures in Namibia) and

Alex sat a little further up. They had been carefully saving all their Botswana coins in a little bag for each evening's gambling.

A French player began hurling coins across the casino floor. After each loss, he would clutch at his hair before manically running around the room frantically screaming for more money from his friends. After six consecutive weeks on the African circuit (Sudan, Rwanda, Uganda, Kenya, Namibia and now Botswana), he had lost the plot. Ironically, on court he was the most conservative, risk-averse player I had ever seen, looping his balls high over the net through fear of making an error. It seemed he found it easier to gamble recklessly in the casino, rather than on court, where the stakes were just too high.

Opposite the casino was a large lounge room filled with high-end prostitutes, wealthy African businessmen and an assortment of older Europeans. There was a sleazy vibe with hazy lighting and smoke lingering in the air. Reportedly, a famous English footballer had recently been evicted from the bar after becoming embroiled in a drunken brawl. Late nights in the Gaborone Sun just seemed to have that kind of effect.

One thing was for sure – if a player wanted to escape the Futures Tour on to the higher levels of the game, then too much time in the Gaborone Sun casino was best avoided. At this point in time, I was so disappointed that I no longer cared.

* * * * *

To take my mind off tennis, I did my first sightseeing in two months when Andrew and I visited the Mokolodi Nature Reserve. People outside of the sporting world would often ask me how much sightseeing I did when I travelled to tennis tournaments. They would never understand when I told them that it was nearly impossible to do the tourist things when on tour. If there were something really special – like the pyramids in Cairo – then players would find half a day and make the effort to visit. However, after a loss, the overwhelming desire was simply to drive straight to the airport and pretend the place never existed.

The journey to the reserve took our taxi past Gaborone's poorest townships. The houses were a disorganised maze of concrete blocks with rusty corrugated walls and roofs. An assortment of coloured clothing hung from makeshift string lines. Unkempt grass blended in with discarded litter.

We passed a huge roadside billboard with the slogan, 'Commit to Zero Transmission Lifestyle – Use a Condom All the Time.' Later on, there was another billboard with the image of a giant condom. 'WEAR IT!' the billboard screamed at passing motorists. Nearly 40 per cent of Botswana's adult population had contracted AIDS/HIV, which made it the number one country for the virus in Africa. At one point during the week, I asked one of the employees in the Gaborone Sun why the staff were all older locals in their sixties. 'Because the middle generation are all dead from AIDS,' was his blunt reply. I stopped asking questions after that.

Before long, we broke through the outskirts of the city and drove through the bush lands of southern Africa. Local African music blared from the car stereo. The reddish-brown earth blended into grass and trees of various shades of green. The taxi eventually made its way to the gravelled entrance road of the reserve.

Our guide was a slim local man in his late 20s. He had an unhurried way of walking that seemed perfect for life in the African bush, and he chose his words slowly and carefully. He led us to an open-topped jeep. Soon we were gradually accelerating along a dirt path out towards a plateau in the distance.

'Although it's a reserve, we don't control the animals,' our guide informed us over the noise of the engine. 'There is an outer fence, but many animals can jump it so they come and go. Leopards have been seen in the reserve.'

The safari car came to an abrupt halt. A large group of baboons crossed the road directly in front of us. Their muscular bodies and huge fang-like teeth gave them a menacing appearance. In the wild, with our open car and our guide's 'we don't control the animals' comment, I had an uneasy feeling of being in the opening scene of some horror film. Andrew asked our guide, 'Shouldn't you have a gun?' He shyly chuckled, but didn't say anything.

The last stop of the tour was to enter the cheetah compound. It is not natural to be entering on foot into an area where there are dangerous, wild animals roaming about. 'You have to be above a metre in height to see the cheetahs,' the guide explained as he led us through the gate. 'Otherwise they might see you as prey and attack you. Children aren't allowed in. Last month I turned my back on them, and one of them slashed me.' I wondered if it would have been wiser to tell the paying customers this after they had finished their safaris.

'And you don't have a gun?' Andrew asked again.

'They don't give us one,' he replied with a smile.

We found one of the cheetahs lying in the shade with a half-devoured chicken lying in front of it. It looked like a cat, only so much bigger with sharp teeth and claws. It stared at me with a blank expression and piercing orange eyes. At this point, I tried to remember if you were supposed to avoid eye contact…or was this with gorillas? Andrew and I got pictures kneeling beside the cheetah, capturing our nervous smiles.

'You can pet the cheetah,' said our guide – the same one who'd been attacked the previous month.

* * * * *

The flight to South Africa, the following day, was on South African Express. It doesn't bode well when your airline sounds like a fast-food delivery service. The alternative was Air Botswana, who had the dubious record of having its entire fleet of aircraft destroyed when one of its pilots went rogue, stole a parked plane, and then ploughed it into the remaining planes. A friend of mine had been working in an international school in Gaborone at the time. He told me that the schoolchildren could see the face of the pilot as he circled the city at ground level – for two hours – before committing suicide. After hearing this story, the fast-food delivery service sounded fine with me.

A twin-propeller aircraft was used for the hour-long journey from Gaborone to O.R. Tambo International Airport, in Johannesburg. The propeller engine whined and hummed. The whole plane vibrated whenever the pilot increased the revs. With only a handful of passengers on board, the stewardess quickly served us a packet of crisps, a small box of juice and a packet of biltong.

After watching Raven Klaasen eat the dried meat for the past month, I was looking forward to trying it. Maybe it's an acquired taste, because I found it the most disgusting thing I had ever tried – sort of like marinated road kill, which I thought could have been a fitting metaphor for how my African tennis tour was looking.

There are so many stories and travel warnings about South Africa, and Johannesburg in particular, that Andrew and I were on edge from the moment we left the airport. It didn't help that it was night-time. Every person we came across was given a second look – did they look like a mugger? It was exhausting to be on alert the whole time.

This wasn't made any better when we got to our hotel near the airport. As we left the foyer to walk to a mall across the road, the concierge rushed up to us, 'Don't walk to the mall. It's too dangerous. You must take a taxi.'

Andrew and I peered down the empty road, then across to the mall a couple of hundred metres away. Everything looked modern and well lit. 'But there's nobody there,' Andrew told the man. 'This is stupid. We could run there before anybody could get close.'

The uniformed hotel employee began to get nervous. 'No, no! Guests must take a taxi – they aren't allowed to walk.' He reiterated again just how dangerous it was…*out there*. Looking down the empty street was like looking across the ocean and imagining a shark lurking out of sight…just waiting to attack.

We returned to our characterless modern hotel and ordered room service.

* * * * *

As early as possible the next morning, we booked a taxi to Pretoria. The scenery turned to pleasant grasslands as the taxi sped away from the dangers of Johannesburg. It could have been easy to imagine we were in Australia with its never-ending countryside and modern highways.

We soon made it to Pretoria, the administrative capital of South Africa. It reminded me of similar bureaucratic cities around the world – Canberra and Frankfurt come to mind. Everything was pleasantly bland (the word *nice* would be fitting). The university had manicured grounds, while the cricket ovals and modern clubhouses were as good as anything found in Australia.

However, there were always little signs of a lurking menace. When the taxi stopped at a red light, we spotted two locals standing aimlessly on the opposite corner of the crossroads. Their clothes were old and faded on their lean bodies, while their heads sported dirty woollen caps. In theory, they could have been students on the way to the nearby university, but hours later they were still there, eyeing the passing cars with a look not dissimilar to the one the cheetah gave me a couple of days earlier.

I knew there was no way I could play, but I signed in anyway. I wanted the excitement of seeing my name in the draw: to be able to say I had played in South Africa. Growing up in Australia, South African rugby and cricket teams were given the highest respect, and I wanted the experience of playing in the country first-hand. I would play a set and then withdraw; it wouldn't blot my record too much.

Andrew drew the South African, Gregg Le Sueur...*again*. In a 64-man draw, what were the odds that he would play one of the Howe brothers for three straight weeks? He was becoming like a family curse.

* * * * *

The next morning, when the qualifying matches for the South African Futures tournament kicked off, it signalled the only week of professional tennis in South Africa for the year. There were no Challenger events, and the once prestigious South African Open had been abolished a decade ago.

'The government see tennis as a white, elitist sport, so it gets no funding,' a South African tennis official told me. 'Five years ago, we had three players in the top 100, and 20 players in the top 100 in doubles. Now there is one player, Wesley Moodie.'

He went on to explain about the government quotas in sport. 'In our cricket World Cup squad, we had seven black players. How can we compete when we are not sending our best players? Don't get me wrong – I'm not being racist – but you tell me, *how* can we compete?'

I agreed that would be truly ridiculous if one of their best tennis players, Raven Klaasen, who is black, didn't get funding simply because he played what was deemed a white, elitist sport.

In a last-ditch attempt to compete, I visited the tournament physiotherapist. 'You must not massage that area. I never touch that area,' he warned me. I had now seen four physios in Africa, and everyone had said something different. 'What I'd like to do is give you a Voltaren injection into the muscle. It'll numb the pain for up to 12 hours.'

He told me he worked with a rugby team where this treatment was commonplace. I declined the injection. At this point in time I was glad I wasn't a rugby player; no wonder so many struggled to walk normally after they had retired. Anyway, to earn an ATP point, I would have to get through three qualifying matches, and then win another match in the main draw. That would mean four injections – one before each match. I told him I wanted to feel the pain – only then I would know if I was making it worse.

I can't tell you much about my match against the Israeli, Liran Levy. It seemed irrelevant whom I was playing as I had no intention of trying to win. In the warm-up, I was hitting the ball great, but as soon as the match started I let every ball go that was out of reach. I stuck to my plan, played a set and withdrew.

I explained to my puzzled opponent what the problem was as we shook hands.

After the match, another young physiotherapist drove me to the Blou Bulle Rugby Club. 'It's one of the best rugby clubs in South Africa,' the physiotherapist explained. 'The top physio there is a guy called Harry. You'll see him about your injury.'

True to his word, the rugby club had state-of-the-art facilities where everything was polished and new. The treatment room overlooked the immaculate rugby ground. The 100-year-old University of Pretoria and a prestigious Afrikaans school were nearby. We were in the heart of the white Afrikaans world, where rugby was its pulse.

When I met Harry, he was just finishing working with one of the rugby players. The guy was so muscular that his whole body seemed to take the shape of a rectangle. His thighs seemed as wide as his shoulders and his neck was as wide as his head. With his crew cut, the guy looked as tough as nails. When I had seen the footballers in Namibia, I had felt the tennis players were physically impressive, but they were *nothing* compared to the brute strength on display in the Blou Bulle Rugby Club.

'Your right leg is one centimetre longer than your left leg,' Harry explained as he twisted my legs through a series of tests. 'Whether this is because of pelvic stresses or one leg is longer, I'm not sure.' He told me the only way of finding out was through an x-ray and measuring the bones. He pushed my leg upwards to test my hamstrings. 'You'll never win a competition for flexibility. I'll send you to a doctor who does sonar and she can see exactly how big the tear is.' He estimated I'd be out for anywhere between one to three weeks.

He had vastly underestimated.

The next journey with the young physiotherapist in his small, white hatchback was to the nearby Jacaranda Hospital. On the way, he explained how difficult things were in his country. 'If you're white, your opportunities are severely limited. You're at the bottom of the list when it comes to jobs. Unless you're the only specialist in your field, then a black South African will get the priority.'

There was no bitterness in his voice, but rather just stating the way it was. It was an interesting comment. Throughout the day I had seen a series of medical professionals and they had all been white. Then again, how tough things were was a common theme I had heard from all young people I had encountered during my time in Africa, no matter what their colour.

Participating in a professional sporting event in South Africa clearly pulled some weight. I was fast-tracked to the top of the waiting list in the private hospital and ushered straight into the ultrasound room. Dr Zanet, the female sports medicine specialist, pointed to the monitor to show me my skin, muscle and intestine.

'This ultrasound machine is the same one we use to see babies in pregnant women.' I found the images of my insides slightly disturbing. I didn't really want to watch, but she kept explaining everything as if lecturing to an intern. 'I can't really see any tear,' she told me as she moved the scanner around. She asked me to strain, and then sit up.

What happened next, I didn't want to hear. 'You see this – it's the intestine. It looks to me like a sports hernia.' When I looked blankly, she went on, 'It's where the ligament is strained and the intestine pushes through. It won't heal. The *only* thing is surgery.'

I had never had surgery before: just the thought of it gave me an uncomfortable, sinking feeling. However, at least I knew where I stood. If I wanted to play on the tour again, I'd need to see a surgeon…and pretty quickly.

I returned to the tennis complex to see Andrew's match with Gregg Le Sueur. They were sent to the furthermost court on the top of a hill to play their first-round match. When I got there, Le Sueur had won the first set. Raven Klaasen, sitting on a wooden bench behind the court, was the only other person in this far corner of the complex.

'Agh, that sucks,' was Klaasen's reply when I showed him the ultrasound images. He read the ultrasound report that stated, 'There is bowel that bulges through the posterior wall...direct hernia.' After two knee operations and a leg half the size of the other, he probably knew the long, hard road back after surgery better than most.

Everyone seemed burnt out. Neither Andrew, nor Le Sueur, could muster the energy of their encounter two weeks ago. Klaasen talked about Gregg's brother who swam with great white sharks off Cape Town and made documentaries about his encounters. To talk about sharks seemed more appealing than watching any more tennis, and no one noticed when the match ended with the South African winning in straight sets. Andrew chatted with his opponent for a while before everyone sauntered off back towards the clubhouse.

I had planned to play until December for the first half of my tour. It was now the end of October. Planned circuits in Iran, and then Sri Lanka, would have to be scrapped. It was with a heavy heart that I logged on to the ITF website and officially removed my name from the entry lists.

6

The Way Back

London

IT WAS a *cold* winter's day in London.

I travelled north on the Piccadilly line, through central London, before changing to the Northern line. Exiting the Hendon Central underground station, I made my way past a row of newsagents and corner shops. A covering of grey clouds obscured much of the clear, blue sky, allowing only a sliver of light to escape through. It was fitting weather for how I felt; after the dread of the upcoming operation was the promise of a return to the professional tour.

This thought pushed me onwards to the manor house at the top of the hill. I arrived shortly in front of a large two-storey house with an enormous Union Jack flag outside and a sign that read 'The British Hernia Centre'.

Upon returning to London after South Africa, I had two choices to repair the hernia. One was the government-funded National Health Service. Any operation would be free. However, the wait could be six months, it would be under general anaesthetic with an overnight stay, and without the option of choosing my surgeon.

My second choice was to pay over £2,000 and see a hernia specialist. I could have the operation within the week, be awake the whole operation, and literally hop on and off the operating table. Their glossy brochure guaranteed a return to sport within a month.

With the pro circuit waiting, I chose option two.

After ringing the bell, a heavy wooden door swung open. A man wearing blue pyjamas and sporting dark stubble greeted me. He shook my hand before speaking in a familiar Australian drawl. 'My name's Kerry. I'm the theatre nurse and I'll be responsible for getting you ready, and just explaining everything you need to know. And I'll be the one to shave you,' he added with a final emphasis. It's not something you hear every day.

As he went through the questionnaire, we talked about how the Socceroos were robbed by the Italians in the recent football World Cup. There's nothing like a national sporting catastrophe to start a conversation. Australians have a national holiday each year to remember the World War One Gallipoli disaster. At Gallipoli, it was arrogant British officers sending Australian soldiers up cliffs into machine gun fire. Now, it was diving Italian footballers finding Aussie legs to fall over.

Kerry went through my 'rehab' programme. 'Because you're relatively young and fit, you're really going to feel it. And because it's on both sides, it'll be double the pain.' When I went to the consultation the week before, the surgeon discovered that I had ripped my abdominal wall on both sides – a bilateral inguinal hernia. The second tear must have happened against Gregg Le Sueur in Botswana.

'For the first couple of days after the operation, you'll be in a lot of pain. Take the painkillers. The key is you have to move, even if it's in ten-minute bursts.' He explained that I would have to move through the pain to stop excessive scar tissue building up. I was given a white bag with a cocktail of strong painkillers.

I undressed in a small room and put on a blue surgical gown. I kept my socks – whether it was the temperature or the nerves, I don't know, but it was freezing in the surgery. The surgeon came and drew two lines on my abdomen with a marker pen. 'This is where I'll make the incisions,' he told me, moving the pen over the lines as if it were a scalpel.

It was a strange feeling to walk into an operating room and lie down on the table; in the movies, the unconscious patient is always wheeled in on a trolley. The anaesthetist sat beside my head. She asked if I had ever had an operation before. 'You look so calm,' she said when I told her it was my first operation. 'But your hands are cold. That's the sure sign.'

I wanted to tell her that she would be cold too if all she was wearing was a thin gown and socks while lying on a metal table. She inserted a needle into my arm. I felt the cold anaesthetic flow around my body and my muscles relaxed. I was enveloped by a blanket of calm in what I can only describe as an out of body experience – I could see and hear the nurses and doctors, but I was floating…far, far away.

A light blue screen was erected about a foot above my chest. I could see the surgeon's head and shoulders moving, but nothing else. The whole abdominal area was shaved and numbed. 'Which side gives you the most trouble?' the surgeon asked. In my light-headedness, I was back in Uganda watching the physiotherapist rapidly poking his fingers in and out of my right side, just before my match with Ed Seator.

'The right side,' I blurted out.

'Fine, we'll start there,' came the surgeon's reply.

The anaesthetist sitting beside me monitored my blood pressure with a little device attached to my finger. Her presence felt reassuring and maternal. Time was difficult to gauge, but shortly the surgeon said, 'We're just inserting the mesh in position now. Give us a big cough.'

Reading the doctor's notes, which arrived in the mail a couple of weeks later, I can report that after the incision, a piece of protruding intestine was surgically removed and repaired. Then a cloth-like mesh of about five centimetres in length was placed over the opening. I felt a slight pull when the dissolvable stitches were being woven through my skin.

'Okay. The right side is repaired,' the surgeon said.

With my mind numbed, I tried to think of something intelligent to say. 'Great!' was all I could manage.

A few minutes later, the left side had been repaired. When they removed the screen I looked down and saw two white rectangular bandages on each side of my abdomen. I was told I could go back to the changing room – and that is literally what I did. I sat up, slid my legs off the operating table and walked away. With no pain, it was hard to believe that I had actually had an operation at all. The surgery rules were that you had to have someone with you for the journey home, and for the next 24 hours. Husbands or parents accompanied all the other patients. Sylvie was far away in Dubai. So, Andrew said he'd fly over in the morning from Frankfurt, in Germany, where he had started a new job. When I turned up for my operation alone, I had to promise the receptionists that my brother was indeed coming. He just considered being with me before the operation a waste of time, so he was in the nearby Hendon Aircraft Museum looking at planes while I was being operated on.

About 30 minutes after my operation, Andrew arrived in the changing room. It was about the same time that I was finally allowed to eat, and a tray with tea and sandwiches was brought in. Although I had been fasting for several hours, Andrew ate them all. At least a benefit of paying for private healthcare is that you can order extra.

By the time the taxi had dropped us back to my flat in west London, I was in fine form. The painkillers were still going strong. For hours that night, I swung my racquet, hitting imaginary forehands and backhands. The surgery's website posted testimonials from old-age pensioners who could play tennis within days of their operation. Some older patients didn't even need painkillers. I didn't bother to read the information sheet that detailed the different stages of recovery – the Australian nurse's warning that I would have double the pain was far from my mind.

* * * * *

The next morning, I awoke lying on my back. Until that point in my life, I hadn't realised that one's stomach muscles were connected to every move the body makes…or tries to make. My bladder was full and the toilet was mere metres away down a flight of stairs. But I couldn't move. Andrew was sound asleep on the floor beside my bed.

It took me half an hour to muster the courage to sit up, and when I did, there was a searing pain in my abdomen and I became light-headed. The meshes would take a couple of weeks to bind themselves into my abdominal wall. Until then, they would move around, causing unbearable pain. Lying in bed, I took every painkiller I could find in the bag they'd given me. Then I stood up, took a few steps…and promptly fainted on the stairs.

After calling Andrew and being (literally) dragged back to the bedroom, I rang the surgery's emergency number. I was convinced something had gone wrong. Instead, they chastised me for taking the painkillers on an empty stomach; the drugs had gone straight into my bloodstream in one, *big* hit.

For the rest of the day, I refused to sit down. I was either swinging tennis racquets or walking around in circles. There was no way I would endure the agony of having to sit up if I could help it. The Australian nurse said to move in ten-minute bursts. I would show him…*I'll do ten-hour bursts instead*.

* * * * *

For the next few days, I experienced what it would be like to be an old-age pensioner in London. I could walk no faster than a shuffle. People would rush past me, and then turn and look, trying to figure out what my problem was. I began to feel vulnerable. If I sensed someone looking, I would start to walk with a slight limp, while at other times I would have conversations on my mobile phone as a way to justify my slow pace.

One day, walking past Hammersmith University, a group of dubious-looking youths kicked a football past me. When I couldn't return their ball, I could hear swearing and threats. I had always considered London a relatively safe city, as far as big cities go. Now I realised how threatening it could be if you looked in any way like a victim.

* * * * *

My recovery went according to schedule. Every morning I awoke to find the pain a little less than the day before. After a week, I removed the white bandages to reveal two fine, red lines about six centimetres long – the stitches having dissolved on their own.

After a fortnight, I went for a light jog. It had been over two months since I could run in a straight line without pain and the feeling was exhilarating.

The next day, I dragged an Australian friend, Mark Robinson, down to a local court on a bitterly cold winter's day. We both wore gloves on our left hands and woollen caps to keep our ears warm. A massive tree had fallen into the side fence after a recent storm and the slightly damp bitumen court made footing difficult. At one stage, local kids from the nearby estate stood behind the fence and threw rocks at us. It didn't matter – my comeback had begun, and that was all I cared about.

Since I had left Africa over a month before, I hadn't touched a racquet. The Stairmaster workouts hadn't done much for my fitness. I now weighed in at 86kg – four heavier than I was in Bangkok at the start of my tour. The hefty bill of my hernia operation had also put a dent in my tennis finances. When a teacher left on maternity leave in my old school in Tottenham, in north London, I accepted the five-month contract until the end of May. It would give me time to rebuild my fitness and finances, and play some smaller-money tournaments before hitting the pro tour again in June.

* * * * *

A month after the operation, I played my first competitive match in a small-money event. The first stop in my comeback was in a town on the outskirts of Frankfurt. I flew across to meet Andrew, who was now working for the European Central Bank (ECB) in the German administrative city. It was February, so the weekend tournament would be held in an indoor complex in the countryside. The lounges were dimly lit, matching the gloom of the winter's day outside.

I entered the men's 'B' division. The plan was to get some easy wins against lesser players. Instead, in under an hour, a local junior had destroyed me on the slick carpet court. The court was so quick that the ball was on to me while I was still preparing my backswing. As if to remind me of how far I was from the Futures circuit, Andrew and I were relegated to the 'B' locker room, far away from the better players.

It didn't get better anytime soon.

In March, I played a series of match play events held in a tennis centre in Sutton, south London. My opponents were junior players – hungry for wins against a higher-rated player. The more wins they got, the higher their national rating and the better the tournaments they could enter. They (and often their parents) were desperate. Bad line calls, all-out aggression and storming off the court rather than losing were common practices. After one loss, I stood at the net ready to shake hands, when my opponent stopped in front of me, began thumping his chest, and then pointed to his entourage in the stands.

Leaving the tennis centre in Sutton in the evening, I would be forced to take a late-night bus through grimy London suburbs, and then the last underground train, arriving home well after midnight. It was tough to back this up every Sunday evening, week after week, but fierce competition going toe-to-toe with desperate opponents was what I needed. I would go to any length to get it.

* * * * *

At Easter, I flew out to see Sylvie in Dubai. There was a Futures event on at the same time, and the desert sun would feel wonderfully warm after the bitter winter months.

The tournament was held at the Aviation Club, near the international airport. It held the Dubai ATP men's event every year in March, where the local sheiks would attend in their white robes and sit under a roof designed to look like a sail from one of their traditional boats. In the 2007 event that had finished only weeks before, Roger Federer had taken the title with a straight-sets win over Russia's Mikhail Youzhny.

I had made some changes to my game so the Dubai tournament would be a good litmus test. I had bought new racquets and got them customised to weigh 360g – about the same weight as Roger Federer's racquet. Gone was the traditional natural gut, and in came the new silver polyester string that brought with it power and topspin. Since my injury, I had hit the gym. Every day after work it was weights, core exercises and skipping. I even started doing push-ups in the sauna after hearing this is what the Austrian, Thomas Muster, used to do when he ruled the tennis world.

I wasn't planning to *just* return to the pro tour; I was determined to come back fitter, stronger, faster than before.

In the qualifying for the Dubai Futures, I lost badly in the second round to a world-ranked Slovakian. I was completely outplayed. Maybe I didn't want to admit it, but little doubts began to creep into my thoughts. Sure, I still had a few weeks to fine-tune my game, but would that be enough time? Improving your game after years at the same level is tough – the improvements are so small that sometimes you don't see them yourself.

Unbeknown to anyone at this moment but the tennis gods, when Roger would return the next year to defend his Dubai title, I would be in the stands to watch his opening match. By that time, my year off from work to compete on the men's pro circuit would be over, and I would know if I had achieved my tennis dreams…or not.

In sport, a year is a long time – *much* can happen.

* * * * *

My return to London coincided with spring. This is often a false dawn in England: everyone looks forward to seeing the sun again after months of gloom, but too often the weather is just as grey and cold as the winter that preceded it.

For me, spring saw a rise in my fortunes. A couple of small-tournament wins in local money events in Wembley and Enfield, in north London, brought some welcome confidence. Wins at any level are like gold dust. To take out a tournament and be the last man standing is priceless – no amount of practise can replicate the feeling. Little by little, my confidence – and game – returned.

During these months, I was still working as a teacher in a tough inner-city school. The two-hour daily commute across London began on the underground, where commuters are crammed into carriages like sardines in a tin. You rarely got a seat and often you would be facing your fellow passengers' armpits as they held on to the overhead handles. This would be followed by a long bus journey down the grim Tottenham High Road. After work, the journey would be repeated, simply in the opposite order.

It wasn't ideal conditions to prepare for a professional sports tour. Yet, every day after work I was training hard. Often, I would run across Hammersmith Bridge into the leafy borough of Barnes. There was a little dirt path covered by trees that ran alongside the banks of the River Thames. After a while, at a junction in the path, I would turn right and make my way past a few rough, bitumen tennis courts towards an oval-shaped athletics track hidden among the trees. Here I would do a series of sprints around the track: starting at 100m, before gradually building up to lung-busting 400m laps.

During one sprinting session, I was joined by a couple of kids who were dragging themselves around. A tennis coach (dressed from head to toe in pristine white) was waiting on one of the bitumen courts with a little basket of balls. He had made the kids (who were wearing jeans) complete a warm-up lap before their lesson. The coach stood with his hands on his hips, waiting patiently as the kids sucked in air and struggled in a mixture of running and walking.

When I finished my training, and walked past the tennis courts, the coach was looking at me with an inquisitive look on his face. I recognised him immediately as Pat Cash, who had obviously dragged his young sons out of the house for a tennis lesson. I gave him a quick nod, before heading back along the little, dirt path beside the river.

* * * * *

After four months of commuting, working and training every day, I couldn't wait to pack my bags and head to the airport.

My farewell after a decade in London was a memorable one. When I walked out of my flat in Baron's Court in the early morning hours, an old lady from the neighbouring building leaned out her window and screamed obscenities at both the taxi driver and myself. The taxi driver looked up blankly. He said it was a disgrace that her family had left her alone in such a big city…where *nobody* cared.

7

In Hannibal's Footsteps

Tunisia

ON THE little, box television, Roger Federer and Rafael Nadal contested the Roland-Garros final. The red clay on the screen regularly broke into white, snowy flecks as the transmission came and went. I sat on one of the single beds – one of the few objects in the sparse Tunis hotel room. The air-conditioning was on full blast to cope with the north African heat. The tiles were cool underfoot.

It was now make-or-break time for my tennis. I had three months to push through to the next level and earn an ATP point, or…that would be it. I had given myself a year, and even with the injury and surgery, a year was a year. That was my promise to myself, so either it would happen, or it wouldn't. At least I could return to 'regular' life knowing I had given myself the chance. But if I could break through, then I'd take my tennis as far as it could possibly go.

With the afternoon to kill waiting for Andrew's plane to arrive, I grabbed my skipping rope and headed out for a light jog. I turned away from the main street into the quiet backstreets where the white, concrete houses soon became worn and shabby. Piles of rubble littered the pavements and broken gutters. A couple of old men sat on plastic chairs, watching as I started jumping rope.

A foreigner doing exercise in their neighbourhood was the perfect excuse for one of the men to approach me. In broken English, he listed my possible nationality, 'Spanish... Portuguese?' I told him Australian. This was amazing enough for him to shout across the street to his friend in Arabic. He then proceeded to take the rope and demonstrate the correct skipping technique. 'Football?' he asked. When I said my sport was tennis, he nodded as if this would have been his second choice. 'Need swim,' he pointed at me. 'Get muscles.'

I left, leaving the men to ponder life on their plastic chairs.

I headed back past the hotel out on to Avenue Habib Bourguiba. The street was a beautiful throwback to Tunisia's French colonial history, with wide, tree-lined boulevards. I continued my run past well-heeled locals sipping coffee, al fresco style, in pavement cafés. Tourists were enjoying ice cream cones during afternoon promenades.

I ran the length of the entire boulevard up to the weird-looking Hotel du Lac. Built in the shape of a two-dimensional inverted pyramid, it seemed to defy gravity as the rooms extended into space with nothing underneath them. Legend has it that in the 1970s, George Lucas walked past the hotel prior to shooting the original *Star Wars* film in the deserts of Tunisia. When Lucas saw Hotel du Lac, it gave him the inspiration for the Jawa creature's desert vehicle found in the opening of the movie. As a *Star Wars* fan, I counted this as a bucket-list moment.

* * * * *

The next morning, Andrew and I left our hotel to head to the city of Hammamet. Rather than take an easy option, Andrew was fixated on getting a van with the locals. He had read about it in another one of his *Lonely Planet* guidebooks. His argument was that these white vans, called dolmuses, would be dirt cheap; they transported the regular Tunisians – the ones without cars and who couldn't afford taxis – around the country. 'We'll see how the real Tunisians live,' he told me.

Yeh…great idea. I'm sure Roger Federer would be doing the same.

We dragged our huge tennis bags around the Central Train Station looking for white vans. No one spoke English and every information desk was devoid of staff. After an hour of aimless walking, we finally found rows of dolmuses in a huge, dirt parking lot a short distance from the station.

'Hammamet?' we asked a driver of a white van. He pointed in the general direction to rows of identical white vans. A few queries later (while dragging all our luggage with us), we eventually narrowed our search down to one remaining dolmus.

These vans were not equipped to transport huge tennis bags. We stuffed them in the final row and hoped this wasn't a popular journey. As our fellow passengers arrived, they would see us, stop, and stare in utter bewilderment at the foreigners with them.

The dolmus wound its way through the streets of the capital picking up other passengers. They too would sit down, realise something was strange, and then turn around to stare at Andrew and myself. It was as if the mere thought that a 'rich' foreigner would choose to travel this way was incomprehensible. I was starting to share their view.

After a while, people started passing money forward to the driver using the other passengers in a human chain. They would then shout out their destination. Their change would be returned to them in the same way, like the passing of a baton in a relay race. When it came to our turn, Andrew passed a note to an old lady in front of us. 'La, la,' she said, waving her hand and laughing. The whole van had now turned around to watch the foreigners. The woman made a gesture with her hand faced downwards.

Andrew looked for the smallest Tunisian bank note he could find and presented it to the woman. 'Na'am,' she said with a smile and passed the note forward. When our change arrived, the whole van was smiling. It felt like we had passed some sort of initiation – we were now clearly one of them.

Our new friends waved goodbye when the dolmus dropped us off in the town centre of Hammamet. It was Friday and the Islamic holy day, so the streets were eerily deserted. An hour later and we still hadn't seen anybody. I was in the middle of asking Andrew if perhaps he should stop reading *Lonely Planet* guidebooks, when a lone taxi drifted through the town. I don't know who was more surprised, the taxi driver or us, but it was quickly summoned and we headed straight to the tennis club on Rue Khaled Ibn El Oualid.

A brick archway was the entrance to the Salle Omnisport club. A huge poster advertised the tournament – a screen print depicting a player hitting a double-handed backhand. The poster's background was a sea of orange and yellow, fitting for a summer clay-court event. Above the entrance, a banner proclaimed with prophetic undertones, 'Welcome players to Second Future of Hammamet.'

The club had a distinctly Mediterranean feel. The clubhouse was a white plaster building, cracked and faded over time from the sun. Club members sat at tables on the front lawn and drank espressos while watching the play. A small, wooden stand ran behind the entire row of clay courts: the space between the back of the court and the seating so narrow that spectators would have to stand to allow someone to pass. For sure, watching the tennis this week would be an intimate affair.

On the show court, two Moroccans ground out groundstroke drills – methodically hitting forehand crosscourt followed by backhand crosscourt. Not a single volley or smash was to be seen. Only at the end did they perform a few topspin serves. Lean and wiry with deep tans and thick, curly black hair, they made sliding on the dusty, dry clay seem so natural that their movement took on an artistic beauty.

Andrew and I were volleying 20 minutes into our practice session. Just the thought of standing in one corner of the court and hitting to the other corner bored me. As for sliding on clay, I had given up trying years ago. Every time I tried to slide into my shot, it would take me a series of tiny steps just to turn around (picture an elephant on ice). I was not lean and wiry with thin legs, and I did *not* grow up on clay.

Around the grounds, Moroccans, Algerians, and Libyans joined the local Tunisian players. A large group of Italians had made the short journey across the Strait of Sicily. There was also a group of Australians in the middle of a three-month overseas tour.

When the draw was made, Andrew would face one of the southern Italians, while I drew a local Tunisian. Without a doubt, they would be clay-court experts. But, then again, apart from the Australians, everyone else in the tournament was a clay-court expert.

* * * * *

My comeback got off to a good start the following morning. Abdelhamid Riani was a typical north African clay-court grinder, so I threw him dying mid-court junk balls and random chip and charges. He looked disorientated, and by the end of the match was hurling his racquet repeatedly in disgust.

It was a relief to get an opening win. My precious ATP point – my 'Holy Grail' – was only two victories away. In many ways, it was so close…yet so, so far. In progressive draws, every new opponent becomes exponentially tougher. By winning today's match, I hadn't just gotten past one opponent – instead, half the draw would be eliminated by the end of the day.

Andrew's afternoon match against Alessandro Torrisi was the final match on the schedule. The clay courts were now dry and dusty with footmarks scuffing the clay after a day of matches. The Italian was the fifth seed in qualifying at number 1,522 in the world. He looked stereotypically Italian, with flowing, black hair and dressed in a white, Italian-designed tennis outfit. He loped around the court as if running frantically would just not be stylish.

The match was so close that it was nerve-wracking to watch. I found myself pacing back and forth behind the court, too tense to sit down. I wondered how coaches manage to sit so passively and just watch. Andrew looked to attack on every ball, while the Italian was content to retrieve defensively, deep behind the baseline. It was clear who had grown up on clay. In the end, Torrisi won 7-6, 7-5. Whether Andrew should have kept attacking, or tried to play more like an Italian, I couldn't be sure.

I had always known I would make a *terrible* coach.

* * * * *

On the courts the next morning, two other Australian brothers were warming up for their qualifying matches. Unlike Andrew and I, who were exactly the same height and weight, the Frost brothers looked completely different.

Leon Frost, the elder by five years, was muscular, had his black hair cut short, and wore sleeveless shirts that exposed gym-honed biceps. In keeping with his appearance, his game was workmanlike, like a blacksmith with a sledgehammer.

The younger of the brothers, Isaac, appeared more naturally talented. Each swing from his long arms produced an elaborate wind up and elastic uncoil from his lanky body. His hair was a mop of curls, giving him the appearance of an Australian surfer.

'We used to live in Townsville,' Leon explained to me. Their home city of Townsville was one of the more northern Australian cities – even more isolated than Gladstone. 'When I was 14, the whole family moved to Brisbane. It was definitely better for our tennis.'

When Leon found out that Andrew and I were from Gladstone, he looked puzzled. 'Are you really from Gladstone? I didn't think *anyone* played tennis there.' He mustn't have been convinced – he asked the same question two more times during the week. I understood where he was coming from: Gladstone wasn't exactly a hotbed of tennis talent.

I felt the effects of playing professional tennis again. My muscles were achy and stiff. It was simply the nervous tension from trying to hit the ball so hard…all the time. I wore the tightest sweatband high around my forearm like a basketball player to ease a sore elbow. Everything on my left side was tight: from my calf, to my hamstring and into my groin. It was ridiculous – I was meant to be coming back stronger, fitter, faster. Now, after one short match at this level, I was falling apart.

* * * * *

In the final round of qualifying, my opponent was Laurent Bondaz, a southpaw from Italy ranked 1,395 in the world. If southern Italians were meant to be swarthy, then Bondaz was undoubtedly Sicilian: a three-day stubble covered his deeply tanned face and black hair covered his muscular legs. One bicep sported a huge tattoo. Unlike Andrew's lean Italian opponent, there would be no loping around the court today. Bondaz was all about power and brute strength.

Bondaz's game was simple to read. He hit a monster forehand that resembled Rafael Nadal's, while in comparison his backhand was a relatively weak chip. The only problem was that I couldn't find it. He was so quick – and the clay so slow – that he hit only forehands. In one point, he even managed to hit a forehand winner from outside the tramlines…on his backhand side of the court.

'You're hitting your forehand too short,' came advice from behind the fence. Andrew was sitting near a group of Italian players and coaches, so it came out as a loud whisper. I thought I heard, 'Hit short to his forehand.' When I did this, the ball sat up and got smacked for a winner. In desperation, I resorted to serve and volleying directly at his backhand. It didn't work either.

In fact, *nothing* was working.

On the wet clay, I was passed like a sitting duck at the net. I ended up losing 6-4, 6-2 and it didn't even feel that close – a clay-court lesson.

After the loss, it was easy to get down on myself. Here was another failure to qualify into the main draw – another week gone with nothing to show for it. Even if I had somehow found a way to beat Bondaz on clay (which looked highly unlikely) there would be even better clay-courters waiting for me tomorrow.

The little voices at the back of my mind were getting louder. Perhaps I *just wasn't good enough* to earn an ATP point. I was just one of many thousands of players caught back in the pack unable to break free.

It was cold comfort that all the Australians also failed to escape the weekend qualifying. The Frost brothers lost to European opponents. Another young Aussie to lose was Joshua Crowe, who was gradually worn down by a Moroccan after two hours of battle. He had won the first set 6-0 with attacking flair. Then the local groundsmen deliberately waterlogged the court, turning the conditions in favour of the north African. Like myself, they would have an entire week to stew over their losses before the next opportunity.

Andrew left that night; he had to get back to Frankfurt and the real world of working for a living. Sylvie replaced him. She had a couple of weeks' holiday from her job with Emirates and would stay with me for the rest of my Tunisian tour.

* * * * *

The rest of the week was idyllic.

A few days were spent under the sun in the five-star Club Aldiana beach resort. There were gardens, palm trees and a golden beach; the food for every meal was amazing. One day at lunch, I overheard an Italian player telling his friends, 'I'm not even hungry, but it's just *so* good!' What was good was that we had only one week at this venue; otherwise players might eat themselves into oblivion.

I put down the racquets for a few days. Instead, I went for long runs beside the ocean, got massages at the spa and did the occasional gym session. During the runs, I gazed out into the blue waters of the Mediterranean Sea and reminded myself that I was doing something special. After all, I was in search of the Holy Grail. I was a man on a mission.

In such an idyllic environment, it would have been easy to abandon the tennis gig and just have a holiday. Instead, I packed my bags and dragged Sylvie into the hotel van for the next leg of the Tunisian circuit. It would take an hour to snake back up the coast, past Tunis, on to the ancient city of Carthage.

* * * * *

Over 2,000 years ago, before the birth of Jesus, Carthage was the centre of a great empire. The legend of Hannibal and his military campaigns originated here, and it took the might of the Roman Empire to destroy it. Today, its ruins could be seen everywhere as the van weaved its way along the Gulf of Tunis towards the tennis club.

In the entrance to the Tennis Club De Carthage stood four stone pillars that were centuries old. The club's intentions were immediately clear; this wouldn't be some modern complex with artificial courts and a clubhouse made of glass and steel. Instead, there were only four clay courts scattered in the grounds among tall trees and bushes. Each court had viewing with concrete steps or a small wooden stand. The clubhouse sat on the side of a hill with its balcony overlooking the courts, where diners enjoyed their lunches while the action unfolded beneath them.

In the clubhouse, a long-haired French player approached me with a springy, bouncy way of walking. He shook my hand, introducing himself as Kevin.

'Kevin's not a very French name,' I commented.

'Ah,' he broke into a rueful grin. 'My mother was a fan of Kevin Costner – the film star.'

We agreed to practise. It was the first of a series of hits where Kevin Benchetrit would become my regular practice partner in Carthage. That was fine with me. He played well on the clay, with long flowing groundstrokes and a typically Gallic flourish at the end of each follow-through.

'I train at Roland-Garros. I have a private coach there,' Kevin told me during a break. 'The French Federation has links with the federation here. They've arranged a wildcard for me straight into the main draw.'

He was looking through his tennis bag while chatting. There were six brand-new Roger Federer Wilson racquets. 'I have a sponsorship with Wilson. I get six racquets, bags and string from them every year.'

I looked at my own new racquets. It had taken a couple of days of my salary to buy them. Kevin was young at 20 years of age and seemed to take the breaks for granted, as if it were natural that everything should be free and easy.

* * * * *

A couple of days passed consisting of morning practices with Kevin, followed by lunches on the terrace with Sylvie. Slowly, other players drifted in for the Friday qualifying sign-in. By the late afternoon, it became apparent that numbers were down on the previous weeks. Two weeks trekking up the Tunisian coast may have been enough for some players, while several European players had club commitments that would guarantee them a bagful of Euros for a weekend club match. Whatever the reason, the queue to register was sparse.

Fortune favoured me as I avoided the handful of world-ranked players in the draw. Only 19 players signed in for the 32-man field. Johnnylad reported to the online community, 'Gregory Howe has a bye in R1 of qualifying.' Even better was a last-round qualifying showdown with an unranked Latvian. This was an opportunity just begging to be taken.

Meanwhile, Kevin's main-draw wildcard failed to materialise. He found his name in the qualifying draw where he'd now have to earn his main-draw berth.

* * * * *

Word in the locker room was that my Latvian opponent was erratic. One of the Australians told me, 'He hits big, but makes a lot of errors – especially off the backhand. Just make a lot of balls.'

On the Sunday morning of my match, I realised that no one had told me the guy also looked like the giant Russian, Marat Safin. He was only 17, but was already tall and rangy with an impressive physique.

Ricards Opmanis travelled everywhere with his mother. She looked stereotypically Russian with her platinum blonde hair. I couldn't imagine travelling with my mother, however, Ricards didn't seem to mind. They ate together for every meal and she was omnipresent attending every practice session, match and anything he seemed to do.

At the start of our early morning match, only Sylvie and the mother were watching (a typical Futures crowd). As the morning went on, club members arrived to join them on the stepped seating beside the court.

The Latvian started *unbelievably* well. He was bombing down huge serves – winning all his service games to love. In contrast, I had to fend off break point after break point. By 4-4 I had been outplayed. Where were all the errors I had been promised? Even his forehand was starting to look like Safin's as I retrieved balls metres behind the baseline.

Perhaps Opmanis's failure to take his chances began to play on his mind. When the deadlock continued, he threw in a double fault and then missed a backhand passing shot. After dominating for the first hour, he had choked; within the space of a minute the match had turned. Looking towards the sky, he let out a guttural roar.

After throwing junk my opponent's way, his game became error-strewn and his racquet thrown regularly. He swore in English, but changed to his native tongue for long dialogues with his mother.

When I served for the match at 6-4, 5-2, it was my time to choke. With the main draw in sight, I *stupidly* changed a winning strategy. I served and volleyed, only to dump volleys and be passed on the slow clay. It took another half an hour of tension-draining energy to edge ahead and finally win in a tiebreak. The feeling was a mixture of excitement and utter relief. I had qualified for my second main draw of my tour to earn another shot at winning ATP points.

As I walked off court, a distinguished-looking, elderly gentleman approached me. He had a dapper moustache, stylishly combed hair, and had donned a sports jacket with slacks – looking like he had walked out of a 1940s Humphrey Bogart film. 'Your temperament was superb – like Federer's. You showed nothing to your opponent, even at the end.' He introduced himself as Harold and warmly shook my hand. He told me how he lived nearby and was a member of the Carthage Tennis Club – his appearance and the nostalgic feel of the club a perfect match.

My Latvian opponent was sitting a little distance away with his mother. She was animatedly talking on the phone, explaining what had gone wrong.

'Unlike him,' Harold said, gesturing to my opponent and raising his eyebrows in a dismissive gesture. 'These eastern Europeans are all the same, constantly throwing their racquet and screaming. You don't see Federer doing that!'

Not surprisingly Harold was Swiss and a Roger Federer fan. Yet, he wasn't always Swiss. He explained that he first came to Tunisia as a member of the Dutch junior team. With this in mind, Harold had taken it upon himself to give some advice to a young Dutch player in the draw. The advice had obviously worked as the Dutchman qualified in Carthage, dropping only five games in his two matches.

When I told Harold that I was playing under Great Britain, he acted delighted. 'Oh, jolly good – all the queen's men and that.' He pointed out that he had a grandiose vision of Englishmen with manners and charm. 'In that case I shall be down to watch you in the main draw.'

The three Australians I had seen last week all qualified, namely the Frost brothers and Joshua Crowe. Kevin had failed to escape the weekend qualifying with a tepid performance against a stocky Italian.

Many players hung around the referee's office watching the chips being drawn and awaiting their fate in the main draw. Not me. I couldn't bear the tension. What was the point? You couldn't will the chips to bring you luck, even though luck meant so much to an unranked qualifier. A bad draw could mean facing a fringe ATP tour player ranked in the top 300 in the world. A lucky draw meant another qualifier or a local wildcard.

When the draw was made, I was already in the player hotel. I only saw it hours later, taped to the noticeboard in the hotel lobby. My heart was pounding as I scanned down the draw. It sunk a little when I found my name and my GBR nationality, right beside the number five seed, Malek Jaziri of Tunisia.

On paper this was a nightmare draw. Jaziri's stock was on the rise and the Tennis Club De Carthage was his home club. I figured my chances of an upset were slim against a player who would eventually become an established pro on the ATP tour.

Yet, there was a possible silver lining to this black cloud of a draw. Last week, Jaziri had been forced to abandon his first-round match with a twisted ankle. He had not been seen practising since. Would he be able to make it on court? Would he try giving it a shot, perhaps withdrawing if it got too bad? If this happened, I would be awarded the match and the ATP point. The tournament director scheduled our match for Tuesday to allow the local favourite more time for his ankle to heal.

All I could do was wait...and see.

* * * * *

I didn't have to wait long. The next morning, I spotted the burly figure of Malek Jaziri entering the club. He was wearing casual long shorts, flip-flops and carried no tennis equipment. The only thing he held was a doctor's certificate. It wasn't necessary; his gingerly gait clearly revealed the state of his ankle. He ambled past on the way to the referee's office to withdraw.

This threw a cat among the pigeons. Jaziri's place in the draw would now be taken by a lucky loser, one of the eight players to lose in the last round of qualifying. It could be one of the local Tunisians, a Brazilian, Latvia's Ricards Opmanis, or my training partner, Kevin. When I later saw Kevin jumping around the grounds doing fist pumps, I figured I would be playing him tomorrow.

* * * * *

The player bus to the club on the Tuesday morning was quiet and tense. Another player must have asked Kevin who he was playing, for out of the corner of my eye I could see him pointing in my direction. 'Il a trente-cinq ans,' I heard him say. He wasn't aware that Sylvie was from Guadeloupe, a French-speaking island belonging to France. When we left the bus, she translated his words for me, 'He's 35 years old.'

I was taken aback. Not that Kevin had discovered my age; he had clearly looked at my ITF player profile where date-of-birth is one of the first things displayed. But rather the idea that being in one's 30s on the Futures circuit was significant, that somehow, I would be a pushover. Was this how the other players viewed me? To a 20-year-old like Kevin, being 35 must have appeared ancient.

Our match was scheduled after Ed Seator's encounter with the Lebanese number one, Bassam Beidas. The Middle Eastern player eventually wore down the Brit with relentless high top-spinning groundstrokes. Seator's face and newly shaven head had turned a shade of red under the midday sun. 'It's so difficult to play against a guy doing that on this surface,' he told me as he walked off court looking drained. 'Good luck in your match. I hope you win.' We were the only two players in the tournament representing Great Britain.

As the groundsmen bagged, watered and swept our court, the side seating was vacant except for Sylvie. Harold had an appointment and apologetically could not attend. He was the quintessential gentleman. Everyone else was either playing or on the balcony eating pasta.

The match began. To stop being overcome with nerves, I hit every shot as aggressively as possible. This seemed to shock Kevin, forcing him on to the back foot. Upon facing the same player that he'd been practising with all week, reality hit and his confidence deserted him. I broke him early in the match and then executed the perfect closeout game at 5-4: every first serve went in and I punched away volleys for clean winners.

I was one set away.

Keep working.

In this position, players know what they *should* do. Push hard to break early, and crush an opponent's spirit, there and then. Perhaps Kevin realised he wouldn't be getting the match for free, for his game and demeanour improved. The water from the groundsmen's hoses had evaporated, leaving the clay dusty. When the afternoon breeze became gusty, the dust began to swirl around, making Kevin's long groundstrokes deadly. He drove the ball with authority to break me in the second set. The match had swung.

At this point, several French-speaking players congregated on the steps. Kevin seemed to draw strength from their appearance and applause; he began to fist pump and move around the court with a spring in his step. In every rally, his feet always seemed to be firmly set on the clay, providing a platform for him to launch his shots.

At my end, I was left scrambling far behind the baseline. What was disconcerting wasn't the fact that the second set was slipping away, but that now I was being comprehensively outplayed. I felt powerless.

When Kevin closed out the second set, he let out a loud 'Come on,' accompanied with a fist pump and skipped to his chair. With his comments about my age coming to my mind, it would be fair to say that I was…*slightly* irritated. However, I had taken Harold's compliments about my temperament to heart, and in his words, 'showed him nothing'.

At one set all, the tournament rules stipulated new balls, and a bagging and watering of the court. The ten-minute break was a perfect amount of time for a player to get it together…or destroy one's concentration. Kevin left for a toilet break. The Tunisian umpire headed to the restaurant. Meanwhile, I left the court and sat alone on a nearby concrete step, speaking to no one, even though Sylvie was seated nearby.

My self-lecture was simple and three-fold. Firstly, I had been waiting for this moment for almost two decades. Secondly, the next 30 minutes might be the best opportunity I would ever get to make an ATP point. And therefore, I vowed to play every point like it was my last, *no matter* what the score.

The umpire returned with a cheese and ham baguette. 'I was getting a bit hungry,' he explained, embarrassed. Kevin returned after receiving encouragement from the now larger group of players sitting on the concrete steps. The court was ready, and the most important set of my life began.

I didn't have to wait long to test my resolve. After breaking Kevin's serve in the first game, my own service game went to deuce. Kevin was pumped. If he broke my service here, his momentum might carry the match away from me.

I pulled out two big first serves – never giving him a chance to get into the point. In hindsight, this was the pivotal moment. Self-doubt seemed to creep into Kevin's mind, preceding the collapse that was about to follow.

When I looked across the net, I could see him trying to loosen his muscles, rubbing his legs between points. He was young and fit – that wasn't the issue, but rather hours of uncontrolled nervous tension had slowly depleted his energy. I won point after point, moving him into the corners as his legs cramped and knotted. At 4-0 down, Kevin virtually gave me the match, pulling up lame every time he tried to run. He limped around the court, throwing his arms up in despair.

When the physiotherapist was called on court, the French players on the concrete steps had gone quiet. There was no way I was going to allow myself to get cold, so I went to one end and practised my serve. Upon seeing this, the umpire put down his baguette, grabbed one of my racquets and proceeded to return the balls to me. 'So you don't have to get them yourself,' he told me. This brought disbelief from the French players assembled on the steps. 'Qu'est-ce qu'il fait?' (What is he doing?) someone asked loudly in a stage whisper.

At 5-0, 40-15 I had two match points. After a lifetime of trying, I was one stroke away from achieving my dream.

I was *deep* in the zone.

I served and volleyed – time for bravery. Kevin ripped a topspin return, curling the ball viciously over the net…to no avail. I hit a topspin backhand half-volley (one of the most difficult shots in the game) that raced off the court for a winner, a cocktail of adrenaline and instinct. I have no idea where the shot came from – Roger Federer would have been proud of it. Kevin started to run, but suddenly stopped dead in his tracks looking stunned.

I heard someone screaming, 'Come on!' In an out of body experience, I realised it was myself.

I calmed down and walked to the net. I didn't want to rub it in to an opponent who had just lost. The umpire called, 'Game, set and match, Howe.' I looked across to Sylvie, who gave me a little clenched fist, hidden from view of anyone else.

In my court-side chair, I draped a towel over my head and savoured the moment. After wanting this for so long, the feeling was one of…*utmost* relief. The feeling of accomplishment would come later, but for now it was as if a weight had been removed from my shoulders. I'm not saying I did a Federer and blubbed uncontrollably, but I got a little misty-eyed (as much as a man growing up in rural Australia could get).

The next couple of hours went by in a blur.

I had a credit of over £100 on my mobile phone. I used it all ringing Andrew in Germany, and then all my friends in London. While on the phone, I saw Kevin sitting disconsolately on a bench – Malek Jaziri sat opposite him trying to console him. Only another tennis player could possibly understand what it meant losing a match when your first ATP point was at stake.

Later, on the bus back to the hotel, Kevin sat morosely, not talking to anyone. We never spoke another word to each other again in Tunisia, which was sad, but I understood. I would see Kevin again at a tournament in west Africa, weeks later. Then, he would bounce up to me and ask, 'Hey man. How are you? I'm alone here. Do you want to practise?'

By then he had put the loss behind him. However, at that moment on the bus, the hole that he had dug himself by perhaps believing that a 35-year-old just wouldn't be competitive looked like it was going to swallow him up.

By the evening, my result had been officially updated on the ATP website. It was quickly picked up by the aficionados:

Steven, 'Gregory made the most of his luck when the no. five seed he had been due to play in R1 pulled out to gain his first ranking point! He's the only British man left in singles outside the UK & Ireland.'

Akhenaten, 'Greg Howe achieves his first ranking point at the age of 35, and in his 78th tournament dating back to 1993. Perseverance pays out in the end. Congrats!'

RobC, 'Greg Howe is the future of British Tennis!'

Steven, 'Oops, it would have been good to look up the ages this week, obviously!'

* * * * *

The atmosphere on the bus the next morning was so much more relaxed. It was round two – the last 16. Everyone had earned at least one ATP point. For most players, they had achieved their goal and everything else was icing on the cake. For the seeded players, they were on their way to go deep into the final weekend.

An Italian player was closely inspecting a designer satchel. 'I own a designer store in Italy. Bags, clothes and accessories – all the best brands,' he informed the French owner of the satchel. The rest of the bus looked on. 'I can tell if it's fake or not. You see,' he pointed towards the inside of the bag. 'It's double stitching, therefore it's real.' Everyone seemed impressed. Only an Italian tennis player could hold a second job as a fashion store owner and expert.

On the bus, I sat across the aisle from the Egyptian ITF tournament referee, Ashraf Hamouda. He explained that he was based in Doha, Qatar. For most of the year, the Qatar Tennis Federation employed him; he ran the season-opening ATP event in Doha. I asked him if having one ATP point would get a player into the qualifying. He rubbed his small goatee while thinking.

'Your chances are good. Often there are byes in the qualifying. The players don't want to spend a whole month in Australia, so they delay their season a week. But then one year everyone turned up and the cut-off was 300 in the world.' He held his hand open. 'You just never know.'

It would take two weeks for my ATP point to become 'live' and for my name to appear on the world-ranking list. When it happened, it would open up a world of possibilities. Only world-ranked players could try to enter the next level of Challenger and ATP tournaments. 'Perhaps I'll see you in Doha,' I told Hamouda.

Until then, I had other things to worry about. In the round of 16, I faced the Australian, Joshua Crowe. As I had lost my hitting partner, I recruited three of the local kids who were messing about on one of the clay courts. We hit in the service box for a quarter of an hour. After securing an ATP point, I was pretty relaxed about things. At the end of our hit, I sorted through my bag of old sweatbands and gave them one each; one of the kids wore a giant green Nike sweatband that seemed to cover most of his forearm.

I was assigned a court midway up the hill. It was a picturesque setting with a quaint wooden stand and bushes adorning each end of the court. Tall trees loomed over the stand. While preparing my bag before the match, birds defecated all over it. Their aim was pretty good considering they sat perched in the branches of the highest trees. If being crapped on was a sign of good luck, then my chances of a win today were looking good.

When Crowe and I tried to enter the court for our match, we were surrounded by a mob of kids. They had taken it upon themselves to get their hats autographed by all the players (perhaps they had seen the idea on television). It was hard not to smile when signing my name – no one usually cared in the Futures.

My Australian opponent was quietly laughing when the hats were thrust in his direction.

*The ultimate fairytale –
Marcus Willis during his 2016
Wimbledon run. (Getty)*

With Kevin Kung after our doubles match in Bangkok.

Opening night drama in Kampala, Uganda. Joe Cooper is far left while Ed Seator has his arms raised.

On centre court in Kampala versus Ronald Semanda. Aly Zaver sits alone in the stands.

Ball boys working the Kenyan Futures in Mombasa.

Andrew on the stadium court in Windhoek, Namibia.

The Howe brothers before our doubles match in the Namibian Futures.

Scanning the draw on the terrace of Tennis Club de Carthage, Tunisia.

The clubhouse at the Northern Lawn Tennis Club, Manchester.

In action in the Senegal Futures in Dakar.

The grass courts at the Pakistan Futures, Lahore. Bogdan-Victor Leonte sits to the left.

Blending in with the locals in Khartoum, Sudan.

I asked a Chinese fan to take this picture after my ATP debut in the China Open. I lost, but it was a great experience.

The 'player lounge' during the Kingfisher Open in Mumbai, India.

On court at the Kingfisher Open – the wall to my right has yet to collapse.

Sylvie in the grounds in Doha at the Qatar ATP event.

The late Federico Luzzi at the 2008 Qatar Open in one of his final ATP appearances.

Troy Gillham in the stands before his match.

Trying to hang in there against Jan Minar in the qualifying for the 2008 Dubai ATP.

In the crowd in Dubai, savouring every moment of being a pro on the ATP tour.

Crowe was doing a pretty good Pat Rafter impersonation. He sported a green and gold, terry-towelling headband and closely cropped hair. Although he was only 18 years old, he had already been training in London for a couple of them. The ATP veteran, Wayne Arthurs, had set up base in Sutton, just south of Wimbledon. It became an informal Aussie training base in Europe where a group of players rented two nearby houses.

Crowe was slowly making his way on tour and was seen as a promising prospect. He had played in the Australian Open qualifying in January, courtesy of a wildcard, and had been world ranked for the past two years. He was now 1,386th in the world...and on the rise.

As the match began, it became clear I was dealing with a different sort of animal. While Kevin Benchetrit and Ricards Opmanis were strong baseline hitters, they gave me time to wriggle free and defend. Crowe *robbed* me of time. Every point he was working hard, being aggressive. As soon as I dropped it short, he would skip around the ball, exhorting with effort, and pounce on it, forcing it into a corner: like being attacked by a pit bull that had latched on, *refusing* to let go.

By now I had assembled a small support group. Sylvie and Harold sat in the back row of the stand. A group of kids sporting multi-coloured sweatbands sat in the front row. After I dropped the first set 6-2, they cheered my winners as I hung on in the second set.

I felt I was being outplayed – yet somehow found myself in a second-set tiebreak. It was as if knowing I would soon be world-ranked had improved my game without me realising. I flicked a couple of return winners to easily level the match: one set all.

I was as shocked as my opponent.

When Crowe faced a break point early in the third set, he looked up at the tall trees. 'Aaaaaagh!' he screamed at the top of his lungs. 'How does this happen?' Still screaming, he was punching his racquet. 'I have one racquet at 50lbs and one at 60!' His face had gone bright red and he stalked around the court in a fury.

I looked across the net, bewildered. I had expected that he'd regroup and take the match away from me. Instead, he had shown me that he was worried.

Perhaps I could win?

Up to now, I was playing free and loose – completely unaware of how effective it had been. This changed the moment I started to think about winning. At break point, I dumped my approach shot halfway up the net. I started to play safe, hoping he would lose the match for me (perhaps another learning opportunity… again).

Shortly after, Crowe won the third set 6-1 to move into the quarter-finals.

Harold approached me, 'Tough luck old boy. I thought you had him there when you won the second set. You should have kept going.' He had age and wisdom behind him. Obi-Wan Kenobi's role in *Star Wars* had been filmed in the nearby deserts, and Harold had a touch of Obi-Wan's mystique about him.

The match was an epiphany of sorts. Was Harold right? Up to now, my only goal was to make one ATP point. I never looked beyond this. How could I when it had been such a struggle to even get close? Now that I had reached this summit, perhaps there were even higher mountains to climb. Perhaps I had sold myself short and I should be looking to move up the ranking ladder, into the bigger events.

* * * * *

At four o'clock the next morning, Sylvie and I left for the airport. When the hotel taxi failed to arrive, a policeman in a nearby patrol car said they would help. They headed out to the nearby highway, lights flashing, returning shortly after with a startled taxi driver in tow.

It was a crazy ending to an intense week in north Africa.

8

In Limbo: In Europe
Norway—Germany

LATER THAT morning, when our plane landed at Heathrow Airport, I hustled through a couple of London Underground rides, a quick shower, and then a bus ride through the leafy suburb of Barnes. I alighted near The Priory rehab hospital. It was a short walk to the Bank of England club where the final round of qualifying for Wimbledon was taking place. I *had* to be there – one of my favourite pros was making a last-ditch stand at salvaging his flagging career.

It has been well noted that the qualifying matches for The Championships are played each year in the middle of a paddock. The paddock isn't even in the same borough as the All England Club. Local university students, who want to earn a little cash, serve as lines people. There are a few metal chairs lying around that one can sit on. For die-hard fans, it is pure heaven. One stands so close to the action that it feels like you are on the court. I could think of nothing better than watching a desperate former top pro, fighting for one last chance at Wimbledon glory.

Fernando Vicente, from Spain, was on the schedule today. I have an affinity with sporting journeymen, and Vicente, who once rose to 29 in the world, was undoubtedly a journeyman. He was also a true artiste: a relic from a different era. His strategy was to hit the most beautiful backhand slice that floated gently over the net...and then scramble for *everything*.

By the time I reached the Spaniard's slice of the paddock, it was also clear he had lost his pace and had developed a piss-poor attitude. After every point, he mumbled in Spanish, looking like he was ready to quit the sport there and then. No wonder he had fallen to 165 in the world. His backhand slice wasn't gently floating, but rather dying in the cold, greasy grass. His opponent, Michael Lammer from Switzerland, laboured away, unable to get any pace on the ball. If he lost a point, he would scream and hurl his racquet in disgust.

'Hey, Greg,' I heard from behind me. I turned to see the familiar face of a British man in his early 40s, remembering his name as Albert. In the past, we had shared a few train journeys heading towards tournaments on the British coast. He was with two teenagers that I would describe as inner-city kids.

'I'm doing a bit of coaching on the side,' Albert explained. 'These guys just started tennis six months ago. We're down here to look at the pros up close.' The two youths looked nonplussed. When Albert asked me how my tennis was going, and I said I just made an ATP point, the older youth responded, 'I'll make points soon. If we play, for sure I'll beat you.' Albert rolled his eyes.

We sat down to watch the fifth set of Vicente and Lammer. The stakes were so high that the tennis was unbearably awful. Lammer would hack the ball at Vicente's backhand and race to the net. 'I saw him play yesterday,' Albert pointed at the Spanish player. 'The same thing happened. After his match, I went up to him to tell him that he had to come over his backhand. He told me he could only hit slice.'

Point after point, Lammer bullishly charged in, only for Vicente to try to out-chip him. 'Hit topspin,' Albert shouted to the player. The former top-30 pro looked sideways at him in despair.

Vicente eventually won 9-7 in the fifth set, mainly because Lammer kept dumping his volleys and smashes into the bottom of the net. A few days later, Vicente won a total of six games in his final appearance at a Grand Slam event.

I left Albert and his students to find my Australian friend and hitting partner, Mark Robinson. Mark was the first person I had hit with after my operation and was one of the guys I called after my match with Kevin Benchetrit. When I found him, he was wearing a woolly hat, scarf, jacket and jeans. The weather had turned miserably chilly. He greeted me with, 'Great job, mate!'

He had called in sick at his architect's firm and had been watching the qualifying since the morning – another aficionado of the game. 'I've been over watching Nicolas Mahut. What a beautiful game – real serve and volley on grass. I really hope he gets through.' Mark explained that he had to go. He was making a tennis comeback and had a match this evening in a local London tournament. Unfortunately, after sitting in the cold all day, he managed to rip his hamstring almost in half.

That was *the end* of his comeback.

* * * * *

After the euphoria of Tunisia, I should have taken time off. However, my flights were booked and paid for, so on Friday morning Sylvie and I boarded a Scandinavian Airlines plane bound for Norway.

Exactly 24 hours before, Sylvie and I were leaving the north African desert heat. Now, the plane descended through the mist and rain towards a thick, green forest near the arctic circle. My logic behind my itinerary was that at least both events were on clay. As the rain pelted down, the chance of an outdoor event looked unlikely.

Everything in Norway appeared to be permanently plunged in darkness. In Oslo Airport, soft lighting illuminated the wood and glass corridors. Everything had a stylish design with shades of natural wood everywhere (like being in a giant IKEA store).

In the airport bus transfer to the city, Sylvie and I were the only passengers. The journey must have taken a long route around Oslo, for there were no houses to be seen – only forest. The pelting rain made visibility through the windows poor as the bus plunged into the gloom.

After half an hour, Sylvie must have seen a touch of worry on my face. 'Is this normal? How long do you think it takes to get to the city?' she asked me. At this point, I seriously wondered if we had stumbled on to a bus heading towards Lapland. Suddenly, with no warning, the bus broke through the city limits and before long we were near our hotel. Perhaps Oslo was a smaller city than I had initially imagined.

With it being Friday and sign-in day, I borrowed a hotel umbrella and headed towards the Frognerparken Oslo Arena tennis club. The umbrella protected my head and little else as the wind blew the rain sideways. I arrived at two rudimentary concrete blocks that served as a pro shop and toilets. A group of players huddled together under a metallic roof, staring at the sea of water that had submerged the complex. Laurent Bondaz, the swarthy Italian, stood with his hands deeply entrenched in the pockets of a thick jacket. His deep Mediterranean tan seemed out of place in Scandinavia. After the sun of Tunisia, perhaps he too was wondering why on earth he had decided to play in this part of the world.

The sign-in for the qualifying was conducted in a narrow corridor in one of the concrete blocks. It was so cramped that it could only fit a couple of players at a time, while the referee's desk looked like a table that had been borrowed from a school classroom. It appeared that the Norwegian Tennis Federation's budget did not stretch to cover the extravagance of furniture... or perhaps they were just frugal people. After signing in, no one hung around.

Except myself.

I was in a strange position. Even though I had earned an ATP point only last week to break away from the pack, this week I would still be an unranked player until my point became 'live'. In Norway, there were four British players with higher national rankings than myself who would take priority. As more and more players dashed through the rain to register, I feared the possibility that I could miss out altogether.

Missing the cut would be a real smack-in-the-face reality check. *Excuse me – big man coming through. Didn't the universe realise I'd made an ATP point last week?*

I hung around in the rain for an hour until the six o'clock deadline. The ITF referee informed me that only 43 players had signed in for the 48-man field. Considering other Scandinavian countries like Sweden and Denmark were so close, I was surprised more players hadn't turned up. I asked a Norwegian tennis official if this was unusual? 'No. The player base in these countries is very small. Apart from the very top players...this is everyone.'

On discovering that I was playing again so soon after Tunisia, even the aficionados were amazed. RobC put it in simple terms when he posted online, 'Greg Howe, playing *again*!'

With some relief, I returned to Sylvie to have dinner in the hotel room. I'd heard that Oslo was exorbitantly expensive (even by European standards), so in London I cooked as many meals as possible, stuffing them in Tupperware containers. We sat in our stylishly modern hotel room, watched the rain pelt against the window, and ate our cold food. Rihanna's new song 'Umbrella' was playing on MTV.

* * * * *

The next morning, the rain came down even heavier. The chance of seeing the sun today looked even bleaker than yesterday. Black rain clouds merged with a sky mixing shades of grey. On the tennis information board in the hotel foyer, a note stated that today's qualifying matches would be held in a nearby indoor complex.

Considering it was the Norwegian summer and I hadn't seen the sun yet, it was amazing how healthy and vibrant everyone looked. At breakfast, the young male and female tennis players (there was a female event running too), all sported glowing tans and wholesome appearances. I heard that solariums were used frequently so that locals could get their dose of vitamin D. Whatever they did, it was working. Everywhere you went in Norway, people looked pretty content with their lives.

The journey to the new tennis centre consisted of a ride on the Norwegian 'T-Bane' metro system, followed by a walk in the pouring rain. Sylvie and I shared the Thon Hotel umbrella. Every room in the hotel had umbrellas for guests' use – emblazoned with 'Thon Hotels' on the canopy. As it appeared to rain constantly in Norway, it was smart advertising.

From the outside, the Oslo Tennis Arena looked like a giant aircraft hangar. Once inside, it looked like a giant aircraft hangar with tennis courts. Spotlights hung from the ceilings, plunging the courts into light, and leaving everything else in darkness. Steel support girders were visible on the wall behind the courts and across the ceiling. Everything from the courts, walls and curtains were a matt, dark green, making the whole place merge into dark shadows.

The opening matches were a fascinating look into tennis in the Scandinavian region. Rangy, blonde players patrolled across the baseline playing controlled baseline games. Everyone had double-handed backhands and slightly mechanical serves, which began each baseline exchange. There were no extravagant flourishes on the follow-through, and no posturing and sulking between points that I had witnessed with players from the Mediterranean countries.

While Swedish tennis was once legendary, and the tour was always populated with the occasional Dane or Finn, tennis in Norway was virtually unknown. This week there were only four world-ranked players from Norway. None of them were to be found in the world top 600. Former pro Christian Ruud was the only Norwegian to break into the world's top 50 in 1995. He seemed to be an outlier, coming from such a small player base in the traditionally winter sports nation.

My opponent in the first round was a Norwegian, Nicholas Bjerke. While he had no ATP ranking, he was relatively high in the Norwegian national rankings. At 18 years old, he was one of the promising juniors that the Norwegian Tennis Federation hoped would make a breakthrough in the pro ranks.

On court, I immediately felt disorientated. I reminded myself why I hated playing tennis indoors: the ball flies through the air before skidding off the court; even though it could be freezing outside, the stuffy air means you sweat buckets; the sound of every shot echoes off the metal roof. The list could go on (I'm sure you get the idea). I would never be stupid enough to willingly enter a professional indoor tournament, yet here I was…playing indoors.

My Norwegian opponent was in his element. The local players played nearly all year indoors. Their games were tailor-made for the sterile conditions. He won the first set 6-2, constantly hitting crosscourt drives that raced off the surface.

Wasn't it only four days ago that I was playing in the main draw of the Tunisian Futures? Now I was getting pushed all over the court on the morning of the first day of qualification. I stepped it up a level, hitting crosscourt on all of the Norwegian's crosscourt shots. It was like playing in some early video tennis game where the ball only went diagonally (and was just as boring). When I squeezed out the second set 6-4, I wondered if I had *finally* discovered the secret to playing tennis indoors.

In the third set, Bjerke must have realised my strategy, for now he began blasting balls down the line. With the change of angle, now I kept seeing a luminescent exit sign glowing in the darkness at one end of the court. How could I have not noticed it before? It had been there the whole match. When the Norwegian pulled ahead in the third set, I had to resist the urge to smash the glowing sign with my racquet.

Bjerke won the final set 6-4 to take the match. If I had to play the match again against the same opponent, in the same aircraft hangar, I am not sure I would know what to do differently.

I swore *never* to play tennis indoors again.

The metro ride home allowed me to mull over the sobering let-down I now experienced. In a way, it was to be expected after the charged emotions of Carthage. That night, I treated Sylvie and myself to the most expensive pizza I had ever eaten (and we ordered the small size). We had no choice – all our Tupperware meals were finished.

To rub salt in my wounds, the following day's play was completed under brilliant sunshine. It was the first time I had seen Norwegian sun. On the clay courts in Frognerparken, I watched Nicholas Bjerke against an Austrian player, having enough time to watch the central European win before my evening flight departed for London.

* * * * *

Back in my London flat in Baron's Court, I had time to decompress away from the tour. During tournaments, you couldn't see the forest because there were so many trees everywhere: flights, airports, sign-ins, practice, and matches… all in a repeating loop. In a blessing in disguise, it rained every day in London, making tennis training near impossible.

Finally, I had a few days to think.

In tennis terms, new doors would open when my world ranking became official. It was now time to consider which direction I wanted to go. Before, as an unranked player, my schedule was simple; out of the numerous Futures events being played that week, all I had to do was balance out which was the cheapest with the best opportunity to get ATP points.

However, with a ranking soon to be added to my name, the tennis world offered a host of opportunities. I was forced to look at the schedule in a whole new light. Once a player was on the ATP rankings, even if it was in last place, they were eligible to compete in any level of tournament – Futures, Challenger, ATP and Grand Slam. As long as there were spaces in a draw, no tournament director could refuse you. It didn't matter if you were (now) a 35-year-old schoolteacher entering the Wimbledon qualifying. If the number of players ranked above you was less than the draw size, then you were *in*.

It was the perfect meritocracy.

What did I want from my time on the tennis circuit? It would be so easy to continue in my comfort zone. I could keep playing the Futures circuit with the hope of grafting out a couple more ATP points to crawl up the ranking ladder. Or was this now time for me to take a risk and move out of my comfort zone? In the top-level ATP tournaments, a couple of qualifying wins could mean a match with a Federer or a Nadal.

Would I even have the nerve to try?

In the back of my mind was an obscure Australian player called John Arbanas. I never knew him, and I only ever saw him practise for a couple of minutes.

However, his story *fascinated* me. In 1992, he was granted a wildcard into the Australian Open qualifying. He had no ranking and was never a top junior, but rather just a very good local player.

For a few days he caught fire, beating three former top pros to make it into the main draw. How did he do it? He never did anything of note after his Australian Open run – not even making another ATP point. It didn't matter – John Arbanas played Grand Slam tennis. It was the stuff Hollywood movies are made of.

My problem was I just had no idea how the big tournaments worked. Player hotels were never advertised for security fears. Where were the sign-ins held? These details were strictly insider secrets.

I decided to ring the ATP headquarters in Monte Carlo; a woman with a French accent picked up the phone.

'Good morning,' I began.

'How can I help you?' replied the woman with the French accent.

'I'd like information on how to enter the qualifying for ATP events?'

There was a pause [I could picture her rolling her eyes], 'Go to our website.'

'I did, but I can't find any details.'

'Are you a player?'

I explained my story of making an ATP point last week, but that I wasn't on the official rankings just quite yet, but soon.

'So, you aren't a top-500 player then?'

'Um...no.'

There was another pause while the woman considered the possibility of my story holding up. 'I'm transferring you through. Hold the line please.'

I was through the first line of defence. Soon another woman with a French accent answered the phone. I changed my line of attack.

'I made an ATP point in a Future last week. When will it appear on the rankings?'

'Normally it takes two weeks, but because it'll fall in the middle of Wimbledon fortnight, it will only appear after the third week.'

'I was thinking of going to the Gstaad ATP event next week. But my point won't have come in by then. Can I still try to sign in?'

'It's up to the tournament.'

'Would I need an approved wildcard?'

'It's not a wildcard. They just decide whether you can play or not.'

'Is Gstaad favourable?'

'I don't know.'

'What is the player hotel?'

'I don't know.'

'Could I get the information sheet e-mailed out?'

There was a pause. Perhaps she thought I wouldn't go away and this was her chance to get rid of me.

'I'll e-mail it to you this once. But in future, you need to pay and register for a log-in.'

This was news to me. I'd never heard of an exclusive ATP site only for world-ranked players. I duly listened to the instructions to fax my passport page and credit card details for the fee.

A couple of days later, my access to the ATP players' site was authorised – opening up a new world of possibilities. I now had access to every level of tournament with details of official player hotels, registration information, player party dates and the provisional entry lists to every tournament in the world. I could check Roger Federer's playing schedule. Just for kicks, I entered my name into the US Open entry list.

You never know.

* * * * *

Back in the real world, I was stuck in a tennis limbo. For another two weeks, as in Norway, I would still be an unranked player stuck at the end of the queue in Futures qualifying events. With this in mind, ideas to play ATP events like Gstaad were shelved. Instead, I flew off to Frankfurt to see Andrew and play a couple of German Futures.

Andrew collected me in a Mercedes hire car from the airport. Our first stop would be the event in Kassel, about a two-hour drive from Frankfurt.

Andrew and I had barely arrived in the tennis club's parking lot when a tall, dreadlocked figure approached us. He wore a matching warm-up tracksuit. 'Konnten Sie Ihr Auto ein wenig bewegen Sie bitte?' he asked.

There was a pause while Andrew tried to translate the German into English. When he realised we weren't locals, Dustin Brown smiled and started again in English, 'Could you move your car a bit, please? I'm just trying to get my van out.' He motioned his hand towards a large, white camper van, parked horizontally in the parking bays.

While the Jamaican-German Brown would eventually crack the world's top 100, now he was still trying to battle his way through the Futures and the Challenger circuits. His ranking was 499 at the time of the Kassel event. With the prize money so paltry at this level, Brown travelled the European circuit in the white camper van to save money, sleeping in parking lots and using the shower facilities in the locker rooms.

The Kassel event was a U$15,000 event, with hospitality; that meant main-draw players got free hotels until the night after they had lost. Brown would be able to collect cash – in lieu of his free hotel room – on top of his prize money, effectively doubling his wages for the week.

The increased prize money meant that the event would be just under Challenger-level status. With more ATP points at stake, the main-draw field was strong. The cut-off for the main draw was 400 in the world, with the number one seed, a German called Dieter Kindlmann, being 294 in the world.

The qualifying draw would therefore be treacherously tough with a couple of Chileans ranked in the 500s fighting to get through. Someone like Germany's Philipp Marx, ranked a top 600 player, would only be a lower-ranked seed in the qualifying section where there was *no* prize money and *no* ATP points to gain. It seemed ridiculous that someone ranked so highly in a major sport could leave a professional event with nothing.

The Kassel tournament had a different feel than other Futures events. The show courts had electronic scoreboards, while rows of temporary seating ringed all courts, making it feel like the outside courts at a Grand Slam event. Mercedes courtesy cars with sponsors' logos plastered on the side ferried players back and forth.

A large sponsor's and hospitality tent sat beside the clubhouse, where well-heeled members were already congregating with their sports jackets and wine glasses.

The queue at the sign-in desk was full of battle-hardened European players. The process seemed full of formalities with a host of important-looking club members sitting beside the ITF referee on a large table. As each player registered, there was a pedantic cross-checking of details, with the club president carefully considering each name and nationality.

When it was finally my turn, the German referee punched my name into the computer. 'You're an old guy, hey?' He looked up with a smug smile on his face. 'Are you a player…or a coach?'

You would have thought the fact that I had been standing in the registration queue with the entry fee in my hand would have given him a clue. 'A player,' I replied.

The referee turned to his colleague, spoke in German, and laughed. I remembered that at Wimbledon, Pat Cash had once called Boris Becker a 'smart-ass kraut'. At this moment in time, I was tempted to repeat Cash's words.

'Well, good luck then,' he replied with a smile, and pushed the sign-in list in my direction. I wished at this point there was a world ranking beside my name. It would have added some credibility. Instead, a British national ranking of 363 brought very little.

As I walked away, I was thankful that I was not trying to bluff my way into the ATP event in Gstaad, Switzerland, this week. If I was being ridiculed for trying to enter a European Futures qualifying stage at 35 years of age, then I couldn't imagine how asking for a place in a European ATP qualifying draw would have gone down. At least the German referee smiled and thought he was being funny. I wondered if the Swiss would have been so humorous.

After three hours sitting in the club café drinking coffee, Andrew returned after checking the draw. God knows how it took the referee that long to pull a few chips out of a bag.

'This is a joke,' Andrew said.

'What do you mean?' I looked up from my third cappuccino. 'Did we miss out?'

'Even worse…I'm playing you in the first round!'

My heart sank. After entering so many of the same events, it was bound to happen sooner or later. Just the thought of trying to beat my brother made me feel ill. I'm sure the German referee had a good laugh over it.

Sure enough, when I checked tomorrow's order of play, Andrew Howe (AUST) was due to play Gregory Howe (GBR) at 10.30am on court five. To rub salt into the wounds, all qualifiers were to be shipped out to another complex, *far away* from the main site.

The aficionados duly noted my match with Andrew, with ForeverDelayed joining in on the humour of the situation when he posted, 'At least one Howe will make the second round.' He continued in a more serious note, 'Just the one Brit has made the trip for qualifying here. Very tough for Greg to qualify here, as in the final round he would have to overcome Philipp Marx, ranked at 595 (the top seed here is ranked at 406, so this is a hell of a Futures event).'

* * * * *

There wasn't much to report on the match.

Andrew and I sat on the same bench and chatted at the change of ends. I couldn't muster any intensity, and neither could Andrew. I had earned my ATP point and I desperately wanted Andrew to break through too. Andrew won 6-3, 6-2 in what was a terrible experience for both of us.

I had more enjoyment playing the role of coach a couple of hours later. Whatever advice I gave didn't work – Andrew went out to a German player in straight sets. We walked straight out to the car park to the Mercedes rental car. Without passing the main complex, we hit the autobahn back to Frankfurt as fast as the Mercedes rental car could go.

* * * * *

My momentum was completely lost. Not surprisingly, as if my body had sensed the let-down, I got a cold. My days consisted of joining Andrew at his work lunch in the European Central Bank. After the tennis circuit, it was a shock being surrounded by bankers and bureaucrats working a nine-to-five day. People were power-dressing with sharp grey suits, and carried themselves with an air of self-importance (it was 2007, still a year away from the world financial crisis where Europe almost bankrupted itself with the ECB at the helm).

The following weekend saw my third, first-round qualifying loss in three straight weeks. Andrew and I travelled to the tiny town of Romerberg. The delight of the remote, rural tennis club in holding a professional event was evident in the effort the club had invested: official courtesy cars, food stalls and free t-shirts made players feel special.

However, staying in the empty player hotel (the German players always commuted from home) near the train station, with only a local Chinese restaurant nearby for dinner, was depressing. When I laboured through a three-set defeat in oppressively heavy conditions, I didn't mind catching the train returning to Frankfurt. The final would eventually be won by the dreadlocked Dustin Brown. He had driven there from Kassel in his white camper van.

On the following Monday, the new post-Wimbledon ATP rankings were released. Roger Federer headed the rankings, followed by Rafael Nadal, Novak Djokovic, and then Andy Roddick. My heart was thumping when I scrolled down the ranking list, past the hundreds of names of professional tennis players. Towards the end of the rankings, I saw my name: Gregory Howe – 1,511.

It was truly a special moment.

Throughout my life, people outside the tennis world always asked the same question – how good a player are you? It was always so difficult to explain where you fitted in among the millions of people who played the sport. Now it would be easy. I was 1,511 in the world.

No need to explain further.

9

The Challenger Tour
Manchester

DURING WEEK 29 of the tennis calendar, there were 14 professional tournaments scattered around the globe. Ten Futures events commenced in locations as exotic as Armenia, Iran and...Joplin, Missouri.

The elite ATP tour had three options to choose from: after Wimbledon, the Europeans could resume their clay-court season in Germany or Holland; in the States, the hard-court swing began in Los Angeles as the tour headed towards the US Open.

My choice was a Challenger level event in Manchester, England. These Challenger tournaments were the bridge between the low-level Futures and the glamorous ATP tour. With U$25,000 as prize money and free hotels for the main draw, Manchester would mix fast-rising young players heading for the big time with ATP journeymen trying to hold on to their careers. For serve and volley specialists, it was a final opportunity to compete on grass after Wimbledon.

The number one seed in the entry list was the giant Belgian Dick Norman, who was flitting in and out of the world's top 100. I had seen him push Carlos Moya at the Australian Open one year. Now at 36 years of age, he was a good example of the kind of player who frequented the Challenger circuit.

The Manchester event was a relic from a bygone era. Since 1880, when it was called the Northern Lawn Tennis Championships, it had been part of the traditional British grass court season. It had survived the change into the Open era, continuing as a major tournament until 1994. In a seven-year period up to that year, its champions' roll call contained household names: Stefan Edberg, Goran Ivanisevic, Pete Sampras and Pat Rafter.

After their Manchester titles, every one of them became a Grand Slam champion. The winners' names gradually become more obscure as the event lost prestige. It had now grown comfortable in its Challenger status – not big – not small – but at least still *present* on the tennis calendar.

Unexpected issues began the moment I prepared to leave my flat in London. Walking past the mirror on the way to the front door, I realised that I was wearing a t-shirt with 'ATP' stencilled across the front. Was I trying to suggest that I was an ATP tour player...around *real* ATP tour players? I changed to a plain black t-shirt instead.

At the Manchester Challenger, there appeared to be a small army running the tournament. From my seat in the Virgin train, a phone call to Madelyn, the transport officer, got me a pick-up at the train station. I was then transferred to Peter who booked me a room. Did I need a physio or practice court? *Not yet, thanks.* I could get used to this: I was so used to doing everything myself on the Futures tour.

The tournament also had a press officer – perhaps the worst job. For the previous three weeks, since Wimbledon had begun, British tennis had taken a bashing at the hands of the British press. This was nothing new. Laying into the Lawn Tennis Association (LTA) had become as traditional as the All England Club's strawberries and cream.

Every year, once all British players had been dumped out of Wimbledon, the press with unabashed relish would attack the LTA, demanding to know why the sport in the country was so bad.

This year all parties took it to a new level. Without an injured Andy Murray to draw the nation's attention, as soon as Feliciano Lopez dumped an ageing Tim Henman out of the tournament, the tennis community imploded, turning on itself. The LTA took the initiative and attacked their own players. Roger Draper, the LTA's new chief executive, told *The Times*, 'You look at some of [them], *they* need a wake-up call.'

Henman himself joined in, with *The Guardian* reporting his words, 'For years we've been far too accepting of mediocrity... we have to be a bit more ruthless, wipe the slate clean and start again.' Henman's assault then turned on the LTA's use of wildcards. He told the BBC, 'If you're any good, you don't need wildcards. You get one at 17, 18...but if you're any good you get into these events on your ranking.'

Much of the public anger seemed to centre on the new, £30m National Tennis Centre in south London. For the LTA, it was the central plank in their battle plan to save British tennis. The press joyfully described it as a 'white elephant' and 'a camel of a building'.

I had my own bone to pick with the LTA. Before Manchester, I had called the so-called 'white elephant' (or 'camel building' – take your pick) to enquire about practising on their grass courts (that were usually empty). After all, I was British, world ranked, and heading to the upcoming Challenger event, ostensibly run by...the LTA.

'I'm sorry – these courts aren't for public use,' a receptionist told me. I complained, was asked for my name, and put on hold. Eventually the receptionist returned, 'The facility is for national squad players *only*.' I should have rung the British tabloids – they would have had a field day with such an elitist comment.

Sitting on the train, my thoughts began to wander. What if I didn't make the cut? I now had a world ranking, but Challenger qualifying draws were tough. Would I too want to be one of those players begging for a wildcard? If I couldn't even practise on my own federation's training courts, then why would the LTA care if I was in the draw or not?

Thankfully the train pulled into Manchester's Piccadilly train station. As promised by Madelyn, a 20-seat bus pulled up to collect me. The driver and I had barely left the station when he was ordered via walkie-talkie to promptly return; an Australian player was arriving via train from last week's Futures event in Felixstowe.

After a couple of minutes sitting in the bus, the familiar face of Luke Bourgeois poked itself through the bus door. I had last seen him in the Gold Coast Futures in Australia the previous year. At that time, he was flying high – Roger Federer's practice partner, working with the legendary Tony Roche and ranked in the world's top 300. However, a year is a *long* time in tennis. The fact that he was back in the qualifying for a Challenger event spoke for itself.

At the start of the year in the Sydney ATP event, he had lost a cliffhanger to Carlos Moya in a third-set tiebreak. He even had a match point of his own, but netted a forehand. After the match, he was quoted in Australia's *Herald Sun*, 'Tennis is a cruel game.'

Beating a former world number one – live on national television – could have been just the break he needed. Instead, a neck injury had led to a dramatic loss of form. He was now 30 years of age, ranked in the 600s and had won exactly three main-draw matches in the last six months. He was indeed right to call tennis a cruel game.

There is no parachute to slow you down when you start free-falling through the tennis rankings. You don't hit the ground; you just fall off the end…into *nothing*.

I had run into Luke Bourgeois at tournaments over the past decade; he was always friendly and engaging. This time though, when I greeted him, he merely nodded and went to sit at the back of the bus. Had he recognised me? Maybe he was just depressed after his ATP experiences to be back in the qualifying of a Challenger event…with players like myself. Seeing me, it must have felt like he'd just lost ten years from his tennis life.

'I just came up from London,' I told him, searching for something to start the conversation. 'It was either the Futures at Frinton or the Challenger here, and I'd never been to Manchester before.'

'Sometimes it's good to go to a new place on the itinerary,' he smiled. 'It's a good way to see the world.'

There was a pause after he finished his sentence. With his 'see the world' comment, I guess he still saw me as someone who was content to play tennis without ever really trying to make it. It was fair enough. I could always go back to my day job if I had to, while players like him had staked *everything* from a young age to make it. There often wasn't a fall-back option.

While he was being cordial, he appeared to be so inwardly focused that merely trying to have a conversation seemed to be a struggle. It was as if he had to force the words out. I began to wonder if the higher the level of tournament one played, the more introspective everyone became in order to conserve energy.

'Are you still in London?' I asked him. I had seen him previously in suburban Sutton, where I knew he trained with other UK-based Australians.

'No. I live in Florida now. Tennis in London became too difficult. It took so long on public transport to get to the courts and the training facilities weren't that good. In Tampa, the weather is so good. There are lots of top players to train with – top trainers too.'

I had so many questions I wanted to ask him. How had Tony Roche helped his game? What was hitting with Roger Federer like? However, it didn't seem to be the time or place. Anyway, why should he reveal their secrets, or even be asked to? Instead we chatted about his brother, who I had met in London playing smaller, amateur tournaments.

The bus soon arrived at the Britannia Airport Hotel – the official player hotel. Bourgeois left with an Australian, 'see you later' before the 20-seater bus, carrying the driver and me, arced away.

Having heard my Australian accent, the driver proceeded to offer an opinion on every sporting confrontation involving Australia and England from cricket to the upcoming Rugby World Cup. He couldn't wait to indulge in the national pastime of using Aussie success as a yardstick to explain why the English are *so useless* at sport.

'It must be some kind of flaw in the national character,' he explained, while glancing at me in the rear-view mirror. 'Maybe we pay our sportsmen too much because every time they win something major, that's it. They never do any good after it. Just look at the World Cup in '66.'

The journey into the exclusive neighbourhood of Didsbury was just long enough for me to ask him if he thought the recent labelling of British tennis players as 'lazy' was warranted.

'Well, I was doing this job last year also. To be honest, some of the British players seemed to be more interested in playing golf than tennis.' Still driving, he turned around to gauge my reaction. 'We had beautiful weather last year. All the other nationalities practised all day long on the grass courts, but I just seemed to be taking the British players to the nearest 18-holer.'

One senior English player seemed to be singled out for most of the courtesy driver's criticism. The player wasn't playing Manchester this week – he had officially retired, telling the newspapers that he had 'stagnated' and was no longer improving.

By the time the bus arrived at the Northern Lawn Tennis Club, the sunshine had broken through the dark clouds, illuminating a small group of immaculate grass courts. With its traditional clubhouse painted white – complete with brown trimmings and a sloping roof – it reminded me of the US Opens of the 1970s, held at the venerable Westside Tennis Club. Strands of bright red seats nestled in front of neatly trimmed bushes.

Four groundsmen knelt on the centre court. They held a taut string to guide their service-line markings. These men had spent the entire summer preparing the five grass courts to the unforgiving standards of the All England Club. After four days of heavy rain, they weren't about to allow players wearing dimpled soles to rip up their precious turf. If the qualifiers wanted to practise, they could 'bugger off' to the artificial Astroturf out the back.

Unlike the traditional clubhouse, the referee's office was the middle of three portacabins jammed behind the indoor courts; the same kind of temporary huts used as toilets at major sporting events. If anyone thought running a pro tennis tournament was glamorous, then they were badly wrong.

Situated in these spartan confines were the tournament director, the referee and the ATP supervisor (professional events always seemed overstaffed to me). The more important the tournament, the more people it appeared to need to make a draw.

'We meet in all the exotic places of the world,' I greeted them with as I walked up the portacabin's carpeted stairs. After having played tennis in Britain for the best part of a decade, I knew many of the officials.

'This year they put us beside the toilets,' said Peter Finn, pointing at the first hut. He was in charge of the 'Control Desk'. I didn't dare ask who had drawn the third and last hut. For one thing, it certainly wasn't the press officer, who was fighting fires in a luxurious room in the clubhouse itself.

'I'm afraid the grass courts are out of action until Tuesday at the earliest. The qualifiers will be going indoors,' Peter apologised.

Wasn't it only three weeks ago that I had sworn *never* to set foot on an indoor court ever again? To be honest, it didn't surprise me – it seemed to have rained every day in England this summer. One of Rafael Nadal's matches at this year's Wimbledon had lasted for five days. In a way, it was my own fault for entering a grass court event in 'sunny' England and expecting to play only on grass.

On the desk there were two sheets of paper: one for world-ranked players and one for those unranked. With great satisfaction, I signed my name on the world-ranked sheet of paper – the number 1,511 following my signature. As the deadline was drawing to a close, my chances of making the cut looked promising. When I inquired, I was simply told, 'All ranked players are in.'

On the two indoor practice courts, there was a noticeable step up in class on display at the Challenger level. Players' footwork and racquet preparation were precise, even slightly robotic at times as the same movement was repeated over and over. No one was screaming or throwing racquets (as often occurred at Futures events). The courts were full, so I headed to the upstairs gym.

A few European players were already there, blending in with local residents who read magazines while going through the motions on the stationary bikes. I recognised one of the players as the German veteran, Lars Burgsmuller.

The last time I had seen Burgsmuller, he had been playing Andre Agassi in front of 10,000 people on Wimbledon's prestigious court number one. Agassi had beaten him in a routine first-round encounter – one of the German's 26 Grand Slam appearances. Around that time, he had peaked at 65 in the world. Now he sat at 277 in the rankings. After not officially entering the Manchester event, he had made a last-minute decision to risk playing his way through qualifying.

Although he wasn't big or muscular, Burgsmuller looked superbly fit. As a sponsored player, he was decked out from head to toe in Fila gear, separating him from the majority of players who wore an assortment of different brands and designs. He went through a series of lower-body exercises on the gym mats, quietly chatting to a giant of a man beside him who was mirroring his movements. Both players were there for over half an hour before heading off to the practice courts. It was a daunting prospect to think that I could be facing either one of them tomorrow.

One of the top British players at the time strolled in. He appeared distinctly underwhelmed as he walked around inspecting the gym equipment. Sporting a beard, a baggy t-shirt that hung loosely over his shorts and slipper-like shoes, he finally settled on the running machine. Whether he was warming up, or warming down, it was hard to tell; he went at a pace somewhere between walking and jogging. After a few minutes, he stopped and headed for the exit looking as uninterested as when he had walked in.

The draw appeared later that evening, pinned up on a noticeboard in the foyer of the Britannia Airport Hotel. I had managed to avoid any of the nightmare scenarios, finding my name paired with one Matt Brown of Great Britain.

Brown had once been as high as 950 in the world. His claim to fame was having once been the national under-16 champion of Great Britain – he had beaten Andy Murray in the final of that year's tournament. Unlike Murray, who had headed straight to the pros, he had chosen the American college route and had just completed his sophomore year at Baylor University in Waco, Texas. He would undoubtedly be a tough player. But at this level, it could have been *a lot* worse.

Later in my room, as I began to settle down for the night, a wedding reception began in earnest in a nearby conference room. Pop music blasted down the corridors, shaking the doors and making sleep impossible. For me, the Challenger level was an exciting step up. I doubt, however, that players like Burgsmuller and Norman – regulars on the ATP tour – felt so thrilled.

* * * * *

Breakfast the next morning was a *quiet* affair.

One by one, players drifted down from their single rooms. The Challenger level gave main-draw players hospitality in the form of free hotel rooms. Unlike in the Futures tournaments, there wouldn't be anyone forced to sleep on other players' hotel room floors.

Everyone had his own form of distraction. A few brought down laptop computers, staring intently at their screens while eating their cereals. The giant European player I had seen in the gym the night before read every article in *The Independent*'s sports section. With the back page completed, he neatly folded the broadsheet twice over before returning to his room. In his entire stay at breakfast, he hadn't uttered anything more than a brief 'hello' to his fellow players. He didn't appear aloof – in fact far from it – but in the quietly tense atmosphere in the breakfast room, conversation seemed somehow inappropriate.

It wasn't until the coach of the Israeli number one, Harel Levy, entered the dining room that the stillness was broken. He moved from player to player, chatting warmly with everyone. He drew players to him as a group formed around one table. It had taken a coach – someone who wouldn't be directly threatening anyone else's chances – to allow the players an excuse to speak to each other.

By the time the bus arrived at the hotel, there was a crowd of players waiting for the trip to the tennis club. I shared the front seat with the driver; perhaps he too felt the opening match-day tension, as he didn't say anything. In fact, no one had much to offer – silence filling the entire journey.

The quietness vanished when I stepped into the small indoor arena. The narrow viewing area was crammed with an assortment of people creating an almighty din. Teams of ball boys in bright red shirts filled an entire corner of the spectator area, while spectators, players and officials fought for the remaining viewing space alongside court one. Any player on this court would look across to see a sea of faces staring at them.

On court one was Lars Burgsmuller. His match against a local player was quick, lasting only 45 minutes. I overheard a nearby spectator comment, 'You can see he's in a different class.' It was true. With his precise footwork, quick changes of direction and ability to rush the net, Burgsmuller quietly and efficiently dispatched his opponent for the loss of just two games.

In the spectator area, I saw the up-and-coming chair umpire, James Keothavong. I had known James when he was a player, long before he had crossed over to a job in the chair. Only two weeks previously, he had found himself in the middle of a public storm. After James had overruled a line judge's call in a fourth-round Wimbledon match between Tomas Berdych and Jonas Bjorkman, the Swede had gone on an astonishing rant. Approaching the chair, he screamed, 'That's why you suck. That's why you shouldn't be having matches like this. You are absolutely useless.'

I told James I had seen the match live on television. 'It happens.' He responded with a smile that suggested he had shrugged the whole incident off. 'The funny thing is that I'd umpired two of his matches in the past and there were no problems. In the last match, he even said "good job" when he shook my hand, so I'm not really sure what he was talking about.'

With his even temperament and philosophical view on things, you could already see why James was heading to the top of his profession (he has since umpired the Wimbledon men's final). In Manchester, he wasn't there as a chair umpire – instead, he was evaluating the other, less experienced chair umpires in the event. As a player, it was easy to forget that there were other people in the tennis world also trying to fight their way on to the ATP tour.

At midday, I found myself walking down a dark corridor behind the courts. My opponent, Matt Brown, followed closely behind me. If Burgsmuller had looked the part in his red and white Fila outfits, both Brown and myself made it abundantly clear neither of us had a clothing contract. I wore a mixture of Nike, Reebok and Diadora. My opponent wore a shirt so green he might have been representing some kind of combined Irish-Mexican football team.

Stepping out of the dark on to the brightly lit court was startling. To look across and see rows of faces staring back was slightly unnerving. A line of ball boys with matching crew cuts stood to attention as we walked past. The moment I sat down, they immediately broke ranks, and with well-drilled precision presented me with a towel and water, before sprinting to their stations in the distant corners of the court.

A full cohort of lines people marched on to the court. The crowd numbered probably no more than 50, yet all available spaces were filled. Surrounded so closely by so many people, I began to have a vague sensation of what it might be like to play an ATP or Grand Slam event.

I was okay; after playing so many matches, my routines were well worn in. I began to appreciate the importance of progressing through the levels of tournaments, so adjusting to linesmen, ball boys and spectators would be a natural process – *no way* was I about to have a deer-caught-in-the-headlights moment.

Ironically, the person who was succumbing to nerves was the chair umpire. He looked middle-aged, and in his regular life most likely held a highly respectable job. However, when he approached Brown and I for the opening formalities, he stumbled over the words. When he tried to toss the coin, his hands were shaking so much it just fell on to the court. I'm not sure if Keothavong would have been too impressed.

Brown was a typically 'English' player – his game honed on the indoor and grass courts that dominate the British game. I'd describe his serve as a *slider*, while both wings of his groundstrokes were hit flat and on the rise. While he moved forward naturally, it was apparent early on that he had a lack of lateral foot speed across the baseline. I wondered if this was the reason why his peer, Andy Murray, had left him for dead in the pro ranks? What works in the juniors, doesn't necessarily work in the pros.

In the opening games, I tried to move my opponent quickly from side to side – à la Andre Agassi – to expose his lack of speed. If I allowed Brown to set up and play his smooth, flat strokes, I'd be watching winners race past for the next hour.

Patterns of play began to emerge. Brown's shots slid off the slick surface, while my spins slowed the ball down. Neither of us was vastly superior enough to dominate the match, and we managed to cancel out each other's strokes. If this had been a football match, it would have been a turgid 0-0 draw heading into half-time.

After a while the spectators blended into the background; changes in ball boys and lines people went unnoticed. At one point, I looked around and realised I had never seen any of the lines people before. When had they arrived?

The first set ended in a tiebreak. In a close match, you have to seize any opportunity with both hands. It could take only one or two points, or errors, to tip the balance in someone's favour. Late in the tiebreak, I missed a forehand – pulled wide into the tramlines. This was all it took to break the deadlock. The tiebreak was gone, and (in hindsight) the match with it.

Packing my gear after the second set had slowly run away from me, I felt deflated. Sure, I had just played my first Challenger event, and I had held my own: in the past, I would have settled for this. But, I wasn't the same player as when I had started my tour. I realised I needed to expect more of myself – to push through on the big points – if I was going to make any move up the rankings.

Gazzpash was sending out live updates from the spectator area to the online community. His final comment on my match with Brown read as follows, '7-6 (4), 6-2. Matt played well and got better as the game went on. Lots of breaks. Matt older than I thought. Was much slower match though than Horgan/Marx.'

I thought about Gazzpash's 'much slower' comment. He had sat through the entire day's play and seen a mixture of ATP pros, local juniors and players somewhere in between, and the thing he noticed the most in our match was the slow pace. I wondered if it was a telling observation. Was it the lack of real firepower – of pace on the ball – that separated myself from the higher-ranked pros?

Some of Gazzpash's other match reports were interesting, 'Got the impression he thought more of himself than he actually is…looked around like he was the big player…got fit G/F!!!…a lot smaller than what I thought…class came through…match was shocking…I think it was finished in 25 min!!!'

If only the national newspapers allowed their reporters that kind of freedom. Gazzpash continued his court-side coverage for the aficionados throughout the week, noting that Lars Burgsmuller won six matches to fight his way to the semi-finals, and that the Israeli, Harel Levy, eventually took the Manchester title. Perhaps he should have gotten a job as a 'court-sider' for an online betting company; during my time at the courts, I couldn't spot him in the crowd as he wrote his reports.

* * * * *

That night, back in the Britannia Airport Hotel, a motivational speaker had replaced Friday night's wedding reception. I snuck in a rear door to join the large group in the conference room. I had expected an impressive man with a penetratingly deep voice pumping up the crowd. Instead, a man who looked like an estate agent drily talked about goal-setting.

I left the motivational talk after a few minutes; I knew what my goals were. When you are on the tour, you had better know exactly where you need to be heading.

10

Chasing *More* Points
Senegal–Pakistan–Sudan

THEY SAY with London buses that you wait an hour for one, and then three come at once. It was the same with my ATP points. After almost two decades of toil to finally earn one precious ATP point, the ease at which they followed was faintly ridiculous.

Something changed, but exactly what?

I flew to Senegal a few days after Manchester, for two Futures events in the west African nation. Within days, it became inherently apparent that it wasn't just one particular factor, but rather a subtle change in everything around me that would help push me up the world rankings.

I noticed the first shift in the lobby of the players' hotel in downtown Dakar. It was my first day in Senegal. As I was travelling alone, I had headed down to the reception with the intention of asking for directions to the tennis club. Standing at reception (also worrying about how to get to the club) was a smooth-looking Italian who appeared relieved to discover a fellow player. He introduced himself as Giacomo, and after a couple of minutes chatting explained he was a main-draw player.

'Do you have points?' he asked searchingly. When I replied that yes, I had one ATP point, he didn't hesitate. 'Let's play doubles this week! Shall we go practise?'

I was genuinely surprised. Did having a world ranking guarantee my pedigree as a player? In the Italian's eyes: yes. He didn't need to see me play before teaming up. I wasn't about to question his logic; I now had a world-ranked doubles and practice partner, and a new level of respect from my colleagues.

My second break came later that evening. At 1,512 in the rankings I would be a seed in the qualifying draw, but nonetheless still back in the qualies. However, when I scanned through the qualifying draw stuck to the wall in the hotel lobby, I couldn't see my name. *Oh my God – I've flown all the way to Senegal and they've forgotten to put me in the draw.*

In a panic, I rang the ITF referee's hotel (referees and players don't stay in the same hotel) to tell him his error. He seemed irritated: they had to take him from his dinner.

'You're in the main draw,' he stated, as if it was obvious. 'There was a last-minute withdrawal in the main draw, and you were the next-highest-ranked player in the qualifying. So you moved up. Congratulations. Okay?'

Hell, yes – this was okay with me. After a year struggling just to escape the qualifying weekend, I was now guaranteed prize money and only had to win one match for another point. If they say having money makes you more money, then having ATP points made making more points considerably easier.

The next shift in thought happened immediately, and came from within. If I was a main-draw player, then what did I care what happened in the qualifying? It became an afterthought. Would Roger Federer give too much of a damn what was happening down in Roehampton in the Wimbledon qualifying? Probably not, and neither should I. All my focus would now be channelled into one match, rather than spread over an entire qualifying weekend.

As if the universe wanted to emphasise my new status even more, in the first round of the main draw I faced an unranked qualifier. I looked across the net and saw the Nigerian, Sunday Emmanuel, nervously begin our match; I knew exactly what he was feeling. I'd been in his shoes the previous year in Namibia against Jurgens Strydom. Then, the burden of trying to break through had been too much – not helped when I looked over the net and, in my mind, saw an accomplished opponent with his world ranking already assured. Now, I was playing that role.

ForeverDelayed on the online forum echoed my change in roles, 'All three [British players] could pick up a ranking point here, as I doubt that Emmanuel and Kante are that good a player, so Howe and Roelants could definitely win their openers.'

Were people now expecting me to win main-draw matches, after winning precisely *one* in the past two decades?

It was a strange match indeed. I was up a set and a break of serve, racing away, when I hit the wall. To be fair, even the African players were affected by the oppressive heat and humidity. At some point, usually around the hour mark, your body overheated with arms and legs losing all power. The problem was that now, a second proverbial wall hit me. I began gasping for breath and couldn't last more than a couple of shots each point. My Nigerian opponent sensed it (to be fair, watching me bent over sucking in air was pretty obvious), and clawed his way back into the match.

The second set tiebreak was a make-or-break affair. I knew it and Emmanuel knew it too. My brain was scrambled and I reckoned I had a few minutes of play left in me. If I lost this set, I'd have to withdraw on health grounds. It was amazing what the promise of a second ATP point could do – I kept on going, point after point.

The Dakar Olympique Club was in the flight path of a nearby regional airport. When a plane came in low, the sound was deafening, blocking out the familiar *thud* of the tennis ball. Even once the plane had passed, the ringing in my ears continued.

'Hang in there, mate!' It came from the back row of the concrete stand where a fellow Australian, Troy Gillham, sat alone. In far-off places, you could guarantee the support of a fellow Antipodean, or Brit, if need be. It was as if the strangeness of the surroundings brought players of similar backgrounds closer together.

At the business end of the tiebreak, the Nigerian's nerves took over. He double faulted at a crucial stage to allow me to edge ahead. All he had to do was start a rally and the point would be his, but his serve floated long. I can still picture the look of horror on his face when he realised what he had done.

On my match point, and facing the Nigerian's second serve, I told myself I was going for a winner, no matter what. My face had gone numb and I was light-headed. Sunday Emmanuel didn't take any risks on this serve and it landed in the middle of the service box. I stepped forward, drove it as hard as I could and watched it skid off the line at the Nigerian's feet. We both looked immediately at the linesman (who had frozen and made no call), and then to the chair umpire who held his hand flat: the *in* signal.

I saw the Nigerian hurl his racquet in disgust and then bend over at the waist in disappointment. Although I wanted this second ATP point so badly, I felt for my opponent (after all, I still had flashbacks from my Namibian loss a year before). I fell to my knees, not in a Bjorn Borg-like winning pose, but rather clutching the net because I thought I was going to pass out.

'Good job mate!' came a familiar Aussie expression from the stands. It was indeed a good job – worth a significant leap up the rankings ladder. I was starting to make my move.

Gazzpash online broke the news of my win, 'Just seen, other result is Greg Howe beat Sunday Emmanuel 6-2 7-6 (5). Greg goes on to play the legend that is Komlavi Loglo!!!'

This was my reward: a match with the number one seed and 359 in the world, Komlavi Loglo from Togo. Gazzpash was correct in the assertion that Loglo was an African legend. He was the highest black African in the world rankings, and would soon represent Togo in the 2008 Beijing Olympics (where he would lose to South Africa's Kevin Anderson).

In the past, I would have given myself no chance. I would have tried, but deep down expected to lose. Now, I was riding high on confidence, and that is a huge weapon to have in one's armoury. Another subtle shift in my psyche had occurred; I was going after one of the best players in the African continent, fully believing I could win.

* * * * *

This being new territory, I made a mistake. On the player bus heading towards Dakar Olympique Club the next morning, I pumped myself up with Aussie rock music…for the entire trip: past the bustling city, past the shanty towns and past the drug-smuggling canoes that lined the Senegalese coast. By the time the bus pulled into the club, I was ready to explode.

During my brief warm-up with Troy, I had to calm myself down. I felt the need to smash every ball as hard as possible. Intensity in tennis is a fine line between being excited, and coupling that with control, so that you can keep it constant throughout an entire match. I had lost control somewhere out among the Dakar shanty towns.

My all-out aggression climaxed at one particular moment deep in the first set of my match with Loglo. Up to this point, I had been slugging it out with him to the extent that he had returned to the African player's default setting – athletically retrieving the ball deep behind the baseline. The Togolese number one was a physical monster; with his muscles and dreadlocks he looked and moved like the alien from the *Predator* films (ironically, he was also soft-spoken and probably the nicest guy on tour). Then, on a break point, he double-faulted. His second serve landed long and the linesman called out, meaning I had levelled the match at five games apiece. To celebrate, I screamed and pumped my fist.

Then I completely lost it.

The small pro-African crowd started shouting at the chair umpire. After what seemed an eternity, he weakly announced, 'Deuce – the ball was in.'

I did my best John McEnroe impersonation. 'You've got to be kidding!' I was screaming so loudly that Troy, far away on the backcourts, later told me he could hear every word I said. The chair umpire looked worried as I approached him looking like some kind of rabid animal.

The chair umpire pointed to the linesman, 'He called it in.' Everybody in and around the centre court immediately turned to the startled linesman who looked like he was about to hide behind his chair. The small crowd was now shouting at him that the ball was in.

'What was your call?' the chair umpire asked the linesman, absolving himself from all responsibility, even though he was the ultimate authority on all decisions.

The linesman by now was no longer thinking about any ball landing near a line, but rather which call would give him less grief. He held his hand flat – *in*.

'Deuce,' the umpire called, with a little more conviction this time.

I looked at the linesman, 'God, you're gutless.'

I continued in an anger-fuelled red mist. Not surprisingly, I managed to lose the match and all composure, but not before I realised I could match it with the higher-ranked players. But how high? I would find the answer to that in the months to come.

Akhenaten posted his match report online, 'Komlavi Loglo's form was once again breathtaking in his 6-4 6-2 destruction of that old warhorse, Gregory Howe of Great Britain. Stylishly, Loglo left the court astride a white stallion waving imperiously to his awestruck fans, as trumpet-players and dancers celebrated the finery of his win. In contrast, poor Howe was left, presumably, to head straight for the knacker's yard.'

* * * * *

As for the doubles events, not only did I get to partner with Giacomo Pirozzi for the first week, but also then secured another world-ranked partner for the second event, in the form of Troy Gillham. I would be lying if I told you I wasn't seeing the possibility of a doubles world ranking too (in doubles, you need two wins and get to the semi-finals in a Futures before you earn ATP doubles points).

For both weeks, things were looking good with first-round wins over African opponents. Yet, for some reason, the universe deemed that my best chance to get a doubles ranking was not to be. Food poisoning for the Italian on the morning of our second-round match ruined the first week's opportunity – he kept throwing up the remains of fish before the match: never a good sign. Then, before our week two quarter-final, Troy got a bad case of dehydration mixed with heat exhaustion. He was adamant he could play and refused to default the match.

'You look awful. We can just stop you know,' I kept telling him.

He refused to listen (after a lifetime of playing doubles with Andrew, I was used to stubborn doubles partners). 'I can play. We can do it,' he told me.

His face had gone pale, and in the space of a morning he somehow looked noticeably thinner. At one point, I looked over and he appeared to be swaying. Thankfully we lost quickly and Troy was admitted to hospital. It took him a few days to recover, which was good; we both had bigger fish to fry in the future.

* * * * *

A couple of weeks after my west African adventure, I started work as an English teacher in an international school in Dubai. It had been a full year since my tour had begun in Bangkok. My money was running out and I wasn't anywhere near high enough in the world rankings for my tennis to be self-sustaining, so my options were somewhat limited. Anyhow, Sylvie still worked for Emirates airlines, so it made sense to base myself in the Middle East and be closer to her.

In my mind though, my tour was not over. I would hold on to my world ranking for precisely 12 months, so my new plan was to combine working a full-time job with the occasional sortie on to the world circuit. I certainly wasn't aware of any other world-ranked professional tennis players trying to juggle a traditional nine-to-five job. However, I could see how it could work with a little imagination, and a couple of days off work… here or there. I was sure the school authorities wouldn't mind.

It was this plan that saw me late one Monday evening, on the rooftop of my building in Dubai, pacing around talking to Andrew on my mobile phone.

'Yeh, I know it looks bad on CNN,' I told him. 'I was just watching it; there are riots and they have now issued a state of martial law.' I paused to look up into the sky, knowing I would soon be flying. 'But I spoke to George Barth today, and he said it's okay.'

It was true. Big George from Ohio was *in country*, out there in Lahore, Pakistan. He said it was fine, as long as you kept your head down. He'd been on the Pakistan circuit for three weeks now and had seen the whole political situation deteriorate. The ITF had deemed it safe for the players…for now, and that was good enough for him. Anyhow, there were ATP points to be earned, so he wasn't going anywhere soon.

George had other, more important, news to share with me when I spoke to him. 'It's the draw,' he told me. I asked him if I had hit the number one seed. 'Much worse,' George continued with a laugh. 'We're playing each other. Well, at least one of us is making points.'

My heart sank a little. I didn't like playing friends: even if you won, it left a hollow feeling. Still, he was right. It was the main draw, and another ATP point and another move up the rankings was up for grabs.

The aficionados saw the contest in a different light:

Salmon, '36-year-old Howe draws the 38-year-old Barth'

Johnnylad, 'Ooh! Hope Greg beats his granddad…and a safe exit from the country.'

* * * * *

A few hours later, at 2am on the day of my match, I landed in Lahore International Airport. It was a crazy schedule, but if

I wanted to work and play, this is what was required: a little imagination. Stuffing all my equipment and clothes into one bag to travel light and fast, this wasn't some long tour of duty, but rather a commando raid of the smash-and-grab type: get in quickly, make some points, then get out quickly before the whole place imploded.

The curtains in the airport mini-van pickup were pulled tightly shut, but peering through the cracks revealed eerily deserted streets all the way to the hotel. Only occasionally another car would pass – whether it was military or another official tourist van was hard to tell in the darkness.

The online community was getting reports from another British player competing in Lahore. Fitzy was updating the situation in what started to sound like BBC reports from a war zone, 'Really I don't want to be outside to *walk into* these free roaming army men, as they probably could just shoot me down without batting an eyelid. Pretty bad out here to be honest!'

Salmon posted in reply, 'Don't worry, you'll be safe as long as you don't go asking for trouble. Howe is due to be in the main draw, but not sure if he will turn up.'

* * * * *

After six hours of sleep, I headed to the club in a three-wheeled motorised rickshaw. These had little plastic flaps as doors, so I stuffed my tennis bag inside and tried to hide behind the doors. Occasionally a person in a passing car (the curfew began after dark) would spy a Westerner in tennis clothes and do a double take, but I made it to the club safely.

I later heard that other players were so convinced I would do a no-show, the number one player on the lucky loser list was already warming up. When I rolled into the club for the first time, just moments before my match, I got some surprised looks. The only player who knew for sure I was coming was George, and he had kept it to himself.

'Hey, Greg,' George called out when he saw me arriving. He was in with the physiotherapist getting some gel rubbed into his back. 'Can you believe it? I bent down this morning and I felt my lower back go.'

'Are you sure you should be telling me this? I am playing you, you know.'

'Ah well,' he continued with a resigned smile. 'We're friends – you'd realise soon enough.'

He was right. On the sunbaked, brown grass courts in Lahore, twisting and bending was required in order to cope with the low skidding ball. At 6ft 5in tall, George's ability to twist and bend wasn't the greatest at the best of times. Now, with his back in spasm, he was reduced to going for broke with his big serve and hope the ball wouldn't come back.

After falling behind in the first set, George shrugged and walked to the net, 'Sorry buddy. I'm calling it a day.' After picking up a point in Africa, George had backed himself to pick up more on Pakistan's grass court circuit. Instead, three weeks of grind amid third-world conditions and political upheaval had brought him nothing but a back strain. On the other hand, I'd been in the country less than 12 hours, and now had my third ATP point. Okay, I didn't have to work too hard for it, but the ATP computer didn't care. When it became live in a fortnight, it'd be worth almost a hundred places in the rankings. I guess this is what you call momentum.

I had arranged to have dinner with George that evening, but he called my room and said he was heading back to the States on the next plane. As it goes with tennis friendships, our paths haven't crossed since, although I did call him one evening when he was in the depths of Africa. But that is another story, way into the future.

Not only did I not have George as a dinner companion, at the hotel buffet I discovered I was the only person in my entire hotel. At U$100 a night for a distinctly average hotel (three stars in Lahore doesn't count for much), all the other players had cleared out. With riots happening nearby and the military patrolling the streets, the place wasn't exactly a tourist magnet either.

After sharing the buffet with the handful of waiters, I headed out to the edge of the hotel entrance to look up and down the deathly, quiet streets. I imagined a state of martial law to be different; it did make me wonder how CNN always made it appear so dramatic.

* * * * *

My Pakistan tournament came to an end the next day when I lost to the giant Romanian, Bogdan-Victor Leonte. I didn't go down without a fight though, losing the first set in a see-sawing tiebreak. I was now regularly playing players ranked in the 300s, and my game was being dragged up to their level of intensity and aggression.

My rise up through the game's ranks had clearly caught the online community's interest, to the extent they were now badgering other players to reveal clues about my identity. RobC posted directly to Fitzy (Andrew Fitzgerald), 'Have you had a chance to chat with Greg Howe? He really seems to be living the dream, playing pro tennis at his age. Does he have a day job, and play tennis as a holiday? Or does he do coaching, and just play when he's at a tournament with his players?'

They seek him here; they seek him there.

My efforts to get back to Dubai that evening, and therefore work the next day, fell apart when the Etihad Airways plane had a malfunction. It sat just outside the departure gate window, taunting the passengers with its immobile presence. With no announcements forthcoming, the aggression from irate passengers was impressive: at least on par with the tantrums coming from many of the tennis players this week.

After sleeping on the floor of Lahore International Airport for 24 hours, I promptly officially re-entered Pakistan, walked around to the ticketing office and bought a business class ticket on Pakistan International Airways' next flight out.

So much for the quick, smash-and-grab, commando raid.

* * * * *

As if to continue my tour of the region's hot spots, a couple of weeks after Pakistan, Andrew joined me as we headed across to Khartoum, in Sudan. I didn't make ATP points (a three-set loss in the first round of the main draw to a giant Russian), but as an experience, it was *out there*.

The player hotel also housed the United Nations peacekeepers. The UN was in the region monitoring the armed conflict heading steadily towards Khartoum. At breakfast, they would self-importantly sit around a big table wearing sleeveless jackets and cargo pants, smoking and deliberating over espressos. Surrounded by players in tennis clothes, the whole scene was bizarre, if not absurd. Dinner in Sudan was just as strange. The menu was always the same: pasta with a bottle of ketchup, or if the kitchen hadn't run out, vegetable soup from a tin.

A couple of days into our stay, Andrew and I were sitting in our hotel room, when he suddenly said, 'There's something weird about this room.' Let's face it; we were near a war zone inhabited by UN peacekeepers. There was something weird about the whole place. But, he was right – the room did have an unbalancing effect.

Then it clicked, 'There's no window!' It had taken us two days to realise it, but a landscape painting was masquerading as a window. The room also had a lamp, but there was no wall socket to plug it into, meaning our room was simply a solid concrete box. After these discoveries, we stayed out of it as much as possible.

On the sign-in day, the player bus had to take a different route because there was a massive lynch mob parading down the main street. A Western primary school teacher had caused religious fury when she inadvertently named the classroom mascot, a teddy bear, Muhammad (unfortunately for her, also the name of the Prophet). The mob burnt effigies of the teacher, demanding she be whipped…or worse.

During practice, play often had to be paused on the courts backing on to the airport when UN military helicopters took off. The dust storm caused from the helicopters' rotors swept across the courts. The white helicopters, with the large initials of the UN stencilled in black on the side, would then hover just above the courts, as if the pilot wanted to watch a bit of tennis.

On one trip to the tennis courts, the player bus took a detour through a poor neighbourhood. I couldn't even call the area a shanty town; there was no town, more of a rubbish dump with spaces cleared for people to sleep in or try to sell things salvaged from the rubbish to passers-by. Little kids played in dirty, brown puddles. For once, the player bus fell into silence as everyone looked on.

I knew poverty existed – I read about it in an article in some newspaper – but to see it in reality was shocking. However, once the bus made it to the tennis courts, everyone's focus comfortably shifted on to hitting the little, yellow tennis ball. To win matches, you need complete focus.

Ironically, after all the threats to life near a war zone, the only security emergency I saw was when Joe Cooper tried to pass through airport security with a backpack full of electronics. Joe – young, fair-haired and very English-looking – didn't fit the profile of an international terrorist. But Khartoum was a place constantly on high alert, and in such an atmosphere, perhaps everyone began to look threatening.

* * * * *

It wasn't my goal to keep on scrambling for points in every country about to plunge into civil war (although a lot of players did this to inflate their rankings). Like all pros, apart from the very top echelon, my schedule had to be a balancing act of smaller events to maintain my ranking, with the bigger events offering a shot at real glory. Too many players ground it out for years on the Futures tour, in their comfort zone, inching their way up the tennis rankings.

They say if you don't escape from the Futures within two years, then you never will. I didn't have two years, so it was time to head to the very top: the ATP tour.

11

Into the Big Time
Beijing ATP

THEY SPOTTED me the moment I left passport control.

It could have been the bright green racquet bag…or the fact that I was a foot taller than everyone around me. A kiosk stood at the foot of an escalator with a large 'China Open' sign erected beside it. Three young Chinese, with the keen alertness of volunteers, stood in front of the kiosk watching for tennis players. They wore matching bright red shirts, while ID badges hung from their necks.

'Welcome to the China Open,' said a slim Chinese girl in her bright red t-shirt. She had left her colleagues at the kiosk as she moved forward in a well-rehearsed meet and greet gesture. 'What is your name please?' she asked, pronouncing 'what' with a noticeable 'h' sound at the start.

In her hand was her list of airport transfers. Scanning down the list, I saw names such as Ivan Ljubicic, Marcos Baghdatis and Jo-Wilfried Tsonga. I pointed to my name at the very bottom of the list. The girl duly crossed it off before clipping the pen back into the clipboard.

'We've been very busy today – over ten players already. Some went to the Holiday Inn and some to the Shangri-La.'

The Holiday Inn had been designated for the qualifiers and the ITF juniors competing in the junior China Open the same weekend. There was a U$75 difference between the two hotels, so I chose the cheaper one. After a couple of days of seeing no other players, I realised even those in the qualifying draw had opted for the main-draw hotel. Perhaps this was a flaw in my thinking; maybe to make it at the ATP level, one had to assume it *was* going to happen. *Why check into the cheap hotel, only to have to move when you inevitably qualify?*

The girl explained that Tim from Taipei...and someone from Singapore had arrived shortly before my flight. Did Singapore have any players? She must have seen the doubt on my face – she claimed she had a bad memory. After checking her list, she remembered, 'Oh, yes. Ivan Ljubicic arrived earlier.' She really must have had a bad memory to forget a hulking 6ft 4in bald-headed Croat arriving in Beijing.

I was escorted straight through customs. The female immigration officers paused their queues of passengers as they tried to recognise the latest tennis player arriving in the city. At the carousel for bag collection, one of the other red-shirted volunteers insisted on waiting for my travel bag. I pointed at a small, grey gym bag that headed towards us.

'Is this all you are travelling with?' the slim girl asked in surprise. 'All the other players have lots of huge travel bags.'

Had I already been discovered as an ATP tour imposter? Were the hospitality girls having doubts about my credibility? While other players were on the tour for weeks at a time, for me this was a weekend sortie. I had taken precisely three tennis shirts, two pairs of shorts and a handful of socks. If I won three matches to qualify for the big time, what would I care? I would just buy more.

The girls led me into the car park where a small, white bus was waiting. On the front windscreen, there was a blue and red ATP sticker. The whole process had been so smooth, that before I knew it, the driver and I had left the airport – heading for the city of Beijing.

It was now well past midnight and the streets were dark and mostly empty. Occasionally we would pass a cyclist riding an ancient bike. Another time a parked police car's lights flashed for no apparent reason. A pine forest raced by the highway, finally being replaced by rows of closed shops plastered with exotic-looking Chinese writing. After the shops began a 12-mile stretch of giant advertising billboards, blocking out the view of the city. With the Beijing Olympic Games less than a year away, much of the advertising promoted the upcoming sporting event. I wondered what the billboards were hiding.

Juggling my two careers of English teacher and ATP pro began earlier in the day. Before my flight to Beijing, I raced into work to teach my early morning classes. Then I sped off towards Dubai International Airport, dumping my car into long-term parking (I was thinking positively) before embarking on the seven-hour flight across Asia.

It was only after much research that I had chosen the China Open to make my ATP debut. Tournaments immediately after a Grand Slam often have weaker draws – the China Open qualifying was taking place at the same time as the US Open Final. Many players simply took a holiday before the build-up to the next major event.

The European winter circuit – held in indoor arenas – was the next focus as the top players aimed to qualify for the end-of-season Masters. Jammed in between the American and European circuits were three hard-court tournaments in Asia and a random event in Romania…on clay. They appeared almost as an afterthought – simply a way to fill gaps in the tennis calendar. What was the point of playing outdoors when the rest of the year's big events were all indoors?

Hidden within a lot of the Asian tournaments' draws were former pros whose careers were in trouble. If they were in the qualifying draws, then they were often making their last stand. Why else would a top professional travel halfway around the world to compete in physically challenging places such as Beijing, Bangkok or Mumbai?

After 40 minutes, the bus wound its way down deserted streets. When we turned into a side street, pulling into the

Holiday Inn-Temple of Heaven, I had arrived into the *big time*.

Well...the big time for the qualifiers, that is.

* * * * *

At around midday the next day, the same bus, with the same driver, returned to the qualifiers' hotel to shuttle players to the tennis stadium. Once again, I was the only passenger. This time, the city was well and truly alive with cars, trucks and swarms of ancient bicycles heaving along the congested roads. A slight haze had enveloped the city, yet nothing like the pollution-induced smog that the Western media had been promising for next year's Olympics.

At the traffic lights for a major intersection, a middle-aged woman on an equally middle-aged bicycle tried to jump the lights. Breaking away from the stationary pack, she hadn't noticed the traffic to the right accelerating towards her. A lorry slammed on its brakes with smoke theatrically pouring from the tyres. The woman froze in shock, before slowly tipping over sideways – all the time rigidly holding the handlebars. An elderly man rushed forward to help drag the woman out of the intersection as the mass of vehicles poured past her. My driver looked at me with raised eyebrows and shook his head.

Arriving at the National Tennis Stadium, our bus was halted at the gate by a mixture of security and Chinese Army personnel. Dressed in drab green military uniforms, they brandished machine guns and held grim expressions on their faces.

One of security guards peered into the bus. 'Tennis bag,' he ordered, pointing to my racquet bag. While the underneath of the bus was searched for bombs, my tennis bag was taken and passed through an airport-style x-ray machine. No one gave me a second look. I guess no one seemed to believe that one of the players was about to blow up the stadium...not until after they had lost, at least.

The driver pointed me towards the giant, bowl-shaped stadium. Once inside, there were signs with arrows directing traffic towards the locker room, press centre, player lounge, centre court and a multitude of other locations. People with an array of different uniforms and outfits crisscrossed in the foyer, heading into the tunnels running under the stadium – like being in some giant ant nest.

Passing through the tunnel, each doorway revealed a different group of people. One room consisted of ball kids with baggy shirts and caps sitting around eating lunch. Then there was a room full of officials wearing beige trousers, followed by the pressroom complete with desks and rows of computers. Only after passing around half the stadium did I come upon the ATP rooms. Two officials blocked the way, with Chinese soldiers stationed at various points behind them. Upon seeing my racquet bag, they moved aside, letting me pass.

I now faced a dilemma. Where was I meant to go? A closed door to my left had a paper attached loosely to it, stating, 'Tommy Robredo – Espana – locker room.' Ahead I could see partially into the player lounge. A huge desk was visible with Western women shuffling papers and looking around with welcoming smiles. It looked *terrifying*. Inside, I knew there would be famous pros that I had followed for years on television. My heart was racing and I needed to find a space to calm down. To my right was the locker room.

I composed myself…and walked through the door.

Two Chinese officials, wearing bright red shirts, sat on plastic chairs – a plastic-looking fern behind them. A white divider blocked the view into the changing rooms. 'Would you like a locker key, sir?' one of them asked brightly in perfect English. I declined his offer – at that moment my racquet bag felt like a security blanket; there was no way I was letting it out of my sight. The same attendant moved aside so I could pass around the divider.

Rainer Schuettler, the German veteran, sat on one of the benches, wearing a pair of white tennis shorts. His upper body looked muscularly taut from hour upon hour of exercise. His square chin sported a couple of days' worth of stubble – a battle-hardened appearance that wouldn't have looked out of place on a German storm trooper in a war film.

As I walked in, he turned and looked straight at me. Without any change of expression, he held my gaze for a second or two, deciding if he recognised the face that had just walked in. When he realised he didn't, he went back to focusing on the floor.

When he was at his peak at number five in the world, Schuettler had the reputation as one of the fittest, hardest workers on the tour. It was reported that in order to psyche out opponents before a match, he would perform agility and footwork exercises in the locker rooms. It was his way of showing that the worse the conditions and the longer the match, the more he would love it.

Sitting in the Beijing locker room, he was now 31 years old. His ranking had fallen to 149 in the world, which meant he had scraped into the main draw as the lowest-ranked player. He had suffered a wretched loss of form – finding himself back on the Challenger circuit and being forced to battle through the qualifying at the recent US Open.

Sitting across from me, he wasn't doing agility drills now. Instead he gingerly bounced on the balls of his feet while sitting, looking as if he was testing them to see if they still worked. He then stood up, wrapped himself in a white towel and headed for the showers. His giant racquet bag and his shoes remained in place on the locker room floor, giving the impression that their user had simply vanished into space.

While Schuettler was in the shower, another player had entered the locker room. I could hear his voice from behind the makeshift screen speaking to the attendants. 'Could I have a locker key, please?' asked the player in a precise, clipped English.

Shortly afterwards, Nicolas Kiefer emerged from behind the screen, heading towards the lockers. He was wearing a baseball cap and a hooded jacket over his tennis clothes. His socks were pulled up high – making his calves look thick and muscular. At 30 years of age he was only a year younger than his fellow German, yet he looked remarkably more fresh-faced and youthful.

It seemed that the Beijing locker room had become a refuge for German tennis players that had fallen on hard times. Kiefer's ranking had also dropped, to 168 this week, after a prolonged absence with a wrist injury. He had been on the comeback trail since Wimbledon in July, when he had fallen out of the ATP world rankings completely. Now his ranking was so low that he had missed the main-draw cut-off in Beijing, only being spared the ordeal of qualifying when the tournament organisers granted him a wildcard straight into the main draw.

Kiefer took his racquet bag out of the locker, carefully locked the metal door, nodded to Schuettler, who had appeared out of the shower, and then thanked the attendants as he left. For a player with a reputation for being arrogant, he appeared as polite as someone could be while remaining sincere.

With no real purpose of being in the locker room other than rearranging my racquet bag, I decided to head towards the players' lounge. This took no more than a few steps, yet I had to pass at least a handful of attendants, security personnel and Chinese soldiers. Once inside the lounge, I was then faced with the ATP help desk women. Looking like they had just been transplanted from Midwestern America, they sat at a large circular desk and smiled helpfully at any player who approached the vicinity of their area. On the desk was information advertising Tuesday's excursion to the Great Wall and the official player party. Golf was also mentioned.

The giant Croat, Ivan Ljubicic, approached the help desk, getting the ladies' attention immediately.

'I'm looking to practise,' said the world number 12. 'Is there anyone available now?'

I stood a short distance away, clearly not important enough to be considered. One of the blonde American women checked a paper in front of her. 'There's no one right now, but Davydenko is arriving later in the afternoon. Would you like me to try to arrange this for you?'

Ljubicic frowned a little. It was hard to tell whether the idea of practicing with the Russian, or having to wait around for him to arrive, troubled him the most. 'No, thanks,' he replied. 'I'll find someone myself.'

Not waiting for him to scan the room only to find me standing there, I quickly left halfway through the conversation to the safety of a giant U-shaped couch. A young Japanese player was sitting adjacent to me. I had never seen him before; I figured he was just a fellow qualifier – so what did I care if he was sharing the corner of the player lounge with me.

On one wall, a couple of workmen were assembling a giant computer screen. Behind me, a row of computer terminals sat unused. Scattered among the couches were more of the plastic-looking ferns that I had seen in the locker room. The entire lounge was quiet with conversations only heard in the background. This inward-looking silence seemed to pervade all areas of ATP life – from the breakfast restaurant, to the player bus, the locker room and now the player lounge. I hadn't had a real conversation with anyone since I landed in Beijing. It was as if no one wanted to speak to a player for fear of breaking their concentration.

The quietness even continued a few minutes later when about 20 Chinese soldiers in single file swept into the player lounge. They separated and moved all around the room, conducting a bomb search. Bins, computer terminals and spaces behind the lounges were all scrutinised. A few of the soldiers were suppressing grins. As the China Open was the last major international sporting event in the country before next year's Olympics, security seemed to be bordering on the paranoid.

I left with the soldiers and headed up the corridor to see the tournament referee. Unlike at Futures events where the sign-in is between five and six o'clock precisely, at the ATP event it seemed rather *laissez-faire*. It opened whenever the tournament director taped a blank piece of paper to his desk. It closed at the ridiculously late time of nine at night. Why a top-flight player would need to arrive at a tournament so late the night before their match is beyond me. Also, unlike the low-level events, in the ATP there was no entry fee. It appeared the entry fee is only deemed necessary for the players who have *no* money…that is, the qualifiers on the Futures circuit.

In the office, two middle-aged men sat behind computer terminals. When I signed my name and nationality, Thomas Karlsberg, the silver-haired tournament director, read out my name and nationality for the other man. Karlsberg was from Sweden, yet he spoke with a refined English accent. He punched my details into the computer, announcing '1,384' to his colleague.

'Do I have enough points to get in?' I asked.

'I have no idea right now – but I don't think last year was full.' This wasn't entirely true as the final qualifying place had gone to a doubles specialist. 'Come back later,' he said with a smile.

With my fate out of my hands, I continued down the polished corridor. Left would have taken me out to the outside grounds, while to the right was the player entrance into the cavernous centre court. When I headed for the door into the stadium, a Chinese soldier moved across to block me.

'I just want to go into centre court,' I told him, pointing to the door. I started to pass by him when he moved to block me again. He had a nervous expression and, not knowing where to look, stared at the floor.

'That's okay! That's okay!' came a voice further up the corridor. One of the red-shirted Chinese volunteers, this time a young Chinese male in his 20s, was running towards us, fearing an incident with a player. 'He doesn't speak English!' he continued loudly, whilst still running.

The volunteer spoke to the soldier in Chinese, who gratefully melted back to his position beside the door. 'He's under strict orders to stop anyone without a pass. Have you gotten your accreditation yet?'

I did my best to look like I knew what he was talking about. Clearly it failed.

'Follow me. I'll take you over to where they are processing them.'

I was led out of the stadium and back to a building near the car park. The white player bus sat parked beside a few limousine-type cars with ATP logos on the side. The red-shirted helper led me through a door where I was suddenly faced with a room full of boys and girls in tennis gear – participants in the junior event.

'ATP player for accreditation!' the helper announced across the room to the other officials. The room went silent and a sea of youthful faces turned in unison to see which big name had entered. I didn't know whether to smile or cringe in embarrassment; I put on my most deadpan expression and headed across the room to get my photo taken. The juniors waiting in a queue for their photos were pushed back so I could be fast tracked.

A short while later, I was heading back to the stadium with a suitably large red and white accreditation badge hanging around my neck. Still feeling like an imposter to this world, I let it hang behind my back out of view. However, I will admit, it felt pretty cool to have a player badge – just like one of the pros you see on television. On it, above the 2007 China Open logo, was a large 'P' – for player – and then my image. In the centre were the details, 'Howe – British – ATP – no. 282.' If anyone accidentally mistook that final number as my world ranking (probably doubtful if they had seen me play), then who was I to correct them?

I passed through the stadium and headed towards the outside courts. Leaving the player exit from under the stadium, I had to walk past security guards and then through a maze of red barriers. The outside grounds looked like a smaller version of the US Open's surroundings. There seemed to be as much space for fast-food stores and merchandise as there was for tennis courts.

Kentucky Fried Chicken stalls competed with Mercedes car showrooms, Samsung stalls and a host of corporate hospitality tents. Rows and rows of red and yellow China Open placards spanned the entire way around the courts in a kaleidoscope of colours. Approaching dusk on the Friday before the tournament, only a few workers and cleaners were present, preparing the stalls.

I headed to one of the far practice courts. The outline of the stadium was in the distance, with rows of flags fluttering on top of its skyline. Just to get a feel of the courts, I went through a series of footwork drills before practising my serve. This was interrupted after a while by a small team of ATP supervisors that were going from court to court – obsessing about the positioning of the Mercedes logos fastened on to the sides of the nets. By the time they had left, the light was fading. I sat alone in one of the ATP player chairs and looked at the view of the stadium's outline against the sunset – doing nothing but savouring the atmosphere.

Upon returning to the tournament director's office, the sign-in sheet was now full with names. 'I don't have the cut-off yet,' the silver-haired director told me, 'but there're lots of players with only one point. It's looking good for you.'

Back in the player hotel, there was nothing to do but wait for the draw and tomorrow's order of play. A handful of red-shirted volunteer girls were stationed in the foyer. They would have to wait around for the schedule, and then players' requests for practice courts, before heading home. It looked a long night for them.

When it approached ten o'clock, I decided to go for a walk. This would be the only sightseeing chance I would get to see the *real* China…outside of the ATP bubble. A couple of left turns out of the hotel and I was on a tree-lined street in the Fengtai District. The dim streetlights cast everything in a soft, yellow glow. On the wide pavement, a group of elderly Chinese danced slowly in pairs. Classical Chinese music emanated around the boulevard from an ancient cassette player standing in the centre of the dancers. A crowd of locals stood nearby watching the performance.

It was then that I spotted my father in the spectators – or someone that was as close to identical as could be. On my father's side, my ancestors had immigrated to Australia at the turn of the 19th century, during the gold rushes. My father was ethnically three-quarters Chinese, making myself three-eighths. After years under the Australian sun, I always thought my father's dark complexion made him look like someone from the mixed peoples of the Seychelles rather than pure Chinese – yet here in Beijing was his doppelgänger.

This minor epiphany made me want to push further down the street. It was then I heard someone screaming. Heads turned as a mentally insane woman headed towards us in a continual wail. She went from person to person, screaming and approaching them with open hands, begging for help. Her victims backed away, unsure of how to respond. Unnerved, I about-turned and headed back to the sanctuary of the Holiday Inn-Temple of Heaven. My experience of the *real* China had lasted about half an hour.

In the hotel foyer, the red-shirted girls apologised for the draw not arriving yet. Texts from Andrew in Germany confirmed that it wasn't on the ATP website either. I went to bed; the discovery of my fate could wait until breakfast, tomorrow morning.

* * * * *

I found my name at the bottom of the order of play – fourth and last match on court two, the mini-show court, 'Gregory Howe (GBR) vs Hyun-Woo Nam (KOR)'

For me, there was a delicious irony in this match-up. A year ago, when my tour had begun in Bangkok, I had watched the South Korean, Hyun-Woo Nam, play in the main draw. Back then if someone had told me I would be facing the Korean a year later in an ATP event, I flatly would have not believed them. Yet now, in many ways, we were on an equal footing.

Okay, I couldn't deny he was the eighth seed in the qualifying draw, was a member of the South Korean Davis

Cup team, and was ranked nearly a thousand places above me. However, in a tournament boasting famous names such as Tsonga, Gonzalez, Davydenko and Ljubicic, Nam from Korea was just another qualifier – just like myself. In my mind, that changed *everything*.

Being the fourth match on the schedule posed a problem. When would I head out to the venue? Too early, and my nerves would be fried from the tension of the stadium. I was desperate to savour the atmosphere of having a player's badge in an elite event, but I reminded myself that I was here to compete – not spectate. Likewise, I didn't want to arrive too close to my match and feel underprepared: or get stuck in traffic and risk a default (just the thought gave me the chills).

I decided that I would go once the second match began. Unfortunately, the mass of technicians roomed under the stadium couldn't get the live internet scoring working. This forced me to continually go down to the foyer and ask the red-shirted girls for the score on court two. A walkie-talkie connected to the help desk in the player lounge relayed the score back and forth. After a couple of visits, the girls would ask for updates as soon as they saw me step out of the elevator. 'Okay, we're asking now,' they would shout across the foyer.

An injury to a Japanese player on court two saw me catch the midday bus to the stadium. For once I wasn't alone. Other qualifiers – a couple of Americans, and a few junior competitors – filled the spaces. At the stadium, the usual assortment of soldiers and security personnel checked player badges. Racquet bags were passed through the x-ray machine and returned in an efficient manner.

Passing through the bowels of the stadium, I could see into the centre court. Directly behind the umpire were three female officials sitting with their backs to me. After each point, they punched the statistics into computers. Beyond them, the three-tier stadium loomed into the sky. There were more flags on top of the stadium than spectators for this first-round qualifying match.

I turned back past a Rolex stand and headed into the players' locker room. The attendants didn't bother looking at me, only glancing at the badge that hung from my neck. Beside the lockers were two American players standing up, looking out a small window to the grounds beyond.

'I just can't sleep. It always happens when I fly this direction,' a burly, red-headed American was telling his friend. 'I need some of those strong sleeping pills – you know the ones.' His compatriot nodded. Neither of them seemed to notice me as I sat on a nearby bench. The red-haired American went on, 'I feel tired now, but I'll be fine once I get going.'

If I were linked to a gambling syndicate, this would have been hot news. It was insider information about a struggling player, moments before a match. I could see now why the ATP had banned all non-players from the locker room.

Looking to warm up, I headed to the outside courts. The merchandise stands were now full of products. On one side of a wall, a giant scoreboard had been erected giving live updates from around the grounds. On court two, the names Rohan Bopanna and David Martin were displayed, waiting for the match to begin. On another wall, an enormous billboard of Ivan Ljubicic showed the Croat stretching for a forehand.

On the practice courts to my left, Ljubicic in person was playing a practice match with Rainer Schuettler. Spectators hovered close to the fence, only metres from the play. In the two points that I saw as I passed, Schuettler managed to dump an easy volley into the net and then shank a forehand into the side fence. Perhaps there was a reason why his ranking had fallen so low.

On the distant court 14, the young Japanese player that I had shared yesterday's couch with, Kei Nishikori, was warming up against a doubles specialist, Ashley Fisher. The rugged Australian had never played a main-draw ATP match, but had won two ATP doubles titles. He would make it three by the end of this week. At 32 years of age, I considered him a veteran, yet I had to remind myself that I was almost four years older than him. About 50 spectators surrounded the court fence. There was no stand for this court, so the mixture of Japanese and Chinese spectators stood or sat on the grass. I felt none of them cared about watching the Australian, only having eyes for the rapidly rising Japanese teenage star.

I spotted a Chinese junior standing nearby with his racquet. 'Are you free to hit?' I asked him, swinging my arm in an imaginary forehand to help get the message across. A huge grin spread across his face.

He nodded and said quickly, 'Okay.'

I asked his name twice, but failed to decipher any of the sounds that came out of his mouth. I put this down to the fact that my Chinese great-grandparents forbid Mandarin to be spoken in their household when they arrived in Australia, meaning that three generations on my father's side spoke only English. It wouldn't matter – tennis's universal language of groundstrokes, volleys and serves was all we needed. Half an hour later I had gotten my warm-up, while my new hitting partner was still trying to get the grin off his face after hitting with an ATP pro (at least the Chinese kid thought I was one).

Back in the players' lounge I found myself sitting in a couch opposite my opponent and his Korean coach. The coach wore a baseball type cap, and a clipboard with a pen sat beside him. I recognised him as the same coach that had watched my match a year ago in Bangkok. Then, I had steamrolled one of his juniors. I wondered what notes he'd made about my game, what his strategy would be today.

We all sat staring at an electronic scoreboard in front of us. The tall Indian doubles specialist, Rohan Bopanna, was closing in on a win against David Martin – a Stanford University graduate. Behind me, Ivan Ljubicic sat in front of a computer terminal with his wife beside him. On the computer beside them, a white piece of paper taped to the screen read 'OUT OF WORK' (times must have been tough in China). The Cypriot, Marcos Baghdatis, could be heard in the background, laughing while a tailor measured him for a new suit. Cleanly shaven and with his hair hanging loose, Baghdatis looked boyishly handsome: a complete contrast to his wild-man, on-court persona.

The scoreboard turned over, flashing a win for the Indian.

In a few minutes, my match would be called from the players' lounge. I didn't wait. Picking up my bag, I headed towards the corridor. I sensed that the Korean player and coach would not be waiting for the call either.

The walk to court two was the longest in the entire grounds. It was a small show court at the far end of the complex. It would take a handful of minutes to get there, but feel like an eternity.

Walking down the corridor after leaving the player lounge, I looked up to see the Spanish world number nine, Tommy Robredo, walking towards me. With my shoulder-length black hair and olive complexion, perhaps Robredo mistook me for a fellow Latin player, for he was staring at me intently, a half-smile starting to emerge on his face. He broke his gaze after a couple of seconds when he failed to recognise me. He then turned and started knocking on the door of his own private changing room.

Leaving Robredo, I continued down the corridor, before turning left out of the stadium. Nicolas Kiefer was ahead of me signing a giant, fluffy and yellow tennis ball for a Chinese fan. When I got closer, the woman thrust the ball and a pen in my direction – demanding my autograph. I carefully signed my name alongside that of the other players, before returning the souvenir ball to the smiling woman. It was my first autograph as a pro on the ATP tour.

I could get used to this.

I headed past the merchandise stalls on the right, and then past the practice courts to my left. The muscular figure of Jo-Wilfried Tsonga was trading groundstrokes with his coach. After years stuck in the shadow of his French contemporaries, Richard Gasquet and Gael Monfils, Tsonga was just starting to make his move. Last month he had broken into the world's top 100, and in Beijing he sat at 60 in the rankings.

Further down the path, the authorities had used metal barriers to separate the players from the fans. When an official with a walkie-talkie spotted my player badge, he moved a couple of fans out of my way, beckoning me to follow him along one side of the barrier. My Korean opponent and coach followed me at a short distance.

The final court before our show court was court 14, where the Kei Nishikori–Ashley Fisher match was coming towards a conclusion. As we passed, the Japanese player unleashed a forehand with an audible *whoosh* as he exhaled loudly. The ball looked like it would hurtle metres past the baseline, only for it to dip viciously and land on the baseline at the Australian's feet. Fisher was rocked backwards as he lost control of his half-volleyed backhand.

Court two – with its four stands surrounding each side – loomed directly ahead. I could see fans scattered around the stands waiting for the final match of the day. I had always considered my tennis more of a journey of self-discovery rather than heading towards any definite destination. Now, I was forced to reconsider this idea. If my destination was 'ATP-land', then I had indeed *arrived*.

Stepping on to the court, I was aware of many things: spectators, lines people, chair umpire, ball kids, service radar gun, and an electronic scoreboard in the corner of the court – the same scoreboard stationed around the grounds, in the player lounge, and on the official ATP website waiting to beam our score around the world in real time.

I chose my seat, sat down on the official ATP chair...and breathed.

Hyun-Woo Nam elected to serve: in such a big match, a clear statement of intent. In the first four points I hit four forehand winners – hit as hard as I could physically manage. It was something that Fernando Gonzalez, the explosive Chilean who would eventually take the title, would have been proud of. I had so much nervous energy that I *exploded* off the ground with each swing. I saw Nam shaking his head while changing ends. Chinese girls sitting in the stand behind me shrieked excitedly after my final winner.

I liked this crowd.

The next 15 minutes passed in an adrenaline-fuelled blur. I had come out too hard, starting in fifth gear and playing way outside my comfort zone. The new balls gripped the brand new hard court – making them pop and sit up in the air. I wasn't used to such conditions. I was swinging too early, muscling the ball and dragging my shots into the alleyways. Where the top players arrived days before their matches to get used to the conditions, I had made a rookie mistake and was now paying for it.

Before I knew it, I was down 5-1. When did this happen? It seemed only a moment ago that I was winning.

Nam had shown his experience by making every ball, allowing myself to gift him point after point. The Korean was a grinder, but without the power to really succeed at the ATP level. His coach was making notes on his clipboard – undoubtedly happy with his player's strategy (of simply putting the ball between the lines).

With the first set slipping away, I decided to test a new strategy. On every remotely short ball, I would bash it at his backhand and rush the net. It was the same tactics I had practised with Andrew, back in Gladstone, a year ago.

What happened surprised even me.

My opponent unravelled, floating passing shots that I pounded away for clean winners. Point after point, the same pattern of play repeated itself – the Korean seemingly unable to cope with attack after attack.

At 5-3, I had a break point to bring the match back on serve. The world number 462 suddenly looked frail down the far end of the court. The break point played to script: I got my short ball, lined up my backhand, and at the last second…changed my mind.

What idiot changes a winning strategy?

Me. I thought I could sneak a cheap winner down the line. I saw my backhand clip the top of the net, a second before I heard a female spectator shriek in horror behind me.

Nam accepted his reprieve to take the first set 6-3.

Sitting down on the plush ATP chair, I surveyed my surroundings during the two-minute break. The mainly Asian crowd were scattered around the show court in groups. I felt they were supporting me more than my opponent; perhaps the Chinese would feel good about seeing a Korean lose. Then again, as the only Brit in the whole tournament, perhaps I was a bit of a novelty. I seemed so out of place on the far side of the Asian continent that even the aficionados hadn't found me.

I counted the number of officials on court – there were nine, including the lines people, chair umpire, and the girls logging in the statistics. I noticed the red uniforms of the ball kids. I saw the electronic scoreboard and the screen flashing up service speeds. I wondered how fast I was serving.

Focus, you idiot.

The second set began. I suddenly realised how much nervous energy I had expended – I felt drained. I had considered myself match fit, but competing at this level was a different ball game. A regular groundstroke at the ATP level seemed to use every sinew in every muscle, turning regular rallies into a test of cardiovascular fitness. Hyun-Woo Nam had been here before with Davis Cup, ATP and Challenger matches under his belt. He had paced himself – like a python slowly strangling the life out of its prey.

On the ATP website, the statistics tell the story. No aces were fired in the match, which lasted for one hour, three minutes and 53 seconds. The Korean won 80 per cent of points on his first serve. I lost 72 per cent of points on my second serve. The electronic scoreboard showed that I had lost 6-3, 6-2.

It was a long walk back to the locker room.

It sunk in that I was now out of the China Open. I rued not making the approach shot on break point, wondering what might have happened had I levelled the match. Yet, I was philosophical about the result. In my first ATP encounter, I had held my nerve in such a pressure-cooker environment, and I had made a player ranked over 900 places above me work hard for his win.

* * * * *

At midnight that evening, I found myself waiting on standby for the red-eye flight back to Dubai. At the last minute I was allocated a seat, rushed through customs, pausing only long enough to give a customs official a tennis ball with the logo 'China Open' stencilled on it.

I arrived back in Dubai in the early morning and took a taxi straight to work. When the second round of qualifying began in Beijing, I was in a classroom in the Middle East teaching Shakespeare to Arab students.

12

Kingfisher Open
Mumbai ATP

I WAS back on the ATP tour two weeks later. After the tour took a one-week break for the Davis Cup, the Asian hard-court swing resumed in Mumbai, India.

This time I wouldn't be alone. After hearing about the lifestyle of the tennis elite in Beijing, I persuaded Sylvie to join me for my second ATP experience. I pictured her sitting in the player box, watching me compete on a show court. Andrew warned me, 'India is not like China, you know.' We'd heard the stories of how hard it was: the poverty, poor food and general chaos. Surely the ATP tour existed in a different world – like a five-star travelling circus.

My determination to juggle two careers continued. After teaching through an eight-hour workday in Dubai, Sylvie and I headed to the airport for the night flight across the Arabian Peninsula and the Bay of Bengal. With the flight due to land in the early morning hours, I figured that I would sleep before daybreak to be ready for the afternoon sign-in. It was a finely calculated plan that started to go wrong the moment we left.

By the time I saw the distant lights of Mumbai twinkling among the city's urban sprawl, it was already four in the morning. The plane had been delayed by a couple of hours – the airline blaming the late arrival of passengers, the

Indian airport system and anything else to do with the sub-continent.

Leaving customs, ATP officials were nowhere to be seen. Instead, a long line of Indians crowded around holding different hotel names printed on paper. Before I had left Dubai, I had e-mailed the official in charge of hospitality twice, finally receiving a reply stating, 'All transport and hotel bookings will be done.'

Half an hour later, after wandering around the airport, I spotted two Indian men in their 20s carrying ATP merchandise bags. Wearing jeans and trainers, nothing else about them looked official. They were emerging out of the darkness of a side car park.

'No one told us you were coming,' the more handsome of the two began apologetically. His black dress shirt was unbuttoned down to his chest, revealing a gold necklace. He searched again through his list of names on a piece of paper that had been folded in his pocket. He listed off the names of the players who had arrived so far, 'Gasquet, Santoro, Kiefer, Schuettler, Nieminen.' When I asked if Lleyton Hewitt was in India yet, he scanned down his list, 'Hewitt – Monday. He's still playing Davis Cup.'

Everything was wet as we walked through the car park. There was a pleasant coolness to the air that had emerged after a downpour of tropical rain. Heavy drops hung on the dark-green foliage while our bags were dragged through puddles in the tarmac. We soon found four Mercedes with logos reading, 'Mercedes – The Official Car of the ATP' and 'Kingfisher Open'. The men explained they thought no more players were arriving that evening, so they sent all the drivers home. Their job was simply to stay out at the airport all night to greet the players as they arrived.

They then displayed a quality that I would see in abundance over the course of my stay in India – improvisation. 'Don't worry. We'll drive you to the hotel,' the gold-chained man explained. It soon became apparent that neither of them had driven a

Mercedes before. They moved from one car to the next trying to decide which would be the best to drive, finally settling on a green one. As all cars were identical models, so I had no idea what took them so long – perhaps an argument over colour?

Shortly after leaving the airport, it also became clear that they were lost. *Really lost.* Mumbai seemed a maze of interlocking streets and roundabouts. At every roundabout, our makeshift drivers stopped the car and shout to taxi drivers, 'Church Gate?' The taxi driver would always repeat the location back to us, and then direct them with a flurry of hand gestures. This had limited success – we saw the same roundabout several times.

Taxi drivers sleeping on the bonnets of their cars, blocking entire lanes, also didn't help their driving. The drivers' iconic Ambassador cars (which resembled fat beetles) were relics from a bygone era when the British ruled India, and Mumbai was known as Bombay.

We seemed to be making progress when the man in the passenger seat rang for directions. 'We're now facing the sea. Do we go left, or right?' He stayed on the mobile phone for the rest of the journey, relaying directions to the driver. Even though dawn hadn't broken through yet, the streets teemed with activity. Lorries, motorbikes, Ambassador cars, pedestrians… and a cow, all flashed by the window of the German luxury car. Each motorised vehicle looked more ancient than the previous one as they poured thick, black smoke into the air.

It was a relief to finally pull into the Oberoi Trident Hotel, one of the most luxurious in Mumbai. What should have been a two-hour flight had turned into an all-night ordeal. Curtains were drawn and the hotel room blacked out as Sylvie and I fell into a deep sleep.

An alarm rang.

I would like to say it was the next morning, but it could have been several minutes later for all I knew. In the pitch-dark, I woke disorientated. Which idiot set an alarm? Where the hell is it? *Oh my God – I've slept through the sign-in!* Then I realised it wasn't an alarm: someone was ringing the telephone.

When I picked up the receiver, a man with an Indian accent introduced himself and his role for the ATP event. I didn't catch either, which was probably a good thing.

'I'm sorry. I hope I didn't wake you.'

There were *many* things I wanted to say, but didn't.

'I'm so sorry,' he continued, extending the vowel in 'soo' (irritating me even further).

'I just wanted to apologise for the mishap last night. I don't know how it happened.'

Neither did I. I'm sure this wouldn't have happened to Roger. Then again, I wasn't a multiple Grand Slam champion. Perhaps Andrew was right – this wouldn't be like Beijing.

'I just want to apologise again,' he continued. Sylvie was mumbling for me to tell him to shut up. 'If there's anything else you need, don't hesitate to tell me.'

I reassured him it was okay, 'No problem.' It seemed to be a common phrase in Mumbai when everything was in chaos.

* * * * *

In the afternoon, I found myself waiting in the lobby for an ATP courtesy car. I was joined by a couple of the Midwest American ATP women. They looked like they could have been a mother and daughter team. Were they in China? They looked familiar, but after a while the women on the ATP tour seemed to blend into the same person – friendly, efficient and blonde. I wondered what their roles were on the travelling caravan that was the ATP tour.

'Are you here for the doubles?' the older woman inquired. Her younger companion beamed a smile, suggesting that my answer could have been the most important thing she had heard all day.

'No. I'm here for the singles qualifying.'

Both women looked puzzled. I could only guess that I looked like a typical doubles specialist. Did I not look young and manically fit? Did it look like I liked the players' buffets as much as the practice court? Perhaps they had a point.

As the ATP courtesy cars pulled up, two other players arrived to share the car with me. Pakistan's Aisam-ul-Haq Qureshi sat in the front passenger seat, while I found myself in the back with Stephen Amritraj of India.

Immediately Qureshi turned around, offered his hand in greeting and introduced himself. He did it with an assured air of self-confidence, but without any trace of arrogance or self-importance. He had the lean physique of a singles player – I could see him playing the artistic, attacking tennis that was so stereotypical of players from the subcontinent. He was currently number 148 in the singles world rankings; in Mumbai, it guaranteed him the final spot in the singles main draw. Playing doubles with the Indian, Rohan Bopanna, he would eventually end the week losing in the final of the doubles competition, collecting around U$6,000 in prize money.

Beside me, Amritraj was just as friendly, although in a less assertive manner. He was thickly set and looked more like a doubles specialist at the ATP level (I guess…like myself). In Indian tennis, his family name was legendary. His father, Anand, was a top-flight player and a Davis Cup stalwart at a time when Indian tennis was flying high on the world stage. His uncle was the famous Vijay Amritraj: top pro, *James Bond* film star and current Rolex ambassador. I desperately wanted to ask him if his uncle Vijay would be present at this ATP event, but I decided against it.

'What is Dubai like? I've heard good things about it,' he asked me after I told him from where I had travelled. I had to admit I'd only lived there for about one month. We made small talk for the rest of the brief journey to the stadium.

Coming from such a famous tennis dynasty in India, I had the impression that Amritraj had been through a lifetime of honing his social skills to the point where he could be pleasant to anyone he met. I'm sure he had forgotten me – and anything we had said – the moment we left the courtesy car.

The tennis club had nothing to do with tennis at all. In reality, it was simply five tennis courts lumped on to the side of an ancient cricket stadium. After leaving the courtesy car, players passed through a gate before being confronted with the outer wall of the cricket stadium on the left, the tennis courts on the right. In an *attempt* at civility, a white picket fence ran alongside the tennis courts. Both the wall and the picket fence had been given a fresh coat of white paint.

Beside the courts, middle-aged Indians drinking tea and reading newspapers sat on wicker chairs under blue and white umbrellas. Towering trees with the most vividly green leaves loomed over the courts, shielding the tennis complex from archaic tower blocks that sat only a few metres away from the side lines of the outer courts. There was so much greenery in the form of trees, hedges and bushes, that it looked like the jungle had exploded within the concrete maze that was Mumbai.

Amritraj walked on to the closest practice court with Jarkko Nieminen, the Finnish number one. As Nieminen was 25 in the world, the difference in terms of rankings was over a thousand places. As they started trading groundstrokes, the gulf in class was evident, but only in subtle ways.

Amritraj could match the Finn for pace, but he was forced to work hard with his shoes screeching on the green hard court. The longer the rally went on, the clearer the hitches in the Indian's groundstrokes became. The hypnotic flow of the ball being sent back and forth ended when Stephen Amritraj shanked a forehand over the side fence into the men reading their newspapers. The next rally would begin, only to follow the same inevitable pattern.

On the adjacent court, Fabrice Santoro was sporting a dull-grey shirt and a luminescent reddish-orange racquet. Nicknamed 'the little magician', he looked anything but little. Muscular and compact, all his power went through his thighs and mid-section. It was almost as if his body could absorb the yellow ball before returning it with a slow, heavy momentum. His unconventional double-handed forehand slice seemed to float through the air, hit the court, and then accelerate away. His fellow Gallic practice partner, Nicolas Devilder, was forever trying to dig out the back-spinning ball from somewhere behind him.

Leaving the training sessions, I headed towards the centre court to see which big names were training there. There was no sound of tennis balls being struck, and I could see why. Three days before the crowds would roll in, only the metal poles had been assembled where the stands should have been. Piles of wooden planks sat scattered on the concrete, still sodden from the morning's rain. Teams of labourers stood around trying to decide what to do first.

Now that I wasn't an ATP tour debutant, I wasn't going to wander around looking lost. I found the tournament director's office and signed my name, nationality and ranking on the sign-in sheet. This week I was at 1,381…having moved precisely *nowhere* since Beijing a fortnight ago. Then it was straight into the accreditation office. Unlike at the China Open where everything was laser printed, my player's badge in Mumbai was a cut and paste job enveloped within a plastic lamination. There were 14 sponsors' logos crammed around the main heading of 'Kingfisher Airlines Tennis Open – Presented by Government of Maharashtra'. Below my photo and name was the identification – 'Player'.

My player badge around my neck, I headed quickly to the empty queue for courtesy cars. I was hoping for a car on my own, simply to avoid an uncomfortable ride with a famous player. The supervisor had other ideas. 'Player Hotel!' he announced loudly in the direction of the practice courts. Before I could escape, Nieminen and another Scandinavian-looking man headed towards my car.

The Finn sat in the front passenger seat: his shirt still wet from his practice session. He turned around, offered me his hand, and with a smile said, 'Hi.' He had that lean, muscular physique that can only be achieved after hour upon hour of playing tennis.

His friend in the back seat was just as tall and lean, but without the muscles. With wavy hair, thin-rimmed spectacles and civilian clothes, he looked an outsider to the tennis world. In the short journey from the cricket stadium to the hotel, he asked about Dubai and its tax-free lifestyle. He seemed far too relaxed to have been a coach; he wasn't self-promoting like a personal trainer. My guess was an accountant, probably a long-time friend of the player, invited over to India to have a holiday… and to keep the player sane.

That evening, I discovered my draw courtesy of the aficionados online. ForeverDelayed had posted, 'British interest in this ATP event, with Gregory Howe continuing his tour of ATP qualies. He plays Tushar Liberhan of India in the first round, with Ti Chen of TPE in the next round (seeds go down to 710 here, so would have been nice to see a couple of Brits try, even though it would cost a lot to get there and back).'

After going under the radar in Beijing, it was only a matter of time before the aficionados tracked me down.

* * * * *

The view from the hotel on match day was not a promising one. Rain teemed down, splattering the windows and obscuring the view of the sea. A group of French players sat in the lobby playing a game of cards; the quartet of Fabrice Santoro, Richard Gasquet, Julien Benneteau and Nicolas Devilder would have made an impressive Davis Cup team. The Germans, Rainer Schuettler and Lars Burgsmuller, sat eating breakfast, with their mutual coach, Dirk Hordorff. Huge racquet bags occupied seats beside them. When I walked past with Sylvie, Rainer Schuettler gave me a second glance – the type when you think you've seen someone before, but you're just not sure where.

Out at the cricket stadium, tennis players, officials, ball kids and spectators stood around staring at the sea of water that covered the courts. The work on the centre court had ground to a halt: a huge, blue tarpaulin having been draped over the wooden steps.

A sign for the player lounge pointed up a flight of stairs in the cricket stadium. A security man was stationed at the foot of the stairs. As Sylvie and I approached, he weakly asked for credentials. 'She's with me,' I replied confidently. He looked unsure, glanced around for help, realised he was alone, and let us through. Bluster and looking important went a long way in India. Before long, players walked past him without even realising he was there. By the end of the day, his job had been reduced to giving directions and telling players to watch the slippery steps. In my entire time in the tournament, he was the only security man I ever saw.

The player lounge at the Kingfisher Open was the concrete steps of the Brabourne Cricket Stadium. As the stadium had capacity for 25,000 spectators, then space wouldn't be an issue. It was a slightly surreal sight to see some of the world's best tennis players sitting in a disused cricket stadium. A couple of large, white tents had been erected on the concrete steps.

There seemed to be some primitive hierarchy happening in the stadium where the players got the prime spaces above the tents. Further along, the linesmen and officials sat in their group. Even further away was the mass of ball kids, sitting beside a pile of black garbage bags. In their red outfits and white socks, the ball kids looked like a flamboyance of flamingos.

The view from the stands was a photographer's paradise. Weather-beaten white buildings surrounded the skyline, their ancient windows looking like something out of a Charles Dickens novel. On the grass oval, several women in brightly coloured saris picked weeds out of the ground. They wore black bin liners around their hips in an attempt to keep themselves dry. From the untouchable caste, their poverty seemed to be etched deep within them; they had deep tans and wiry, thin bodies after a lifetime of manual labour.

History was also etched within India's first permanent sporting stadium. Like watching an old black and white recording, one could picture a cricket Test match being played just after World War Two, a football match between India and the Soviet Union in 1955, or India's first prime minister, Jawaharlal Nehru, delivering a political speech in

1960. One thing was certain – those heady days were now long gone.

Buffet lunch arrived in the white tents. Nicolas Kiefer wasn't scared of the local food – leaving the tent with a huge plateful of rice and curry. Some of the Indian players weren't holding back either. Many of the best local players were slightly heavy, while one player had a big belly and was at least 20kg overweight. He must have had the best hands in the business to hold a ranking in the 600s. Before long, he had lost complete control at the buffet lunch.

At any moment, the sun could have appeared and play commenced. What were some of the Indian players thinking? They all had qualifying matches scheduled. If they were asked to play anytime soon, they would be vomiting all over the court. I stuck to the soup.

The renowned chair umpire, Gerry Armstrong, sat a short distance away from me on the concrete steps. There was just nowhere else to sit. When he finished his plateful of curry, he scraped the scraps into a plastic container. It was absurd to think this was an elite tournament on the ATP tour.

The group of French players passed by. Richard Gasquet was heading back to the hotel, tired of the rain. 'Pourquoi tu retournes a l'hotel?' asked Julien Benneteau. Benneteau continued, with Sylvie quickly translating for me, 'Why are you going back to the hotel? It's boring back there – there's nothing to do. Stay here.'

Shortly after, the loudspeaker system announced that play for today had been cancelled. This sparked a mad scramble for the courtesy cars. Within a few minutes, all the players, officials and ball kids had vacated the stands, leaving Sylvie and myself alone with a few servants cleaning out the tents.

Later that evening, desperate for some exercise, I went to the gym in the Oberoi Trident hotel. Paul-Henri Mathieu was already there, halfway through a session on the rubber mats. It looked like a well-rehearsed routine as he moved from one exercise to another without break or conversation. He then spent an eternity stretching his hamstrings – his foot propped up on a windowsill for support.

Nieminen and his friend also entered the gym. Nieminen nodded when he saw me, while the friend said hello. The Finn also went through a similar routine of floor exercises and stretching. Everything had an attention to detail. It occurred to me that my entire time on the lower-level Futures tour, I had only gone to the gym when I was injured. On the Futures tour, I rarely saw players doing this much physical work away from the court.

* * * * *

Scanning the newspapers at breakfast the next morning, the *Mumbai Mirror* ran interviews with the Germans, Nicolas Kiefer and Rainer Schuettler. Looking for controversy, the headline ran, 'I Don't Agree with the Quota System'. This stemmed from the demand by the Asian Tennis Federation that 25 per cent of the draw for all Asian ATP-level events had to be held for Asian players. It seemed a *ridiculous* request, going directly against the meritocracy that was integral to the tennis circuit. Kiefer was quoted, 'You have to work hard to win matches. It's not a gift.' Perhaps he had also seen the local players at the buffet yesterday.

Another sub-heading quoted Schuettler about his role as President of the ATP Player Council, 'Difficult to change things in ATP: Schuettler'. His discontent was evident when he said, 'It's like a political job. So, I quit and now I want to concentrate on my game…I'm not getting any younger.' After falling out of the top 100, it was probably a wise choice.

The British double specialists, James Auckland and Ross Hutchins, were also having breakfast. It was somewhat of a surprise to hear their distinctly British accents at the buffet. I assumed I was going to be the only player representing Great Britain on the Asian circuit. In contrast to the singles players who seemed to spend their entire time in complete concentration, the doubles specialists looked like tourists on holiday – constantly chatting and laughing, enjoying each other's company.

Out at the tennis courts, there was a hive of activity with ball kids, officials and players preparing themselves. A worker used a blowtorch on the stands around centre court, sparks flying into the outside courts below.

The top seeds in qualifying were warming up. The Italian, Davide Sanguinetti, was hitting groundstrokes with the smoothest swing I had ever seen. His strings were strung so loose that every shot produced a soft thud as the ball trampolined off his racquet. With career wins over Federer and Roddick, finding himself in a qualifying draw on the subcontinent must have been a sobering experience.

On another court, Lars Burgsmuller was fine-tuning his attacking game. Since I'd seen him in Manchester, he'd won precisely two matches on tour. Like Sanguinetti, he too was now in his 30s and making a last attempt at resurrecting his career. He would fail to escape the qualifying, losing later in the day. Both men would be officially retired within the year.

To warm up, I went for a run. Running alongside the cricket stadium, I passed the outside courts, the centre court, and then a huge hospitality tent before the wall turned left. Something *felt* wrong. When I looked around, I saw Indians wearing work clothes passing by; I had run out on to a main street without knowing it. Pedestrians were staring. It must have been a bizarre sight to see a professional tennis player warming up as people went about their daily business. There had been no security at the gate to stop me – anybody could have walked in off the street.

My preparation for my upcoming match ended up with me hitting balls against the wall of the cricket stadium. The two designated practice courts were jammed full with main-draw players. It was not ideal, but in India, *nothing* was ideal.

Beside one of the courts, an Indian woman was watching the action intensely. I figured she would be the mother of one of the Indian players. When I asked her which player she was supporting, she paused for a moment. 'Neither – my daughter is on the court as a ball kid. I'm watching her.' She pointed to a distinctly non-athletic teenage girl struggling to catch a loose ball. In the oppressively humid conditions, many of the ball kids appeared to be already flagging in the first match of the day.

After a couple of hours of play, the two Indians on my court had finally run themselves into the ground. The consolation for the loser was that they wouldn't have to play again that afternoon. To make up for yesterday's loss of play, the tournament director scheduled back-to-back matches. Perhaps he needed to run around in the oppressive humidity to understand what he was asking of the players.

When I went to sit in my court-side chair for the start of my match, the umpire approached me, 'You can't wear that cap. It has two logos on it. ATP rules stipulate that you can only have one logo.' He was English – clearly a stickler for the rules. I took the hat off to search for the two Nike ticks. 'There's one on the back.' He pointed to a minuscule logo that I swear I had never seen before.

'But I wore the same hat in China two weeks ago, and no one said anything.'

He shrugged, 'Well, that's the rules. Do you have another one?' I searched through my racquet bag and found an old, beige baseball hat. 'That one's fine.'

I wanted to point out that it was okay for someone to use a blowtorch above our heads, but it wasn't okay to wear a logo the size of a thumbnail.

In the warm-up, it was clear that my 20-year-old opponent, Tushar Liberhan, wasn't a stereotypical Indian serve-and-volleyer. Lean and wiry, he played a modern baseline game based around a two-handed backhand. At 857 in the world, he had only narrowly missed out on being a seed in the qualifying draw.

My lack of court time in India showed in the opening game. The courts were lightning fast. When a ball slid off the court unexpectedly, I top edged it straight up into the air, watching it sail on to the centre court. The workers on centre court threw the stray ball to a fellow labourer perched at the top of the stand, who relayed it back to us.

While I struggled to adjust to the conditions, my opponent was pouncing on any short ball to race around his forehand and launch a winner. His footwork was precise and his strokes a little more fine-tuned than mine. Everything was frustrating – even the brand-new Kingfisher Open towel was fraying and leaving my face and arms covered in white fluff. *Did anything work properly in Mumbai?* When Liberhan won the first set 6-2, it was an accurate reflection of how the match was going.

Top-flight players walked along the alleyway beside the court. I wondered what they were thinking when they paused to watch a point or two. I can think of no better motivation to play quality tennis than have the best players in the world watching.

Even though Liberhan was over 500 places higher in the world rankings, the second set became an evenly matched, tense struggle. A newspaper cameraman set up a huge lensed camera on the side of our court. Not to be outdone, Sylvie sat beside him with her smaller camera. I thought it strange that no one questioned her, but then I remembered there was no security with any clout to ask her to leave.

Suddenly, there was a loud bang.

Players, spectators, ball kids and officials all stopped in their tracks. Had the centre court collapsed? The experienced Brazilian ATP chair umpire Carlos Bernardes – roving the grounds – rushed across with a walkie-talkie held up to his mouth. Players came over from the practice courts to see what had happened. It soon became clear that the solid six-foot-high wall that separated our court from the adjacent court had collapsed. Nothing was holding it up, so it simply fell over with an almighty *slap* to the ground.

'Oh my God. That could have killed someone,' our chair umpire blurted out while staring at the fallen wall. Luckily, no player, linesman or ball kid was near the wall at that time. What a way to end one's playing career – being crushed to death by a wall while playing an ATP event in India.

'Let's all move to the other side of the court,' the English chair umpire told everyone. For the rest of the day, there was the absurd sight of Indian workers at each end of the wall holding it upright.

After the delay, at five games each, I sensed an opportunity. My opponent had slightly lost his rhythm. Before either of us knew it, with a couple of flicked return winners, I had taken the second set 7-5. Following the live scoring, Johnnylad announced my achievement, posting, 'Howe took a set in ATP qualies! I think James Ward should be here...could have qualified.'

By the third set, I was so drenched in sweat that the balls from my pockets were leaving wet skid marks all over the court. Every time I swung for a shot, a spray of perspiration sprayed all over the court. Sweat was even coming out of my shoes.

'Could you not put the ball in your pocket? Can you take it from the ball boy for your second serve?' the umpire requested. It was fair enough – the heavy, wet balls were affecting the play, leaving wet marks on the court after every impact.

The turning point in the third set was a long, gruelling rally. It ended when I simply could not move my legs anymore for a wide ball – dumping the ball into the bottom of the net. The continual loss of fluids had finally taken its toll.

After two hours of play in oppressive conditions, I ended losing in three sets. Although it was disappointing to be out of the tournament again at the first hurdle, I had given everything. With a set under my belt this time, I was getting closer to securing a victory on the ATP tour – dragging my game up to the required level.

Liberhan had to play again a few hours later against a seeded opponent who had received a first-round bye. Not surprisingly, he lost to Ti Chen of Taipei in two easy sets. There would be *no way* he could have recovered to play a second match on the same day.

As an interesting footnote, Ti Chen went on to qualify and play Lleyton Hewitt in the main draw in Tuesday's night match. If I could have won three matches, it would have been me playing Hewitt on the newly completed centre court.

Now, that would have really been something.

13

Beginning the Season
Doha ATP

EVERY YEAR, after a six-week end-of-year hiatus, the ATP tour begins again in January. Players are fresh and motivated. A bad year, injury, loss of form, or a slide in the rankings – all can be forgotten with a great start to the year. It's where out-of-season training counts – journeymen and rising stars hope to catch a big-name player searching for fitness and form. There's a special energy in the air; everyone starts with a clean slate.

There were three ATP tournaments that would open the 2008 season. Adelaide, in Australia, would attract the Australians to Lleyton Hewitt's hometown, while Chennai, in the south of India, and Doha, in Qatar, could be used as a transition for the European pros on their way to the Australian Open – the first Grand Slam of the year. Doha was by far the biggest of these events. With over a million dollars of prize money, the draw boasted the likes of Andy Murray and Stanislas Wawrinka. As the Qatari capital was a short flight across the Arabian Gulf from Dubai, it was also my return to the ATP tour.

Andrew and Sylvie joined me on the trip. My plan was to enter Doha quietly, without all the ATP fanfare and pressure. This idea fell apart the moment we descended the steps from the plane. On the tarmac were ATP officials with a sign, 'ATP

– Visas'. We were whisked away in a special bus to a small glass conference room, crammed with other players and hangers-on.

As soon as we entered, everyone in the room turned towards us. A group of Spanish players sat on one row of chairs, while three Koreans sat closest to us. Tommy Robredo (world number ten) was standing near the far glass wall. He paused for a moment to see who was entering. We hurried to the only three seats available, next to the Koreans. 'We should have just gotten tourist visas,' Andrew mumbled to me under his breath.

Shortly after, an immigration officer made an announcement. There was a burst of Korean from beside us as they tried to translate the message. The player in the group was Hyung-Taik Lee. Currently ranked 51 in the world, the veteran had been on tour for over a decade. How on earth had he survived for so long on the ATP tour without a command of the English language? Despite English being the unofficial language of the tour, neither the player, nor his coach or personal trainer appeared able to comprehend the information.

While the Koreans sat quietly with arms folded, there was juvenile laughter from behind us: it seemed someone in the Spanish group was trying to grab someone else. Perhaps this wasn't so different to the Futures tour after all.

The same official returned a while later with a passport. 'Mr Robredo,' he announced formally over the room. The Spanish world number ten had left the room. 'Tom-mee…Tom-mee,' cried the Spanish coach. Robredo jogged over to the official with springy steps. He even made collecting his passport look impressively athletic.

The egalitarianism of the immigration room disappeared once passports were returned. The Spanish and Koreans were whisked away in Mercedes luxury cars to the five-star Marriott: the main-draw hotel. They would be staying near the tennis complex on the upmarket end of the corniche. Meanwhile, Andrew, Sylvie and myself were led to an odd-shaped white bus for our trip to the Al Seef Hotel.

The designated qualifiers' hotel, the three-star Al Seef was closer to the airport than the tennis stadium. With its art deco Arabic style and combination of beige and sapphire blue, it looked as odd as the bus. It was no wonder that qualifiers in ATP events were so desperate. Qualify, and you get free nights in the Marriott: lose, and it's a week in the Al Seef. Perhaps there was a reason the airport was so close.

We quickly left the Al Seef for the journey along the corniche. The skyline of skyscrapers loomed over us as we pulled into the Khalifa International Tennis and Squash Complex. The stone white walls of the stadium court matched the white buildings of the surrounding neighbourhood. Date palms dotted around the grounds gave the complex a deliciously exotic Middle Eastern feel.

On a far practice court, Murray was sparring with Wawrinka. The unique purple and green court was ringed with a dozen spectators at most. Up close, watching two of the best players in the world standing toe-to-toe was awe-inspiring, with the yellow tennis ball looking like a tracer bullet being fired back and forth.

Wawrinka's explosive upper body uncoil on his backhand wing was matched by Murray's heavy weight of shot on his two-hander. The rally reached dizzying speeds when Murray ripped a forehand into the net; he leant back, looked to the sky and screamed in mock anguish. Wawrinka turned to his coach, both of them smiling.

At this point in his career, the Swiss was only 36 in the world to Murray's ranking of 11. Yet, in the baseline duels that were unfolding, it was interesting to note that Wawrinka seemed to be able to match the higher ranked player's strokes blow for blow. It was no surprise that when both players faced off again in the final seven days later, the match would end in a three-set thriller.

On the neighbouring court, the giant Belarusian, Max Mirnyi, was training with his father. Nicknamed 'the beast' due to his impressive physique, one only had to look at his father to see genetics at work. Dressed in a full tracksuit, he was as tall as his son, with square shoulders and the size of an ex-athlete. He dropped tennis balls in front of his son as Max belted ball after ball into the distance. Once as high as 18 in the world, Mirnyi was fading fast. At 152 in the world, he would require a wildcard into the main draw in order to avoid finding himself with the qualifiers playing on the weekend.

Heading back to the rooms under the stadium, an assortment of players were making their way past the ATP ladies on the front desk. The whole set-up was much smaller than in Beijing. Upon entering the foyer, a corridor ran left and right, while glass double doors opened straight on to the centre court. I headed towards the tournament referee to find the familiar face of Ashraf Hamouda, the same referee from the Carthage tournament in Tunisia.

'You made the trip,' Hamouda said as he looked up from his laptop.

I was looking at the referee trying to figure out what looked different. 'You shaved your beard!' He rubbed his smoothly shaved chin while smiling. Seeing the referee from Carthage, where I earned my first ATP point, brought back a flood of good memories. 'Whenever I see you, only good things happen,' I told him. I just hoped that his missing goatee beard wasn't part of his lucky charm.

Scanning down the qualifying sign-in sheet, I could see familiar names: Christophe Rochus, Wesley Moodie, Alberto Martin, George Bastl – all were respected professionals who had been top 100 players. There was also a smattering of players from Qatar, Syria, the UAE and Oman.

I added my name to the list with the ranking of 1,299. It was a satisfying feeling to see my name quietly moving up the rankings. Looking at the rankings of the players on the sign-in list, there were several pros ranked in the top 200. However, there were also many players behind me in the rankings. My chance of making the cut for my third straight ATP tour event was looking good.

When the sun began to fade behind the city's skyscrapers, the temperature dropped sharply with a real chill in the air. It was ironic that players headed to the Middle East to escape the European winters, only to find that the desert nation's winter winds and evenings could be just as bitterly cold. The only kiosk in the grounds was a frozen yoghurt stall – the *last* thing anybody wants when your lips have already gone numb. Luckily, they had an espresso machine that was doing steady business.

Andrew and I stocked up on takeaway coffees and headed towards the practice courts. We chose one of the show courts with rows of seating behind each end of the court. The Islamic call to prayer wailed across the grounds as we started our warm-up.

Andrew and I had been practising for the past couple of weeks in Dubai. He was starting to hit good form. Next week, he was heading to the Americas to play the Central American Futures circuit, before going on to Colombia. I had tried in vain to persuade him to try his luck in Doha. 'If I had points, I'd play. I don't have points, so I don't deserve to play at this level,' was his reply. I saw his point. Without a world ranking, you would be begging the tournament director for permission to play – he wanted to enter on his own merits.

Our friend Ahmed Abdrabuh was in the same situation. Although Syrian, he lived in the Qatari capital with his family. We had known Ahmed for years after seeing him in numerous Middle Eastern tournaments. Still trying to develop his game, his successes were often limited. Yet, with boundless enthusiasm and a great attitude towards life, he threw himself into all levels of competition. He had added his name to today's sign-in list and spoken to the tournament director, hoping to find himself in tonight's draw.

Later that evening, the draw was posted on the ATP website. Ahmed had gotten his wish to play after being awarded a wildcard, drawing the former number 57 in the world, Wesley Moodie of South Africa.

I couldn't bring myself to look, instead asking Andrew to find my name. 'Here you are,' Andrew told me with glee. 'Do you want to know?' I ran through the list of established pros in the draw. 'He's the number six seed and 199 in the world,' Andrew teased. 'You wouldn't have heard of him – Sergiy Stakhovsky of Ukraine.'

I agreed with Andrew – never heard of him. After searching through his results, we found that Stakhovsky had lost to Andy Murray in the US Open junior final four years before. There was an image of him and Murray holding their respective trophies. Maybe this wasn't so bad. In Manchester, I had lost a close match to Matt Brown – and he had *beaten* Murray in the British under-16 junior finals. Perhaps it wouldn't be too tough after all.

Meanwhile, on their internet forum, the aficionados discussed my draw...among other things:

Wolf, 'Gregory Howe playing qualifiers. He plays Sergiy Stakhovsky in R1.'

Sheddie, 'Howe must be one rich geezer.'

Steven, 'He scored ranking points in Tunisia, Senegal and Pakistan last year and I assume he's funding himself – maybe the need to be able to fund himself explains why he's playing more overseas tournaments in his mid 30s. His best performance last year, however, was probably taking a set off a young Indian now ranked in the 700s in Mumbai qualifying last September.'

* * * * *

Seats in the player bus the next morning were at a premium. The final player on board was the number one seed in qualifying, Federico Luzzi, from Italy. Realising that all the spaces had already been filled, he struggled with a small seat that unfolded into the aisle.

At 129 in the world, he was tantalisingly close to the main draws in Doha and the Australian Open. A few more places higher in the rankings, and he would be assured of *big* prize money and a shot at the *big* stars. For now, he would have to go through the qualifying like everyone else on the bus. With jet-black hair that fell to his shoulders and high cheekbones, he was strikingly handsome – like some Latino movie star.

At the tennis club gates, the bus was halted by security. The official demanded to see credentials and player badges. Players shouted back that they weren't available. 'We have matches – let's go,' came a voice from the back of the bus. The security official was at a loss. If he let the bus through, he would lose face – an unthinkable scenario for a macho Arab male. He puffed out his chest. In the most authoritative tone he could muster, he instructed nobody in particular, 'Okay, today – but tomorrow, we check. You get passes.' There was sniggering as the bus – full of equally macho Italian and Arab tennis players – was let through.

My match with Stakhovsky was scheduled for ten o'clock in the morning. Kicking off the day's proceedings on the first day, of the first tournament of the year, had a nice ring to it. We would literally be starting the 2008 tennis season.

The grass was still wet with morning dew as Andrew and I headed to a far practice court. Ahmed, who was scheduled for the second match on a show court, joined us in the warm-up. The ATP ladies were in place early: assigning practice courts, tins of new ATP Head balls, towels and water. They worked long hours, arriving early and leaving only after the final night match.

The court in the morning played nothing like our previous evening's hit. The balls refused to bounce above hip height and were oddly slow; it was as if the newly laid court surface had too much rubber – killing all pace and bounce. 'These courts are weird,' Andrew shouted across the net. 'Maybe the balls are dead.' We checked the balls, opened a second tin, and continued to watch balls plop past at knee height.

This new surface would be an ongoing controversy throughout the Australian summer circuit. For the past 20 years, the Australian Open had used the Australian-made Rebound Ace surface. This meant all lead-in events would have to be held on the same surface. However, there were always problems with the court getting sticky in Melbourne's heat. Coupled with criticism from Lleyton Hewitt that it didn't suit his game and that he'd had a 'gutful', the authorities caved in and abandoned the Rebound Ace.

Unfortunately, their decision on the new court surface seemed to have backfired. For a start, they took their business to an American company. 'We've lost our Australian-ness, our uniqueness,' Paul McNamee, the former tournament director, told the *New York Times*. To make matters worse, the new Plexicushion court was so slow it suited the Europeans more rather than the Australian players. In the same article, former great Mats Wilander said, 'I just don't know what they were thinking; this is the worst hard court they could pick for Lleyton. The ball pops up and doesn't penetrate.'

I had a Lleyton Hewitt counterpunching kind of game. That didn't bode well for my chances.

When I walked on to the match court, the officials, ball kids and my opponent were already in place. Stakhovsky, dressed in an all-blue outfit, leant on the net post, swinging a leg back and forth; just under his kneecap, a white tape ran around his knee. When I got closer, he looked across and gave a nod in my direction.

As the chair umpire went through his pre-match speech, I stole a glance at my opponent. He had a modern player's build – tall, at least 6ft 4in and lean. When I won the toss, I didn't hesitate, 'I'll receive.' There was no way I wanted to gift a top player an early break because of my own nerves. His service game would give me time to settle down. Perhaps he was nervous too? He would be expected to crush a player over a thousand places lower than him.

The court had no seating or stand. A full team of lines people, ball kids, chair umpire, and officials recording statistics, were all crammed within the wire meshing, making the court feel small. Sylvie sat on an outside bench. Andrew was too anxious to sit – instead hiding behind a pair of date palms. A few other spectators stood around the court, but at this time in the morning the grounds were mostly empty.

The scoreboard lit up. Howe and Stakhovsky flashed up in yellow, both with zero besides our names. Live scoring had begun, beaming the score around the world in real time. I wondered if any of the aficionados were following. It would only be six in the morning in the United Kingdom, but these were die-hard fans so it was possible.

Stakhovsky rocked back, stepped forward, drove up…and got the 2008 season underway. I had faced big servers over the past year on tour, but I wasn't expecting this. The ball *exploded* off the court; it had so much weight that it twisted the racquet in my hand. How had he done that? His service motion was so smooth that it had appeared effortless.

I retreated a couple of steps further back to return the next serve: the linesman behind me now within touching distance. When the ball rocketed past, I turned to see the linesman perform a last-second evasive action – the ball narrowly missing him before thudding into the back fence. 'Stand behind your chair,' I advised him. I had heard the story about a linesman being killed by a Stefan Edberg serve; I didn't need a decapitated official on my conscience.

On my serve, the Ukrainian simply chipped his return deep into the centre of the court, glided across the baseline and started the rally. I was getting *nothing* for free. On the low-bouncing hard court, everything was coming into his hitting zone. He had a game developed on slick indoor courts where – on both wings – he stepped into each shot with long flowing swings, launching balls into the corners of the court. I was being sent from one side to the other before watching the inevitable winner scream by.

With a break of serve up his sleeve, my opponent was going in for a quick kill. I could feel it. He moved further up the court, taking away time, increasing the pressure. Soon he wasn't trying to work the point – instead going for the winner as soon as he could. The intensity coming from across the net was on a new level that I hadn't experienced before.

After 15 minutes, I was down 5-0.

For the first time in my tour, I was actually *worried*. I was going out in a hurry with nowhere to hide. If I couldn't stop the onslaught, the match would be gone in half an hour. A giant scoreboard in the centre of the grounds updated all the courts.

Did I want to be the first loser of the year?

'Attack, attack.' Andrew's voice came from somewhere behind the date palms in a stage whisper. When I glanced my eyes across, he made a pushing gesture with his hands – signalling to get to the net. Then he turned around and pretended to be watching another court; none of the six officials on the court had heard or noticed.

On my next service game, I scraped enough points together to finally have a game point. As I hit a second serve, my opponent back-pedalled to set up for a big forehand. I watched helplessly as the ball landed a good inch inside the baseline for another winner.

'Out!' came a shout from behind me.

Stakhovsky suddenly sprung back, taking two enraged steps towards the umpire. The call was so late that he had already turned to walk to the other side. The umpire was nodding. I was caught still staring at the spot where the ball had landed. Quickly I headed for my towel, trying not to look guilty. At this point I was desperate – I'd take anything to get on the scoreboard.

'Game: Howe. Stakhovsky leads 5-1,' announced the chair umpire.

For a split second the Ukrainian thought about challenging. Instead he turned, threw a dismissive hand in the direction of the umpire and walked away. I guessed he thought the first set was his – which it was a few minutes later.

My learning curve was rapid. Even against other highly ranked players, I had time to work my way into the point. Here, there was no time. If I wasn't hitting a forcing shot, I was dead. I realised I had better find some chinks in the Ukrainian's armour...and quickly.

I held on to my opening service game by hustling. Stakhovsky was a tall man who needed to set up his feet and wind up with long backswings. If I could keep him moving, he was less effective off balance. To win the game I ripped a backhand crosscourt – his running backhand passing shot crashing into the net. 'That's it,' I heard from out near the date palms.

I started to adjust to the service bombs he was sending my way. However, I still could make no impact on his first serve: into the corners, it was an ace. Even if I could block it back, he was all over the net with superb volleys, always punching away a winner.

Stakhovsky's second serve, though, was a slow high-kicker. On the new Doha courts it sat up nicely for my two-handed backhand. I could jump into it, creating small windows of opportunity where my opponent was momentarily on the back foot. Out of nothing I manufactured two break points – a tiny glimmer of hope to claw my way back into the match.

Who was I kidding?

I never even got a look at either serve. Stakhovsky showed his class by finding two big, sliding first serves into the corners when he needed them.

In my tennis bucket list, to play a top pro in an ATP event ranked highly. Sergiy Stakhovsky fell into this category. The second set proved something – for short bursts, I could stay with a top player off the ground. But, without a big first serve, I would *never* be able to survive at this level. There was just too much pressure every time I tried to hang on to my service game. In the second set, I won two of my service games, and lost two. It was as simple as that.

Sometimes match statistics don't tell the true story. In my match with Stakhovsky, they were spot on. The match lasted precisely 41 minutes. The final score was 6-1, 6-2. I wasn't so much disappointed at losing the match – instead slightly relieved that I had escaped with three games.

By the end of the match he had won 23 out of 24 points on his first serve. On paper, it seemed ridiculous. How could I win only *one* solitary point against his first delivery, especially as I thought of my return of serve as my best shot?

On his second serve, though, I won 47 per cent of the points – a fair return. In contrast, I got most of my first serves in, but could win just over a half of them. If I'd learnt anything from the match, it was that spinning a safe first serve in at this level was a complete and utter waste of time.

Stakhovsky gave me the locked-thumb handshake and a nod. His year was off to a good start. Exactly two months later, he would win his first ATP tour title in Croatia, beating a host of established pros; he was on his way to a career high of 31 in the world, amassing over U$4m in prize money along the way.

Andrew's post-match briefing was as brutal as usual, 'Your serve's crap…this is an ATP match – you can't do that here…I thought you were going to be hit by his serve…standing so close…so defensive…were you trying to slow ball him…this is not the 1980s you know.'

It's hard to argue when you just lost a match lasting precisely 41 minutes.

We headed over to one of the nearby show courts. Ahmed had just walked on court for his match against the big-hitting South African, Wesley Moodie. I wasn't sure if I would even describe this as a David versus Goliath – more like the Christians being thrown into the lions. It would take Ahmed a monumental effort just to stay in touch with a player who was an established pro on tour. Yet, he was ready to fight – and in a one-on-one contest, strange things can happen.

A few dozen spectators sat scattered around the two stands. Most of them were ball kids who were having a break from their duties – snacking on crisps and soft drinks. A few expat Filipinos had arrived for a day watching tennis, taking advantage of the free entry. No one was paying too much attention to the players getting ready.

Ahmed won the toss and immediately chose to serve. If he was going to bluff, then he had to bluff with confidence, even if it meant revealing his slow spinning serve straight away. While his serve might not get attacked at a lower level, now it looked like it could be ripped to shreds. As Ahmed served, I could see the South African's eyes visibly widen – the fluffy, yellow ball wobbling into his strike zone.

What happened next was fascinating.

The crowd focused, looking forward to the bloodletting. In a can't-lose match, Moodie's hand froze; I had never seen an ATP pro so tightly wound with nerves. He dumped his return feebly into the bottom of the net, hitting a forehand with an ugly Eastern backhand grip. Normally faced with high-speed encounters, Ahmed's serve was like a baseball pitcher's knuckleball.

Unwilling for the same thing to happen, Moodie chipped the next return safely into the middle of the court. The match had been reduced to something one would see in the juniors. Ahmed pushed his groundstroke invitingly back over the net, teasing Moodie to attack. The South African charged forward, wound up his backswing, and promptly shanked his forehand into the side fence. 'Out!' called the linesman. The crowd sniggered. Moodie paused for a split second, unsure of how to react, composed himself and retreated to the baseline.

Just when it looked like Ahmed could hold on to his opening serve, his inexperience showed. On each serve, he took a step forward before hitting the ball. At the ATP level, there was a linesman planted on the baseline, looking only for foot faults. Now, point after point was surrendered as Ahmed's foot stepped across the line. Four points later, when Moodie was awarded the game, Ahmed angrily swung his racquet at the linesman on the near baseline. The linesman held a palm upwards – bewildered at why the player would be angry with him for doing his job.

Up a break, the South African visibly relaxed. His serve had such venom and pace, that on one return Ahmed caught it late, driving the ball towards the umpire's chair. Rarely would he have faced such a serve-and-volley barrage as this. Ahmed's one chance to hang in the match had gone…there wouldn't be another one. In the ATP qualifying, no one took their foot off the gas. The established professional players simply saw the win, and the quicker the better. Thirty-seven minutes later, the match was over, with Moodie securing tennis's version of a whitewash – a double bagel.

For the record, Ahmed's match wasn't the quickest. Philipp Davydenko, nephew of world number four Nikolay Davydenko, lost his match a minute faster. It relegated my loss to the third fastest of the day.

On the adjacent show court, Federico Luzzi, with the matinee idol looks and the number one seeding, was in trouble against a fellow Italian. His long hair was pulled into a high ponytail, secured in place by a pink hairband – something a young girl might wear. Everything he did seemed to be clashing. His classical all-white outfit ended abruptly with a pair of dark-grey tennis shoes, while his classically styled game was at odds with his increasingly erratic behaviour.

He appeared in the throes of a meltdown. After one unforced error, he mocked himself by rehearsing the shot with all the form of a complete beginner. He postured, screamed, held his head in his hands, looked to the heavens, and then finally, caved in the head of his racquet. I had heard Luzzi once described as 'a man on the edge'. After capitulating in the third set, it looked as if he was about to fall over that edge.

From the back of the stand, I watched him forlornly leave the court. He walked slowly, head staring intently at the pavement in front of him, still holding the smashed racquet. Passing a waste bin, he carefully placed the racquet head first into the opening, before disappearing down the side of the stadium.

Luzzi had star appeal. Even on a backcourt in Doha, he was compelling to watch. He would have been perfect as a top player in the heady days of the 1970s. I made a note to follow his progress in Australia and beyond.

What I wasn't expecting was such a tragic downfall. He failed to escape the qualifying in the Australian Open. Shortly after, he was banned for 200 days for innocuously (but stupidly) gambling on tennis matches. It seemed a harsh penalty for bets worth only a handful of euros. Worse was to follow. I opened a tennis magazine later in the year, only to find a short brief about his death, due to leukaemia. The whole chain of events was hard to comprehend.

Following the Italian on the far court in the Khalifa International Tennis and Squash Complex, a match between two true journeymen had begun. It was an aficionado's delight – the kind of match that is often played in front of a handful of spectators. It was between George Bastl, of Switzerland, and Alberto Martin, of Spain: both fine examples of where grit, perseverance and discipline could take you. Neither man looked blessed with natural talent – but they were maximising what they had.

Bastl's claim to fame was being the last man to defeat Pete Sampras at Wimbledon. He was all muscle, huffing and puffing around the court, attacking the net at every opportunity. He was the protagonist – *always* forcing the action. His foil was the diminutive Spaniard. Once a top 40 player, Martin was what you get if you hit five hours a day, every day of your life: the quintessential grinder.

Martin eventually prevailed in a match heading towards the three-hour mark. Some 180 points were played – every one of them earned through sweat and graft. Both men were fighting to revive their flagging careers and the desperation showed, making it utterly compelling.

* * * * *

Our return flight to Dubai was booked for Monday evening. It meant Andrew, Sylvie and I would be able to watch the official opening day's play of the Doha ATP event. The most significant moments occurred in both the opening and closing minutes.

The little magician, Fabrice Santoro, and Andreas Seppi, of Italy, opened the day's proceedings on centre court. Entrance was free. It was hard to tell whether this was to entice more spectators, or simply because Qatar had so much money they didn't care. Either way, the centre court was empty. A dry wind cut through the air, making the shade uncomfortably cool.

Seppi started his 2008 season by promptly dumping four serves in a row into the middle of the net. Had there been any crowd, there may have been jeering. It seemed to be symbolic of how some of the pros treated the early season events – simply a way to blow away the cobwebs.

By the evening, the temperature had plummeted in the desert nation. We sat in the stand of the furthest outside court, watching 'the Beast', Max Mirnyi, play one of the last singles matches of his career. He played a terrible match against Hyung-Taik Lee, of South Korea. It was hard to tell if he was angry, frustrated or just plain resigned – his facial expression never changed. It was as if he was playing by numbers. Once Lee had negated all his set plays, he had no options left and the match quickly ran away from him.

I returned to the ATP ladies in the foyer of the stadium, ordering a courtesy car to the airport. The only other person in the foyer was Mirnyi, waiting for his doubles match to be called. I could feel his eyes fix on me as he swung his racquet… over and over again. It was difficult to tell what he was thinking – his countenance was still set in his game face of brooding intensity. He could be the nicest person in the world, but having someone nicknamed 'the Beast' staring at you at close quarters was slightly unnerving.

It was a relief when the ATP ladies announced the courtesy car had arrived. 'See you in Australia,' both ladies chirped. Unfortunately, I wouldn't be joining the tour heading 'Down Under'.

'Yep, see you there,' I replied. They were so friendly, I didn't have the heart to tell them otherwise.

14

Living the Dream
Dubai ATP

IN THE 2008 Australian Open Final, Novak Djokovic defeated Jo-Wilfried Tsonga. The Frenchman was the surprise package of the event – finally bringing together all his weapons in a destructive run through the draw. The two biggest names in tennis, Roger Federer and Rafael Nadal, were dumped out in the semi-finals. I watched the whole event on television – far from Australia, with the detachment of a living-room spectator. It made me feel disconnected from the tour; they could have been playing on the moon for all I knew.

In a normal year, after Australia, most of the tennis elite would have headed back home before amassing for the American hard-court swing in Indian Wells, California. However, 2008 was anything but a normal year.

The world was in the middle of an orgy of easy money, greed and financial recklessness. The economic bubble had grown to epic proportions – and the biggest bubble was in my new hometown of Dubai. A third of the world's construction cranes were in the Middle Eastern city. Just lying down on my living room sofa, I could see eight cranes through the window, perched atop half-built skyscrapers.

The city had exploded in size. Ordinary people were making crazy money – buying mansions that hadn't even been built, flipping them the next day for a profit. You didn't even need money: banks would lend any amount. Different banks simply meant more available loans and more houses to buy... and flip. Dubai was determined to show the world *nothing* was impossible.

This included their ATP tennis event. As a Gold Series tournament (now called a 500 event), it ranked under the Grand Slams and Masters events. Whereas these top events were compulsory for all top players, the Gold Series and below were not. The best they could hope for would be for a couple of the elites to play their tournament.

Not Dubai.

Through appearance fees, they would simply buy every top player; rumour had it that Federer's appearance fee started at $1m. Was it true? Did anybody care? In 2008, money was *no* object.

Las Vegas was holding a tournament the same week. How could it compete? Even the American number one, Andy Roddick, opted to travel halfway around the world to play in the Middle East rather than Nevada.

The cut-off for the 32-man draw was 36 in the world. It would be the strongest, most elite entry list for any regular tournament that year, or the decade for that matter. Tsonga, the hottest new player on the block, wasn't playing. At 38 in the world, he hadn't made the cut. Marin Cilic, the giant Croatian ranked at 45, found himself in the qualifying draw: surely the only time ever that a top 50 player would have to go through qualifying for a middle-tier ATP event.

So, where did this leave me?

By March, I had lived in Dubai for six months, juggling my teaching career while travelling to ATP events. This tournament would be different. This time the show was coming to me. The Dubai ATP would be held in the Aviation Club – a private club where I was a member. It felt like the best players in the world would be playing in *my* backyard. However, I had to wonder – would there be a place for me? The qualifying draw in Gold events allowed only 16 players, and the players were already confirmed. The sign-in was only to make a list of alternates in case one of the confirmed players didn't show up.

At midday on the Friday I had arranged a practice session with my fellow Queenslander, Troy Gillham. I had seen Troy sporadically throughout my tour: Bangkok, the Gold Coast, and all throughout Africa. By the end, we had become firm friends – playing doubles together in Senegal, sightseeing and joining up for dinners while on tour. When I moved to Dubai, it was only natural that he would become my regular practice and doubles partner. We had won so many local doubles titles in the past months that I had lost count of both trophies and money.

Troy had a rugged Australian serve and volley game – based on his idol and another Queenslander, Pat Rafter. With his dangerous serve, great volleys and athleticism around the court, I thought he had a top 500 game. During training, when he was on, I couldn't stay with him. Not even close. He had been tearing up the local UAE money circuit, beating highly ranked players and raking in more money than he could ever hope for on the Futures tour.

Yet, for some reason, he just couldn't translate this into success in the pros. In Kenya, I saw him reach the quarter-finals. A breakthrough into the top 1,000 in the world looked a formality. However, match after match, he got caught in protracted rallies with baseliners, getting pushed deep, when all his weapons were near the net. Travelling on his own, with no coach to see the same pattern emerging, he had gotten stuck.

In his mind, Troy's tennis career had two scenarios: either he would make it, or he would not. There was *no* middle ground. With no tangible progress in the rankings, week by week, the pressure inevitably increased.

During a practice session the previous year, we chatted about our plans. About to embark on my ATP journey, I tried to persuade Troy to join me. It would have been great – someone to practice with and support and motivate each other. I told him the story of John Arbanas, the unranked Australian who had gotten hot for a few days to qualify for the Australian Open. Perhaps we could do the same. What could take years of hard grind on the Futures tour could be done in a handful of days on the ATP tour.

His mind was set, 'I need to put myself under pressure – real pressure. Maybe I've been too easy on myself.' He had planned a gruelling three-month Futures tour around the world. In his mind, it was now or never. 'I can't use my parents' money forever. Either I make a breakthrough on this tour, or I'll have to start supporting myself.'

I followed Troy's results. Ten tournaments without a break are like running a marathon every week – the longer it goes, the slower you become, until you hit the proverbial wall. When it involves travel across four continents, then just keeping sane would be a challenge in itself. Not surprisingly, he won precisely one main-draw match in the entire campaign, earning a solitary ATP point. He had put himself in a make-or-break scenario, and in his mind, his tennis dreams were over. He would play the local events, start coaching and think about his future.

Now, as we met in the foyer of the Aviation Club, there was a renewed sense of purpose in his movements. He was feeding off the energy of the ATP tour. I sensed he was daring to wonder if he would be given one final shot at a pro career.

Life-size images of Roger Federer and Rafael Nadal decorated the foyer. Burly Arab security guards blocked every possible corridor. The ATP ladies had been stationed in one of the squash courts – sitting behind cubicles in a U-shape. We were assigned practice court number seven – ironically our regular court – and given a couple of cans of practice balls each and Dubai Open towels. By the end of the week, we would each acquire at least a handful of these.

We were directed towards another ATP lady at a nearby desk. 'If you get into the qualifying draw, come back for your food and drink vouchers. Also, players will get one free massage, and there's an allocation of tickets for the stadium, but you can only collect them on the day.' In her American accent, she wished us 'good luck'.

A sign with an arrow pointed down a corridor towards the locker room. On the left wall hung the racquets of past winners – Thomas Muster, Nicolas Kiefer, Fabrice Santoro, Roger Federer and Rafael Nadal. In their glass cabinets, the strings of the older racquets had frayed and split over time.

The history of the tournament was literally engraved in the nearby locker room. On the dark wood of the locker doors, legends from the past had their names etched into silver plates, screwed into the wood. Stefan Edberg's locker was in a far corner, fitting for his reserved, understated manner. Ivan Lendl's name could be found in the centre of the locker room – the master of his universe.

Today, I dumped my belongings in Wayne Ferreira's locker – the other club members had beaten me to all the good lockers.

On the way to court seven, we paused to watch Rafael Nadal on practice court eight. Uncle Toni was selecting balls from a brown cardboard box and feeding him one by one. His nephew would retreat a couple of small steps and drive the ball into a corner – the ball audibly thumping into the back fence.

Watching one of the most destructive hitters of the ball in tennis history, up close, on a backcourt with no one around was, initially, slightly underwhelming. Only when I watched the ball closely did I see its vicious spin – I felt I could hear it hum as it tore over the net. A couple of hours later, Nadal was still out on a remote practice court, driving forehands with the same ferocity.

In the Dubai ATP tournament, spectators were restricted from watching practice courts. Whether it was for security reasons – or just to keep the players happy – was unclear. Surely enough, when we reached court seven, the court was nearly completely enclosed with a dark green meshing. Only a gap a few metres wide provided a view to the outside world.

As it was Friday and no matches had begun, security didn't bother stopping the public. A few people wandered over from the nearby Irish pub to watch Troy and I practise. One Western expat brought his glass of beer over with him. He must have assumed the tournament was a safe zone from Islamic Sharia law's strict stance on alcohol. They watched for a couple of minutes before sauntering off in the direction of Rafa and Toni.

After our practice, we headed to the alternate sign-in, a five-minute walk away in the Al Bustan Rotana hotel. This would be the same Al Bustan hotel where, two years later, an alleged elite Israeli team assassinated a Hamas military commander. Undoubtedly, it will be turned into a film someday. Eleven Mossad agents — some disguised as tennis players — used fake passports to gain entry into Dubai before drugging, electrocuting and strangling their victim in room 230.

This day in the Al Bustan, the only people who wore tennis clothes were Troy and I. The huge marble foyer was deserted. In a small office under a staircase sat Gerry Armstrong and the tournament director, Ed Hardisty; the room was bare, except for a wooden table and a blank piece of paper. No other players had bothered to travel to Dubai with so little chance of playing. As I had three ATP points to Troy's two, I was designated as 'alternate one', with Troy 'alternate two'.

With nothing to do until the qualifying draw was made, Troy and I headed to a Japanese restaurant beside the Aviation Club. To stop ourselves agonising over whether we would make the cut, we joined the hot topic of discussion in Dubai at the time, flipping real estate and making fast money. Poring through the local newspaper, the *Gulf News*, we looked at the hundreds of off-plan offerings. Should we buy a villa on Tiger Woods's golf course, or an apartment in the Trump Tower? In Dubai in 2008, *anything* was possible.

How about playing in the most elite tennis event this year? Why not?

It was past ten at night when we ventured back to the ATP information room on the squash court. The desks were vacant and the television monitor showed an empty stadium. Troy looked around for the draw.

'Hey, you're in!' He was pointing excitedly at the information board.

Sure enough, at the bottom of the draw under 'Last Direct Acceptance', was the information, 'Gregory Howe – 1,312'. With such a small qualifying draw, a possible showdown with Roger Federer or Rafael Nadal was only two wins away. I later discovered that due to a last-minute withdrawal, Marin Cilic had moved into the main draw. Instead of playing Cilic, Jan Minar from the Czech Republic was now playing Gregory Howe. I'm sure Minar would feel the quality of opponent would be...roughly the same.

Before I had even driven home, the aficionados online had begun commenting on the draw:

ForeverDelayed, 'The strongest ATP event of the season also has one of the weakest qualifying fields of the season, but there is British interest with Gregory Howe making the trip and sneaking in as an alternate. He's got ninth seed Jan Minar (CZE) (promoted to a seed after Cilic made the main draw) in round one.'

Johnnylad, 'If only Boggo [British number two – Alex Bogdanovic] was there ...'

Steven, 'Yes, down in that section with Sirianni would be nice!!'

John, 'Would you rather he go out early to play this? Challenger semis or chance to get into one of the biggest ATPs of the year?'

As with Doha, I guess it was again up to Andy Murray and myself to keep the British flag flying. I wondered if he even knew I was there?

* * * * *

On match day, I drove my Ford Focus to the Aviation Club, parking in the members' dirt car park. Roger Federer also drove his car to the club – a Mercedes – parking it wherever he damn liked. Later in the week, a security guard made a complaint that someone had parked on the pavement. It was made clear to him that the car was Roger's, and that he could do whatever he wanted.

My match with Minar was scheduled for ten in the morning. That meant arriving early to sort out accreditation and re-stringing. I'd had a sore wrist since my match in Doha with Sergiy Stakhovsky. I hadn't felt it during play, but afterwards there was a pain that lingered for the following couple of months. I had decided on a last-minute decision to use natural gut – the cow's stomach lining softening the impact of the ball.

In the club's foyer, the three re-stringers were frantically threading strings back and forth. I knew them as the club's local tennis coaches, from India.

'I need this done – I'm on at ten,' I told the closest stringer. He looked at me in despair, his eyes glancing at the pile of racquets and the growing queue of players behind me. Feliciano Lopez's blue Babolat racquets sat on the desk with a reel of string.

'I have to do these first,' the Indian re-stringer replied. I was being treated like a club member, not an ATP player.

'He has a match. He has priority,' came a voice of authority from a nearby official.

The Indian coach with the stressed expression looked at me. 'I'll try,' he said weakly.

As I wrote my surname on a slip of paper, I became aware of a tall European player glancing at my writing over my shoulder. He saw me looking, and smiled knowingly. I figured it was Jan Minar. In such a small draw full of regular ATP tour players, there were only a couple of unknown faces, so Minar must have deduced he would be playing me.

With an hour to go, I jogged a couple of laps around the stadium. This meant running through the outdoor seating of an Irish pub, past a fish and chip shop, a Costa, and a Mini Cooper stuffed with tennis balls. The merchandise and corporate stands had already opened. For them, the event wasn't beginning, but rather at the midway mark after the women's event had started a week earlier.

Spectators had already started to filter in for the women's final between Elena Dementieva and Svetlana Kuznetsova. A few fans were waiting for the men's qualifiers to begin, but this was not a traditional tennis crowd who knew anything beyond the stars on centre court. Most were heading to the pub or for an early morning coffee in Costa. A couple of people looked at me in bewilderment as I ran past, as if surprised to see a tennis player.

Back in the locker room, the players for the first four qualifying matches were preparing for battle. The ultimate journeyman, George Bastl, was changing into his tennis clothes. Beside him, a pale bandana lay ready to add the final touches to his ensemble. The powerful figure of Viktor Troicki, from Serbia, sat on a bench, slowly winding a pale blue grip around the handle of a racquet. He appeared in some kind of hypnotic trance, looking at the grip, but his thoughts far away. The Serbian doubles specialist Nenad Zimonjic was in a far corner near his opponent, Jan Hernych.

Exiting the locker room, I came face to face with the principal of my school, a British woman in her 50s. We looked at each other, unsure of how to begin. I wasn't prepared for these two different spheres of my life meeting. A couple of weeks before, she had called me into her office to explain some teachers had complained that it was unfair that I was being allowed to take time off to play tennis. Weddings were allowed, sick grandparents for sure, and even a marathon was deemed an acceptable reason for the occasional day off – but tennis?

'I'm here to get my nails done in the spa,' she started, breaking the uncomfortable silence. 'Oh, are you playing?'

'I'm just about to play the biggest match of my life,' I replied.

'Jolly good. Good luck then.' She was sincere, but still off-balance.

I wondered if it occurred to her how unusual it was for one of her teachers to be competing in one of the biggest events on Dubai's sporting calendar? Probably not. To be fair, she wasn't alone in her inability to understand what I was trying to achieve.

When I told one of my colleagues that I played tennis all over the world, a confused look crept across her face, 'Do you mean you go to these countries and hit against a wall?' At this point, I realised the only wall I was facing was the one I was hitting my head against trying to explain to academics about my tennis.

I waited behind court eight while the other players filed past. They were playing on the outside show courts where there would be spectators. I had drawn the court that was hidden behind temporary huts, close to the pub.

A team of ball kids had entered from another exit and was busy preparing the players' areas, unfolding towels and selecting drinks from the refrigerator. The officials came in their matching outfits, followed by the chair umpire and my opponent with an official escorting him. The ball kids lined up and waited to attention until we walked past.

Minar was tall and lean with a distinctly central European look about him. At 200 in the world rankings, he was at the peak of his career after years of toil on the Challenger circuit. His younger brother, Ivo, had been a top 100 player in the past, so perhaps he felt he had a point to prove later in his career.

Viewing for court eight was limited so Sylvie and Troy were forced to lean from the side of the nearby stand to see around the side fence. It was clear the event didn't see the qualifiers as worthy of the public's interest: entry to the outside courts was free, and it remained that way for the entire week.

My opponent won the toss, served and promptly held his serve to love. The ATP site listed Minar as 186cm – exactly the same height as myself – yet he looked so tall and imposing, pounding down heavy first serves. He was almost the same ranking as Sergiy Stakhovsky when I played him in Doha, but Minar's game wasn't as explosive or intimidating. Whereas the Ukrainian was looking to blow his opponent off court, my opponent today was moving the ball around looking for openings. On every point, he was slowly turning the screw, giving away nothing and patiently hitting crosscourt. I won my opening serve, but only after being forced to save break points.

It didn't take long for Minar to realise he could attack my second serve – a slow kicker that never kicked very much. As soon as I missed a first serve on the advantage side, he would back away and position himself in the tramlines, bluffing that I couldn't sneak a ball down the middle. He was right, and after my serve I would look up to see him winding up his forehand ready to launch a winner.

I was hanging on for dear life. Ten minutes into the match I had already faced five break points. On the sixth, I double faulted – the pressure finally too much.

I was now down 3-1, playing catch-up with a highly fancied opponent: the worst position to be in. Troy was clapping loudly, never once hinting at any disappointment at not playing himself. The aficionados on the internet were following my progress, watching the score slowly ticking over, posting updates on their forum.

The pattern continued. Whenever he found himself in trouble on his own serve, the Czech could always escape with a big delivery down the middle. I held to move to 4-2 but a few minutes later I was locked in another rearguard effort in saving break points again. I ended up saving ten of them during the match, with Minar becoming visibly irritated with my ability to wriggle free. However, constantly coming from behind is too difficult to do for an entire match.

Eventually, I was broken to lose the first set 6-2.

With a set under his belt, Minar loosened up and moved his game up another gear. When an opponent is slightly better in all areas of the game, it becomes an effort to string four points together to win a game. I earned three break points on Minar's serve in the second set but that final point to make it count always remained elusive.

On the internet, the aficionados were monitoring the live scoring:

Jamatthews, 'Gregory 2-6, 0-3. Is his career prize money really $1,191? I think you might get more than that losing first round qualies here in Dubai.'

Wolf, 'Howe lost 6-2,6-1.'

Johnnylad, 'I'm amazed he won three games! Minar must be kicking himself about that!'

Jamatthews, 'He almost won a fourth. The scoreboard changed to 3-1, but then it went back to 3-0, deuce. Minar eventually broke for 4-0.'

I lost the match, earning (as Johnnylad helpfully pointed out) just three games: yet I felt that so many of the games were close. As against Stakhovsky in Doha, my lack of a killer first serve had been telling. This time I managed *one* ace, to bring my total number of aces in four ATP tournaments to five. It wasn't exactly a John Isner or Goran Ivanisevic statistic.

For years and years, like so many players, I had spent hours grooving groundstrokes. Yet, at that moment in time, sitting on the ATP chair out on court eight, I would have traded all the nice feel and smoothness of my forehand and backhand for a rocket of a first serve. If only I could go back in time about 20 years and know what I knew now.

The ball kids stood again in their line and applauded Minar and I as we left the court. I headed up to the stands, behind where Viktor Troicki was muscling his way to a first-round victory.

'Unlucky,' Troy offered. 'You made him work for it. He was getting a bit pissed at himself out there.'

It felt good hearing it. True – I had made my opponent work hard, but the outcome of the match had never been in doubt. Before the tour, I had wanted to know exactly where my game stood among the pros. After four ATP tour events, and the last two against high quality players, I found out I couldn't compete with the top 200 players. They were out of reach.

After showering, Troy and I collected our meal vouchers and headed into the players' area. Most of the world's tennis elite was sitting around having lunch. The Spanish sat in a group: Rafael Nadal, David Ferrer, Fernando Verdasco, Juan Carlos Ferrero and Feliciano Lopez. They seemed to dominate the lounge, comfortable with each other, conversing in Spanish.

'Excuse me sir…your shoelaces.' I looked over to see one of the Indian waiters pointing towards Andy Murray's shoes. The Scot had entered the lounge, clearly enjoying the feeling of walking around with loose shoelaces. Murray looked back, replying, 'Oh, thanks,' before continuing on. He was polite, but felt no need to explain himself.

Andy Roddick was helping himself to the food in the buffet. He acknowledged the waiters, thanking them as he moved from station to station. I would describe the American as a mobile tank with the physique of an American football linebacker. Wearing a baseball cap and a plain t-shirt that hung from impressive shoulders, he stood apart from the Europeans with their warm-up jackets and tight-fitting Italian-designed tennis outfits. He sat down alone, looking around, perhaps wishing there were some other Americans playing.

I wondered where Jimmy Connors was – the legendary American was coaching Roddick at the time. Later in the week, Roddick announced that he and Connors had split. Roddick told the BBC, 'When I am going from Australia, to Austria, to California, to Memphis, to Dubai, it becomes difficult.'

Maria Kirilenko was the lone female player in the lounge. Although she had lost a week ago in the women's event, she was dating the Russian, Igor Andreev, so she was hanging around with him. The media were portraying her as the new Anna Kournikova – the *new* hottest body in tennis. She would soon be seen in a swimsuit for the *Sports Illustrated* magazine. Today, she wore a skimpy shorts and singlet combination, but no one in the packed room of alpha males bothered to even glance in her direction.

On a far table were the local Emirati players. I knew them fairly well, playing them several times already on the local money circuit. The number one local, Omar Behroozian, had damaged his knee playing football. Ranked as high as 805 in the world, he had played in the main draw of the Dubai Open nine times as a wildcard, competing against the likes of Tim Henman, Younes El Aynaoui and Dominik Hrbaty.

With Behroozian's injury, the Emirati wildcard into the main draw this year was Mahmoud Nader Al Balooshi, the unranked Emirati number two. It was one of the quirks of holding ATP events in exotic countries with no tradition in the game: an unknown and unranked player would be in the same draw as Federer and Nadal.

The aficionados had spotted the Emirati's entry, with John commenting, 'Take a look at the local wildcard, Mahmoud Nader. I can't even find an ITF profile on him. According to the ATP site, he hasn't even played before. I just can't believe that a guy who's never played an ITF could be given a wildcard into one of the biggest ATPs of the year. Can anyone find anything on him?'

Nader was a solid player having competed for years on the UAE Davis Cup team, but I feared what might happen if he drew Federer or Nadal for a centre court night match. He escaped facing this prospect in the afternoon's draw, instead finding his name positioned beside a qualifier.

Troy had returned excited after a quick trip to the referee's office. No one had seen the Pakistani Aisam-ul-Haq Qureshi for his afternoon match. Rumours circulated that he had missed his flight, meaning Troy would take his place in the qualifying draw if he failed to appear. This was confirmed moments later when an Egyptian ATP supervisor bellowed across the lawns to Troy, 'You're in, you're in!' The supervisor ran many of the local tournaments, and he seemed even more excited than Troy at this latest development.

It transpired that Qureshi had been the victim of miscommunication. When he had won a Futures event in Dubai, he'd been promised a wildcard into the Dubai ATP. As he was 132 in the world and already within the cut-off for the qualifying draw, he assumed, logically, that it was for the main draw.

His flight was booked for Saturday evening. When he discovered in the morning that he was actually playing today in a qualifying match, he was still at home in Pakistan.

Troy tried to organise a last-minute practice court. The ATP lady looked at the sheet filled with names. 'Well, I can always ask Roger if he's willing to play four to a court.'

'No, no,' Troy said quickly, starting to laugh at the suggestion. 'Don't worry, we'll find a court.'

'Are you sure? You have a match,' the ATP lady replied in a serious tone.

Now that we were being treated like ATP players, we couldn't handle it, still feeling like imposters in such an elite field. We left, heading to the outside courts in search of an empty one.

Troy's match was against a Lebanese wildcard, Karim Alayli. Alayli was a great guy – a regular player on the Futures circuit in this region where both Troy and I knew him. Rumour had it that he was from an important family in Lebanon and that he had used his family connections to secure his wildcard. It seemed how this part of the world worked. Ranked 1,495 in the world to Troy's 1,401, it was a great opportunity for both of them. The winner would be guaranteed five ATP points, and U$1,650.

Troy's match with Alayli began on court two, one of the outside courts played in front of a 1,000-seat stand. Wesley Moodie warmed up with Paolo Lorenzi, of Italy, on court one, while another local Emirati wildcard played a Russian player on the adjacent court three. Spectators sat scattered around the concrete steps of the stand.

With so much at stake, both players' nervousness could be seen from the stands. Troy gave clenched fists to pump himself up, while the Lebanese picked at his strings to keep calm. With the first set locked at 4-4, Ilie Nastase and Mansour Bahrami entered the stands and sat in the front row. They seemed to have a vested interest in the Lebanese player, watching him intently as if evaluating his game. When Alayli sprayed a return wide on a crucial break point, Nastase raised his hands in an open gesture of confusion and disgust, questioning how such a wasteful error could happen on such a big point. Both Nastase and Bahrami left shortly after that – they had seen enough.

After just over an hour, Alayli played the big points better to beat Troy 6-4, 6-2. Perhaps Troy wanted it too badly, had too much pressure riding on the outcome of this one match, for he looked so much more tightly wound than his opponent.

'I'm grateful for the opportunity,' Troy told me after the match, 'but I'm disappointed I couldn't win. I had a great chance to win. Now Karim has five ATP points and a shot to qualify.' The elation he had felt only a couple of hours before had vanished. Winning the match would have opened the door to more opportunities; now there was nothing except coaching to look forward too.

* * * * *

On Monday, after work, I returned to the Aviation Club where the first round of the main draw was scheduled to begin. I had barely arrived and gone inside a café when a strange thing happened. I was standing, quickly scanning through a newspaper, when I heard someone say, 'hi'. I looked up to see a man – Afro-American, maybe in his 30s and well dressed in casual designer wear – standing close by, smiling and waiting for a reply.

'Are you a player?' he asked. He was still smiling, revealing Hollywood-white teeth.

'I was in the qualifying,' I replied.

'That's strange. I've never seen you before,' he went on. He was completely at ease talking to a total stranger. 'I thought I knew *everyone*.'

At this point, I was starting to wonder if I was being hit on. It seemed a conversation for the sake of conversation – leaving me wondering what his agenda was.

'I live in Miami. I hang out with Marat Safin, Fernando Verdasco and a few of the other players – I party with them when they're in town. They're great guys.'

There was a momentary pause, as if to allow me to digest this information. Around his neck hung an official pass with the words 'Player Guest' printed under his smiling photo. At the bottom of the pass was a row of colours, showing full, unrestricted access to all areas of the tournament.

'Oh, yes,' he said when he saw me looking towards his pass. 'I'm here in a player's entourage. I'm always on tour and different players get me passes.' With this, he smiled, told me it was nice to meet me and that he would see me around, and left to go talk to someone else.

The brief interaction was a superficial, and wholly unnerving experience. Unlike other fans who collected autographs, my new *friend* appeared to collect tennis players. Is this what the top players had to deal with on a daily basis? I wondered how many other hangers-on there were lurking around the ATP tour. I left the café...quickly.

In the locker room, the main-draw players were preparing themselves for their matches. Feliciano Lopez was staring closely into a mirror – not because of vanity, but rather inserting contact lenses. Like many of the top pros, he was such a physical specimen that it was reassuring to know that in some small way he was not perfect.

Behind the locker room in the Aviation Club was a smaller room with a cold pool, Jacuzzi, steam room, sauna and deck chairs. While I was relaxing on one of the deck chairs, Novak Djokovic walked in wearing only knee-length Lycra compression pants.

He spent ten minutes alternating from the cold pool to the Jacuzzi – immersing himself from the waist down. Alone, without his coach or trainer, he appeared completely focused on what he was doing – meticulous in his preparation.

I had seen Djokovic several times in the locker room by this point. Often, he would be walking around with a towel around his waist after a shower, talking to anyone who wanted a moment of his time. As this was a private members' club, then this ranged from older, local Emiratis who wanted his thoughts on Dubai, to kids who wanted an autograph. He seemed to somehow gain energy from these interactions, appearing to genuinely like talking to ordinary people.

In Dubai, he was the most outgoing personality in the locker room – in a mostly subdued environment where players quietly went about their business. Many of the top players used their entourage as a shield, separating themselves from any unnecessary interactions. Their different approaches were not necessarily better or worse – they were individually simply doing whatever they had to do in order to get in the right frame of mind for their matches.

After the locker room, I headed to the outside courts where Jan Minar was taking on Igor Andreev, the world number 34 from Russia. With his muscular, high-tempo game, Andreev took well over an hour to wear the Czech qualifier down. The difference was a break of serve in each set – that was all. For much of the match, Minar held his own with the Russian number three, matching him blow for blow.

Sitting in the stands, I felt no different than the other spectators. Had I really played Minar only two days ago? I tried to picture myself out on the court with Andreev, something that would have happened if I had won two matches.

Using my player pass to get past security, I left to go find the office that dealt with prize money. Inside was a man from Dubai Duty Free – the sponsors of the event. 'Which currency do you want – dirhams, dollars or euros?' he asked me as I signed beside my name.

'Dollars.'

I wanted the official currency of the ATP tour. The man handed over U$870. It was the full amount, Dubai being a tax-free country.

The crowd was starting to file in for the evening session. There was a palpable excitement in the air. In a first-round clash, Roger Federer was facing Andy Murray. Even though Murray was 11th in the world, the top eight players had taken all the seeded places, leaving the Scot as a dangerous floater.

Outside the stadium, desperate Western expats, still in their business suits, were trying to buy people's tickets. The asking prices rose steeply the closer it came to the starting time, with some tickets passing hands for U$400. I'd bought two tickets weeks ago at the original price of U$20. Sylvie was flying with Emirates, so I gave my spare to a work colleague for free. There was no way I was willing to risk being caught scalping the ticket while being a player in the tournament.

Federer was at the peak of his powers, virtually invincible in winning three Grand Slams the year before. The mere chance of him being dumped out in the first round was unthinkable; it had happened only once before in the previous five years. Yet people were sensing an upset, and were willing to sit in the stairwells if necessary to witness it.

During the match, I looked back upwards into the rows of people to see Minar in the crowd. He was sitting beside a fellow qualifier, the Australian Joe Sirianni. They each had a pint of beer in their hands, thoroughly enjoying the boisterous behaviour around them.

The tie was on a knife-edge for hours – the atmosphere electric. When Murray served for the match in the third set, the crowd were baying for blood. Faced with second serves, Federer refused to play safe. He skipped backwards in order to launch big forehands – backing himself with a champion's mindset that he could hit winners. When he drove the ball into the net on match point, the shock on his face matched much of the crowd, unable to comprehend what had happened. For Federer, it was that he had missed; for the crowd, it was that he was out on the first day's play.

After Murray's on-court interview, I left the stadium and made my way towards the locker room. It was like following the destructive path of a storm. Throngs of fans outside the stadium were still buzzing with excitement, checking their photos on their phones of Federer stalking past them after his shock loss.

I realised that the world number one was ahead of me – just out of sight. I passed a line of middle-aged Swiss fans, decked out in red shirts with white crosses on the chests. They looked a little stunned, their heads turning towards where their national idol had disappeared into the clubhouse. 'He doesn't have the greatest sense of humour sometimes,' said one of the women, absent-mindedly still holding a little Swiss flag in her hand. It was possibly a little unfair. Was she expecting Roger to crack a joke on the way past?

At the rear door to the clubhouse, the muscular security guards were listening intently to their earpieces. 'No members are allowed near the locker room. You got that!' shouted one guard to his colleague stationed at the locker room entrance. I flashed my player pass – the guard focusing his eyes on the photo, and then up to me.

I wasn't sure what to expect. Was Federer smashing racquets...destroying locker room doors? I walked through the door trying to act as disinterested as possible. There was no destroying of objects, but he looked seriously pissed. I *liked* that – I liked that a lot. Here was a guy who had already won 12 Grand Slams. He could have easily taken his appearance fee, had a bad loss in a run-of-the-mill event, and said...who cares. But he was seething, and in my book, that showed he cared – that he was genuine.

Federer had clearly been fuming in his immediate post-match press conference. Around the world, every major newspaper the next day dutifully reported his comments, 'He stands way behind the court. You have to do a lot of running and he tends to wait for the mistakes of his opponent. I gave him the mistakes but overall, in a 15-year career, you want to look to win a point more often, rather than wait for the other guy to miss. Who knows, he might surprise us all.'

I changed and headed upstairs to the gym. I needed to release the nervous energy of being a spectator, but more so, I wanted to still feel like a player in the event. I sat on an exercise bike. Through the window in front, I could see the lights of stadium court in the distance.

When someone else joined me on the exercise bikes, I looked across to see Murray. He had appeared with his coach, Miles Maclagan. He pedalled slowly, warming down from his match, still in his tennis clothes. For about ten minutes he quietly discussed his play with his coach. Late at night, there was barely anyone else in the gym except the three of us. It was fascinating to see the player: away from the centre court, the noise, the battle and the crowds.

The spectators who were in the Irish pub that backed on to the stadium court would still be talking and thinking about Murray's victory. They would probably imagine the player out on the town celebrating. I doubt any of them would picture Murray, an hour after the match had ended, sitting on an exercise bike in a near-empty gym facing his own reflection in the window.

* * * * *

In the final, Andy Roddick played Feliciano Lopez. I didn't watch it. Instead, Troy and I were training on an outside court. Tomorrow, the ATP road show would pack up and leave town, leaving the Aviation Club as just another club – Troy and I, just regular members.

Long after the final ball had been struck, and long after Roddick had raised the trophy and the crowd left the stadium, I remained out on court.

Not that long ago, I had been a teacher in London dreaming about playing on the tour. Then, I was a 34-year-old, wondering if I was good enough to earn a world ranking. I *never* ventured beyond that. If someone had told me that I'd play a few months on the ATP tour among the greatest players in the game, I flatly would not have believed them.

The lights in the empty stadium were still burning brightly, illuminating the dark desert sky. At some point, the lights would be turned off. I *knew* that. But until they did, I was living *my* dream – a pro tennis player on the ATP tour.

Postscript

'There are too many players trying to compete on the professional circuit; too few players are breaking even; and the age of these players is increasing.'

ITF, 2017

MY TIME on the pro tour happened the best part of a decade ago. In any sport, this is a significant amount of time – enough for a generation of players to change and a sport to evolve. Considering this, the world of men's professional tennis looks remarkably similar today as it did back then. In 2007, I sat in a Tunis hotel room and watched Rafael Nadal and Roger Federer in the Roland-Garros final. A decade later – the two are still squaring off in Grand Slam finals and are dominating the circuit.

* * * * *

Several of the players I encountered along the way in the lower echelons of the game have risen on to the ATP tour, and are currently having fine careers. They are making money from the sport, appear on television playing on the ATP tour and in the Grand Slams, and are recognised by fans – all benchmarks of having 'made it' as professionals in the world of tennis.

While some of the players I encountered were almost destined to reach the top of the game – their success most likely no real surprise to anyone (including themselves) – a handful of others somehow broke free from the pack after years of toil in the minor leagues. For me, their successes in the Grand Slams are all that much sweeter considering I saw first-hand the struggles they went through just to get there. For where they succeeded, tens of thousands of other aspiring professionals fell by the wayside.

For all the players I played during the tour, the most impressive was the tall Ukrainian, Sergiy Stakhovsky. He had such a smooth, effortless power coupled with an intensity that I could literally feel standing on the other side of the net. He won his maiden ATP title within a couple of months after our match – clearly a player heading to the top of the game. When he reached a career high of 31 two years later, his career looked ready to explode.

However, since then, with the exception of a four-set defeat of Roger Federer in the 2013 Wimbledon Championships, Stakhovsky has been somewhat of an underachiever. By the end of the 2017 season, at 31 years of age, he has fallen outside of the world's top 100 and has been forced back on the Challenger circuit.

Dustin Brown, the tall half-Jamaican, half-German player, whom I had seen trying to move his camper van from the car park during the Kassel Futures event in Germany, has also had his moments of spectacular glory. With his breath-taking shot-making (or recklessness, depending on one's point of view), Brown, like Stakhovsky, has saved his best for the biggest stage, blowing away the likes of former champions Rafael Nadal and Lleyton Hewitt in separate Wimbledon Championships. After spending the first seven years as a tennis professional struggling in Futures events, he has spent the next eight flitting in and out of the world's top 100. If I ever run into him again, I'll ask him if he still has his camper van.

Kei Nishikori, whom I saw as a lowly ranked qualifier in the 2007 Beijing ATP, rapidly moved through the rankings to a career high of number four in 2015. In Beijing, he was 17 years old – just one of 32 other qualifiers whose tennis future was unknown. When I walked past Nishikori's court in his match against the Australian Ashley Fisher, I saw him hit only one shot – a wickedly explosive forehand. I would be lying if I told you I saw top-five potential based on that shot alone. In hindsight (where everything is obvious), it was noticeable that Nishikori did have an extra gear – another level of fast-twitch explosiveness – that no one else in the qualifying draw possessed.

I often wonder how my tour would have turned out if Malek Jaziri's ankle had healed itself before our first-round encounter in Carthage, Tunisia. Against the burly Tunisian, on clay, on his home courts, I would give myself a snowflake's chance in hell of beating him. If I hadn't gotten my first ATP point then, perhaps I would have never become a world-ranked pro and this story would have turned out very differently. Now that Jaziri has become a permanent fixture in the world's top 100 after years in the Futures, I see him regularly playing on television, and every time I do, I quietly thank my lucky stars that he withdrew that day in Carthage.

In January of 2014, I turned on my television to see Raven Klaasen in the doubles final of the Australian Open. When the cameras closed in on the South African, I was looking at his legs to see whether they were now the same size (thankfully they were). Although Klaasen lost his first Grand Slam final, with Eric Butorac of the USA, he has had many other successes in making a fine career for himself as currently one of the world's best doubles players. When I spoke to Klaasen during my African tour of 2006, he was surviving on biltong and appeared uncertain if his damaged knee would ever allow him to play again. Of all the players I met on tour that 'made it', perhaps Klaasen had the toughest journey. I take my hat off to him.

The last I saw of Luke Bourgeois was when he was leaving the player bus in Manchester. While the Aussie phrase 'see you later' usually isn't said literally, I did expect to run into him further down the line. This never happened as he retired from the game two months later, unable to stop his slide down the rankings. I wonder if things could have turned out differently if he had only won that match point against Carlos Moya. Are the margins at this level so fine that 'making it' could come down to one solitary point? It's scary to think so.

Many of the players – back in the pack – whom I encountered on the Futures tour are still out there, chasing ATP points and living the dream. My good buddy, big George Barth from Ohio, earned an ATP point in 2013 in the east African nation of Burundi. When I saw the result on the internet, I tracked him down in his hotel room to congratulate him. At 44 years of age and ranked 1,799 in the world, he was – at the time – the oldest player on the ATP rankings. I recently heard him give a radio interview in America about his experiences on the Futures tour.

Kevin Kung succeeded in his plan to attend an Ivy League school in the States, graduating in 2011 from Columbia University in New York. While pulling 12-hour days as a trader in an investment bank in Hong Kong, he earned a world ranking, played ATP qualifying events and represented Hong Kong in the Davis Cup. That he could do all of this didn't surprise me – I've never met such a focused person in all my life.

I have continued to run into Joe Cooper over the years – usually in the most obscure places around the world (Dublin, the Sinai…you get the picture). Having set up his own online business, Joe is back on the tour, and is currently working his way up the world rankings as a doubles specialist. In the 2016 season alone, he played 29 Futures tournaments – the sign of a *real* journeyman.

His fellow English travelling partner, Alex Johnston, severely damaged his knee after his African tour and was out of the game for two years. On his return, he couldn't get out of the Futures qualifying draws and he finished having never achieved a world ranking.

* * * * *

In 2010, Stephen Donald and Jason Stoltenberg featured in a television programme about the poor state of Australian tennis. It ran on national television as part of the award-winning *Four*

Corners series, led by investigative reporter Debbie Whitmont. Donald was cited as the prime example of a promising young player ruined by Tennis Australia, having retired from the game at age 19 to return to school.

Chatting to Donald off court, I found him intelligent and articulate. It seemed wrong that a young man in his position should feel they have to quit school early in order to succeed as a pro tennis player. The pressure to win, knowing there was no back-up option, must have been intense.

Isaac Frost, the younger of the two Australian brothers whom I saw in Tunisia, was hit with a provisional world-wide ban on July 2, 2017 after being implicated in a match-fixing scandal. He had risen to 458 in the world before injuries saw him slide back down the rankings. When I met him in Tunisia, Isaac was an intelligent 18-year-old who had the option to study full-time at university. If he had gone down that route, he might now be several years into his chosen profession instead of having endured a decade of toil and financial uncertainty on the Futures and Challenger circuits for seemingly nothing. Has he completely lost direction and been abandoned by the tennis world? If so, it's a heavy price for a 28-year-old to pay for following his dream – I hope he gets a second chance.

* * * * *

The past decade has seen the rising stock of Great Britain in the tennis world. For so long the butt of endless ridicule, tennis in Great Britain is flying high – no more so than in the 2016 season. At various times that year, GBR owned the singles world number one spot (Andy Murray), the doubles world number one position (Andy's older brother – Jamie), and were the defending Davis Cup champions.

However, one is never sure if this is what the British tabloids truly wants, or needs, to sell newspapers. At the end of their stellar 2016 season, one *Daily Mail* headline ran, 'British Tennis *has to* Capitalise on Andy Murray's Success'. Has to...or what? There lurks the lingering feeling that behind all the success stories, the British press is patiently sharpening the knives waiting for an inevitable British capitulation somewhere down the line – preferably during the Wimbledon Championships.

A couple of years after my tour, I was playing an event in Chennai, India. After my match, an older Englishman wearing tennis clothes approached me, and introduced himself as Paul Hutchins. A former British Davis Cup player and captain, Hutchins was head of men's tennis for the LTA during the years of my tennis tour. He told me he had followed my name in the ATP qualifying draws, adding that if I was ever in London, I should contact him to come down and train at the National Tennis Centre in Roehampton.

I had always assumed that I had gone under the radar – with the exception of being tracked down by the aficionados online. To realise that the person responsible for professional tennis in the country had been monitoring my results was humbling. As for the invitation to train down in Roehampton, maybe the LTA wasn't so bad…sometimes (for the record, the National Tennis Centre as an elite training base was scrapped in 2014).

Like the LTA in Britain, Tennis Australia has also managed to salvage some pride in recent years, although at what cost to the nation's sporting psyche is anyone's guess. In a nation whose identity is so interwoven with its sporting heroes of the past, the emergence of Nick Kyrgios and Bernard Tomic has caused much soul searching in the nation 'Down Under'. Their erratic behaviour has caused generational rifts, claims of racism with comments like 'go back to where their parents came from' from former sporting greats, and uncertainty by the sporting establishment as to how to deal with them.

What is significant is where Kyrgios and Tomic do come from – crowded metropolises like the hedonistic Gold Coast and the nation's capital, Canberra. The Australian sporting public had better get used to such personalities, for the possibility of another country boy like Rod Laver developing their game and emerging from the rural towns of Australia is unlikely, if not impossible. The Lavers and Emersons are ghosts of the past – possibly never to return.

Tennis in sub-Saharan Africa has lost momentum since I played in the continent in 2006. In that year, a host of African nations held Futures events: Sudan, Rwanda, Uganda, Kenya, Ghana, Namibia, Botswana, South Africa, Nigeria and Senegal. A decade later, the number of countries holding pro events was down to four. One of the top African players in recent years, Zimbabwe's Takanyi Garanganga, put it succinctly when talking to *tennis.com*, 'There were a lot of tournaments back when I started. But now…you can count the number of tournaments they have in the palm of your hand. That's kind of declined. It's terrible.'

One of the taboo subjects on the tour (especially among the Futures players) is money – not prize money, which is transparent and in the public domain, but rather where players get their money from to travel in the first place. Playing on the tour is expensive: flights (which even the top players have to pay for), visas, hotels, food, entry fees, re-strings…and these are just the necessities.

For my year on the tour I spent roughly U$23,000. Out of this, U$8,000 was on flights alone. The rest was hotels, tennis expenses and my hernia operation. Sure, I could have done it cheaper – played in one region, travelled and slept in a van, and crashed on the floor in other players' hotel rooms – but it wasn't like I was marching off to the nearest five-star hotel if the player hotel was poor. In return, for the same period up to the Dubai ATP tournament, my prize money was a whopping… U$1,944.

I knew where my money came from – I was older and had a job. So did big George Barth. For a few of the really promising juniors (like Stephen Donald), their national tennis federation bankrolled them. In return for funding, results are expected… and quickly; there will always be another promising junior player coming along if you can't make it. For the rest, it's most likely the 'bank of mum and dad' providing the financial support. A top coach once told me that the Futures tour is a 'millionaire's playground'. He had a point.

As an interesting aside, I recently found a list of the all-time ATP prize money leaders since the advent of the pro game. Heading the list was Novak Djokovic with U$104,927,878. A *little* further down the list…at number 6,062 was one Gregory Howe.

Changes in the game will soon make it impossible for anybody to replicate what I did – namely become world ranked while playing part-time, and then fast tracking my way into ATP events with such a low ranking. It was as if players like myself had found a loophole in the system that was deemed unacceptable. In 2016, the ATP cut all ATP qualifying events to 16-man draws, in order to improve their 'quality'.

The fait accompli will occur in 2019, with the ITF's decision to effectively cut the Futures from the professional tour, thus ripping up four decades of a meritocratic system. Futures events will no longer give ATP world-ranking points and their qualifying draws will be limited to only 24 spots, favouring juniors, and forcing most older players out of the game. The rankings will be stopped at 750 in the world.

Recently, one higher-ranking ITF official told the *New York Times*, 'There is a large group that are semi-professional, and I don't expect them to stay on the [new] transition tour.'

Why not?

One of the official reasons given by the ITF is that there are 'simply too many' players competing at a professional level. *Too many players competing?* Is this a bad thing? I couldn't imagine FIFA coming to this conclusion – deciding to cut most of the professional leagues around the world on the basis that there were simply *too many players.*

I'm sure the tennis authorities have their reasons. After all, they conducted comprehensive player pathway studies and analysed data from stakeholders (Oh, do you mean players and officials?). But this is the world you create when bureaucrats are given the keys to the kingdom.

This is not *my* world.

It would be a shame if pro tennis lost its romance – you know the type – where a Marcus Willis ends up playing Roger Federer on Wimbledon centre court. Or a schoolteacher competes in ATP events on his weekends.

* * * * *

I continued to play after the 2008 Dubai ATP event. During my summer holidays, with the threat of my ATP points about to disappear from the computer after the allotted 12 months, I summoned everything I had in a last-ditch attempt to hang on to my world ranking. In the thin air of Tehran in the Islamic Republic of Iran, I fought through two main-draw matches to make the quarter-finals of a higher-level Futures event. It earned me three ATP points and a career high of 1,222 in the world.

The resulting discussion about the Iran Futures tournament from the aficionados online was…interesting, to say the least:

Steven, 'Taking their lives (also Myles Blake) in their hands …'

Salmon, 'Further strengthens my belief that Howe is based in the Middle East! Good luck to both guys.'

Vandenburg, 'How old is Howe?'

Steven, '36 if I remember right. Well, the danger of being arrested and held as a spy was worth it. L32: Gregory Howe (1472) beat (WC) Omid Souri (Iran) by 6-3, 7-6 (3).'

Freerider, 'Well done Howe.'

Salmon, 'Yay! Another point for Howe.'

ForeverDelayed, 'Howe gets another point…although unranked Iranian WC's are the kind of draw you dream about in 15K events.'

Vandenburg, 'lol. So what's the crack with Howe, is he some old man trying to live the dream that he should have done in his misspent youth?'

Happycynic, '36 = old man? Makes me positively geriatric at 39…Hell let's face it, 21 is quite late in the day as a pro sports person getting established in Futures, old man! Andy was in the top-ten ATP by then. Anyhow, I am happy for him. Live the dream. His money, his life.'

Nicknack222, 'I'm pleased for Howe; he seems to be a true workhorse, going to all these slightly mysterious countries. I do agree with Salmon, that he must live out there, or know people or something.'

Freerider, 'My theory is that he is an oil executive or something who just works on a laptop time to time, hence why he's in the Middle East. But that's just my theory.'

Steven, 'No, he's what you might call a "late Bloomer"! It took him 14 years of trying before he got his first ranking point. Howe also plays on the UAE tennis ranking circuit, where he is one of the top players – that's probably why he likes to have a ranking point or two, to maintain that status.'

Nicknack222, 'That's a pretty good theory. Would explain why he does have the money to travel to other countries outside of that area. I did hear somewhere, that he was a coach for a long time, back in Derby, but I'm not 100 per cent sure.'

Talp, 'We should make a petition for him to get a Wimbledon wildcard: lol.'

Nicknack222, 'Another great idea. He competed in the senior Wimbledon last year I believe.'

Vandenburg, 'I believe it's some kinda tax dodge situation, he has to spend X amount of time a year abroad in the Middle East.'

Nicknack222, 'A possible answer there. The possibilities of him having a job over in that area, or something, whether it would be a family or some other commitments could be another reason.'

Steven, 'Maybe the LTA should send everyone to Iran... Howe has only gone and beaten Krkoska (ranked 904) to make this at age 36 the first tournament he has ever gotten more than one ranking point from. Hope for us all who are already ancient in tennis terms.'

Wolf, 'That is the result of the year from a British player right there.'

Akhenaten, 'Wow! That's brilliant! Superb from Greg!'